REFLECTIONS

From Nancy,
With best wishes—

Harry Mark Petrakis

March 28,
1985

**a writer's life
a writer's work**

PETRAKIS
REFLECTIONS

a writer's life
a writer's work

Lake View Press
Chicago

*For my granddaughter Alexis Petrakis
and for all my future grandchildren.*

Design by Larry Smith
Americom Type & Design
Chicago, Illinois

Lake View Press
Chicago, Illinois

Stelmark

Foreword

A little longer than twenty years ago, after suffering for two years as a junior-rank speechwriter for a steel company in Pittsburgh, I returned to Chicago with my wife and our three sons. We moved into an old house on the South Side of the city with a plan that I would make my first efforts to live as a free-lance writer. The confidence for such a hazardous venture hardly seemed justified on the basis of a couple of short stories and a first novel I had published, but I had grown desperate to prove to others and to myself that it could be done.

We lived in that house for about a year and a half but we never were the only tenants. Our family shared those quarters with pigeons cooing their reveilles at dawn under our eaves, with ubiquitous squirrels in the attic, and with creatures of indeterminate species in the basement.

Existing for that first year on the dinners and, sometimes, the loans of family and friends, in that house, late one night with my wife and young sons asleep, I wandered like one of Seneca's prologizing ghosts, pondering my fears. In the labyrinth of darkness that begins at midnight, I wrote a letter to my family summing up my life at the age of thirty-eight. I tried to explain those things I had come to understand about myself and to apologize to them for the tensions and insecurities I had inflicted upon them. The letter began:

> I have chosen this night of wind and unrest to write this letter to you because I hope that if I write from my heart, through the flurry of words, you may see the measure of my longing and my dream. That is all you might ever have from me in place of any legacy of material possessions I would be able to bequeath to you.

Twenty years and nine books later, a tumultuous period with our nation having endured three dreadful assassinations, a bitter, divisive war and numerous public upheavals, as a foreword for this book I take inventory once more. Not so much for my sons, who are grown men now no longer at the mercy of my fitful dreams, nor for my enduring wife of nearly thirty-seven years, who has probably resigned herself to sharing the capers and capsizings of the writer's life. I am now addressing my friends, old and new readers, and, to an extent, myself. On the thumbscrew of sixty, not old and yet no longer able to claim middle-age, like a portly climber of mountains, I pause here for breath. Perhaps I will be able to gauge the terrain I have ascended and estimate the distance I remain from the elusive peak I understand and accept now I may never reach.

For these past twenty years I have managed the prodigious achievement of surviving as a free-lance writer on a battlefield strewn with the carcasses of noble and talented scribes. That survival wasn't quite accomplished by writing alone, but also by numerous lectures and readings before colleges and clubs across the country. From my father, who was a Greek Orthodox priest, I inherited a certain resonance of voice and, from my Greek ancestors, some sense of tragic and comic dramatics. These lectures and readings along with the writing provided us an integral means of survival.

There were many hours of pleasure and satisfaction during these readings and at the writers' conferences where I taught as a writer-teacher. In addition to meeting many comrade novelists and poets, I shared the dreams and aspirations of young men and young women and, often, older men and older women. Having struggled for many years to achieve some skill at my craft, there was a gratification in helping others clear the clutter from their words and articulate their own visions.

In those early years there were less beneficent aspects of the lecturing. Looking back on them I remember an endless succession of desolate hotels with musty lobbies inhabited by listless loungers who sat staring out upon the forlorn streets an Edward Hopper might have painted. Then there were the drab motels with names like the sections of cemeteries, Sleepy Hollow and Shady Rest. In tiny rooms that contained the aggregate loneliness of men and women who would remain forever unknown to me but who had slept on the same lumpy mattresses smelling of sin and futility, I listened in the unsleeping night to the fitful beating of my heart.

Yet, each time I came home from my journeys, the lonely

travels were forgotten when I returned to my typewriter or when I assembled with my family around our table. Those reunions were times of laughter, love and the warm fragrance of foods. Later, with the house grown dark and quiet, lying beside my wife in our bed, solaced by her closeness, I came to understand how other beds were simply an exile from my own.

But the lecturing and readings were merely a corollary. My main occupation and source of income continued to be the writing of my stories and, over the years, through fitful starts and stops, I managed to do that. Slowly and arduously learning my craft by writing and revising endless times, I came to understand the onus of delays and adroit evasions the writer must always combat in maintaining discipline. I became crafty as an old wolf in finding ways to avoid the writing that another part of me longed to do. Yet, despite the obstructions, I finished in the first years of the 1960s some stories and books. There were the novels *Lion at My Heart* and *The Odyssey of Kostas Volakis* and a collection of short stories, *Pericles On 31st Street*.

Any writer who has written and had several books published comes to understand the ephemeral quality of publication. Books are published with some small flurry of activity, a few good and bad notices, some letters from old and new friends, and then the book disappears, driven from bookstore shelves by the need to make room for other new books. The returns in economic terms are insufficient compensation for the effort and time. Having once dreamed of fame and wealth through my books, after several of my books had been published I had to take what consolation I could in believing that many fine writers died poor while waiting for posterity to applaud their contribution to the literature of the ages.

Perhaps this moderating of my early expectations mollified my tensions, as well. If I wasn't going to become wealthy and famous through my writing, I might as well try to relax and enjoy it. Perhaps the years of traveling, talking, meeting different people had also provided me additional insight into the diversity of human beings. Perhaps the death of my father after a long, debilitating illness and that experience of love, loss and grief had, after a number of years, been absorbed into my spirit, as well. I had begun to see how often the apparently undistinguished life contained the epic of classic destiny. I was finally ready to understand and create a character like the questioning, assertive Leonidas Matsoukas in my novel *A Dream of Kings*, who had divine as well as human adversaries.

The writing of that novel provided me, to a greater degree than any writing I had done before, the joy of being attuned to one's work. I felt myself part of some luminous confederacy that encompassed all the good poets and artists who had ever lived, an affiliation linked to some divinity in heaven or on earth. At odd times during the days and nights I worked on the book, words and phrases and scenes flew into my thoughts, seemingly unrelated to characters and scenes in the story. After a while I understood with a feeling of bewilderment and awe that another more profound force than my own was directing my vision. The life of that book became more real for me then, while eating, drinking, walking and talking seemed a ghostly charade. I finally understood the emotion Martin Buber called "the holiness of an active relationship with God."

When *A Dream of Kings* was published I had the astounding experience of watching it become a commercial as well as a critically successful book. A book club made it an alternate selection, a paperback house bought the reprint rights, and, for twelve weeks it nested in the list of national best sellers, dissolving my younger conviction that such exalted categories belonged to writers who had, in some scornful way, "sold out." The book was, finally, also sold for a film and I traveled with my family to California to work on the screen play. For eighteen months, while living in several luxurious houses with fruit orchards and heated pools, we basked in the Hollywood sun like poor heirs bequeathed an unexpected inheritance.

But that whole experience of the writer in Hollywood, so poignantly and precisely recorded by many other writers who had made the same journey, proved depressing and disappointing. In my relations with studio executives and with one or two stars, I passed from anticipation to futile efforts at accomodation and then resignation. Although I did not understand it at the time, a substantial part of the problem was my own stubborn refusal to accept that the novel and the film were separate arts. As a novelist who felt my own words and scenes were inviolate, I failed to empathize with the actor who must find a way to speak those words and with the director who had to fashion scenes that utilized action or silence.

So, for all these reasons, I came to understand that while

talented artists and technicians might fuse their forces creatively to make films I admired and enjoyed, I preferred the individual art of the novel and the short story.

I brought my wife and our two younger sons (the oldest boy, Mark, away at college) back to the middle west. Although our home had always been in Chicago, the spaciousness of California left us with a longing for a less crowded environment. Using the loot acquired from the sales of *A Dream of Kings*, we purchased a house in northwest Indiana overlooking the sand dunes and Lake Michigan, just across the water from the misted neighborhoods of my childhood in Chicago. Living in that house which was exposed to the sun and sky and wind allowed me to watch and ponder the luminosity of dawn and to experience, as well, "the fabulous, formless darkness" of Yeats. There was the miracle of spring turning all around us into summer with its jubilant medley of crickets and birds. Within the clasp of autumn and winter I could sit before my fireplace, watching the glowing embers with that nostalgia for youth lost and yet savoring earthly enjoyments. If one were to ask me then what I wished to do with my life, I would have answered like Lear "to pray and sing and tell old tales."

In that timeless landscape of sky and water, I began to assemble the essays that became *Stelmark*. I burrowed like an archeologist into my past, exhumed the bones of the dead I had loved, felt once more the proddings of guilt and remorse, of sadness and joy. I reflected on all my blunderings and flounderings, the endless small and large failures of which I had been guilty. I recalled the times I had spoken that I should have been silent, the times I had been silent that I should have spoken.

In the process of refashioning the memories into words for the pages of a book, I think I came to understand a little more of myself than I had known before. In writing of my father, my relationship to him, I think I extended the boundaries within which I try to understand my sons. By recording the fevered addiction to gambling I had endured as a young man, I think I understand a little more about the compulsions to different forms of bondage the young people feel driven to make today. There are no final answers, but things are made clear. Every calamity opens a perspective on the human condition if we but have the sense to comprehend it.

In finishing *Stelmark* I had a consoled feeling that I had exorcized the past, laid my ghosts to rest and by admitting my laments and failures rendered them less painful. If I could not be young (I am not even sure I would want to be) I had reaffirmed for myself once more that the important thing is to strive to become one's self, a lifetime's task, and to come to a kind of tenuous maturity that means accepting the earth and our place upon it.

Prologue

Nostalgia is something I have always known. Although I have never been to Crete, the island where my father and mother were born, the constellations of my childhood shimmered with stories of that tragic and lovely land. For many years I believed that when I finally made the journey to Crete for the first time, it would be a jubilant homecoming for a prodigal or an exile.

I am no longer sure when I make the journey of what I will find. The years have made me understand that we remain wanderers, in transit all our lives, seeking a haven that somehow remains just out of reach. Or is the answer simply that I have lost the faith of childhood?

Once I felt I belonged indelibly to that island where tall cypresses cast long shadows across the graves of my grandparents and great-grandparents. The songs, tales, ballads, and proverbs passed from my parents to me.

I knew the myths that were steeped in blood. On that dark, mysterious island, Minos reigned; his wife was possessed of a demon-driven lust for a bull, and that union gave birth to the Minotaur that the king imprisoned in the labyrinth. Theseus came and killed the monster, fleeing to freedom following Ariadne's golden thread. From that island, Idomeneus, Prince of Crete, set sail for Troy to join the Greeks in avenging the flexuous Helen.

If the myths sometimes seemed spectral, the Cretans of my childhood abounded with energy and life. The white-haired old men from Sfakia dancing on the holidays, their bodies grown stiff and brittle to bend like ancient bows but still possessed of an awesome grace. The Cretan girls, hair black as raven's wings, faces serene as madonnas even as their bodies moved with concupiscent flame. And where they walked, the old women, eyelids sprinkled by black sand, hovered nearby. In their timeless knowledge of suffering in a world of men, from the pain of recurrent childbirth, to the toil that thickened and wearied their bodies and spirits, they knew youth, beauty, and love would all someday settle in the inexpiable embrace of death.

What does it mean to say that one's roots are sprung in a particular section of the earth? Are not countries much the same, trees and mountains, sea and sky? What foolishness to claim greater resonance for one patch above all others. From such allegiance bursts the madness of war. Yet, from the love of his land, a poet's song comes as well. Near the end of his life, Nikos Kazantzakis, the greatest of the modern Greeks, could write of his island birthplace in this way:

"I hold this Cretan soil and squeeze it with ineffable joy, tenderness and gratitude as though in my hand I were squeezing the breast of a woman I loved and bidding it farewell. This soil I was everlastingly, this soil I shall be everlastingly. O fierce clay of Crete, the moment when you were twirled and fashioned into a man of struggle has passed in a flash."

An enigma for me in my childhood, the feeling of exile and separation from a land I had never seen, and an enigma for me now. For until I understand I am not sure where I belong. Born in Missouri, America my home, the island of Crete remains to haunt me. Perhaps that is the way it will always be.

From this island, Crete, my father and mother with four of my older brothers and sisters emigrated to the United States in 1916.

I

I have seen an old brown and faded photograph of my father and mother with four of my brothers and sisters, a photograph taken a few months before they came to America. My father sits imposingly in a large, highbacked chair resembling a Minoan throne, my mother and the children clustered around him. He wears a tall black stovepipe hat, common to Greek Orthodox priests of that period of the First World War, and a long black cassock covering him from neck to ankles. Even seated he gives the impression of height and strength. Above the glossy abundance of his beard, a quality of arrogance molds his face. He was thirty years old when the photo was taken, in splendid health, and possessing an unflinching conviction that he had been consecrated to elevate the lance and the cup and the Holy Grail containing the ever-fresh blood of the Saviour. He had not yet been assailed by illness and age, and was still unblighted by the dark knowledge that if a divinity shaped our ends, that divinity might still be powerless against injustice.

My mother is a small, handsome woman with thick long hair swept back into a bun and bound with a pair of pearl-rimmed combs. The combs are not visible in the photograph, but having seen them often later, and having been told by my mother that she brought them from Crete, I know they must be there securing the soft, heavy strands of her hair. (As a child I took them once from her dresser and with a strange warm excitement slipped them into my own hair, where they glittered like a pair of small fragile wings.)

But most significant are my mother's eyes. Despite the four children she had borne, her eyes in the photograph exhibit an innocence, a serenity curiously remote from the shadows and tensions I remember years later. Her eyes changed as she traced a furrow in suffering in the way a farmer traces a furrow in a field.

My mother's maiden name was Christoulakis, and she came from the village of Nipos not far from Rethymnon in Central Crete. Before she was born her parents had three children, two girls and a boy. All three died before they reached the age of three. When my grandmother became pregnant for the fourth time, carrying my mother, she and my grandfather prayed fervently that if the child lived they would consecrate its life to St. Stellianou (Stanley or Stella) and offer an icon to the church in honor of the saint. My mother was born and they christened her Stella.

The threat of early death seemed about to repeat itself once more. When my mother was about two, she became seriously ill. Crete had few doctors, but my grandfather heard of a French physician visiting in Rethymnon. He traveled by horseback to the city and pleaded with the doctor to alleviate the malady that devoured his children. The doctor, moved by my grandfather's pleas, returned to Nipos with him and diagnosed my mother's illness as typhoid fever. He offered scant hope that the child would survive.

My grandparents prayed to my mother's patron saint and placed small icons in the four corners of the child's sickroom.

The entire village took up the cause. An icon of St. Luke in a nearby monastery was reported to have supernatural power. A petition was presented to the Turkish governor in Rethymnon for permission to carry the icon to my grandparents' house. Permission was granted and early one morning, led by a priest and a coterie of acolytes, everyone in the village able to walk moved in a chanting procession to the monastery. They carried the icon back to my mother's room. While the villagers assembled around the house and prayed, my grandfather raised my mother in his arms.

"Come, child, kiss the icon and it will make you well." My mother claims to this day she remembers those words spoken to her, and the cool feel of the icon under her lips. Afterwards, miraculously, she recovered. (Through the power of the icon and my grandparents' faith, my mother says.)

My father's grandparents came from the province of Sfakia, one of the most rugged and inaccessible regions of Crete, a place of stark gorges and steep canyons. Under Venetians and, later, Turks, the Sfakians remained their own law. They descended in bands to raid the foreign garrisons and then retreated to their mountain strongholds, setting up ambushes for any troops foolish enough to pursue them. They were like a tribe of pagan warriors, constantly at war, living by brigandage, smuggling, and piracy. When they were not raiding and harassing Turks, with equability they plundered villages of other Cretans, or fought and killed each other in vendettas as bloody and savage as those of Sicily and Corsica.

By the end of the nineteenth century the unceasing rebellions, warfare, blood feuds had decimated many of the families. The arable land had been laid waste, the flocks scattered, houses left in ruins. Infelicity and bitterness drove families to emigrate to other sections of Crete. In one such move my grandparents settled in the village of Villandredou, a fertile, sun-soaked oasis high in the mountains above Rethymnon.

My father, one of five children, removed from the environment of vendettas and warfare, funneled his energies into another battleground. He studied for the priesthood, completing his theological studies in Rethymnon. Afterwards, caught for a moment by uncertainty, he delayed his ordainment, considering as an alternative studying music, because he had a strong, resonant voice.

When the Bishop of Rethymnon learned of my father's hesitation, he called him into private council and reminded him sternly that the Orthodox Church had been the means by which the faith, tradition, and language had survived under the Venetians, Franks, and Turks. Seeking a life outside the church, the Bishop said, meant my father was shirking his sacred responsibilities to his land, family, and the hallowed dead. As for his voice, bestowed upon him as it had been by God, the Bishop said, let my father use it in the chanting of hymns to the glory of God.

Ashamed of his contemplated dereliction, my father agreed to accept ordainment. Since young men entering the priesthood were only permitted to marry if they did so before ordainment, the Bishop recommended a lovely girl from a prosperous family that, by sheer chance, happened to be related to him.

My father did not have anyone special in mind and trusted the matchmaking propensities of his prelate. But the capricious belle (missing her chance to become my mother) would have none of the shabby habiliments associated with a parish priest's wife and vehemently refused.

The Bishop was outraged, but, unwilling to surrender a reliable prospective bastion of Orthodoxy, settled quickly upon Stella Christoulakis, now seventeen years old. He wrote the young girl's father (a first cousin of the Bishop) asking him to anticipate the visit of a young man named Mark Petrakis, of a reputable family and destined for the service of God. Still rankling over the earlier rejection, he included a somber warning about the shortage of eligible young men and the emotional instability of young girls grievously infected by the cursed epidemic of French novels.

Less than a week later, my father, accompanied by a close friend, traveled on horseback to the village of Nipos. After stabling their horses they sent word, respectfully, to my mother's father, asking to be received. My grandfather formally invited them into his parlor, spoke of various inconsequential topics, when my mother entered carrying a tray of coffee and sweet loukoumi. Neither my father nor my mother appeared to have been struck by love at first sight.

"She was very short," my father said, years later, about his first impression of my mother. "The top of her head would not have reached my armpit. And she had a certain defiant air that suggested trouble for any man who gave her orders. But she had an attractive face and fine thick hair. I thought she would do as well as any other girl."

"He was tall and very thin," my mother recalled. "With a countenance like a mournful deacon. It was as if a smile cost him money. But he was very polite and had sensitive eyes. I thought a few years of good meals would fill him out."

That evening the engagement was sealed pending the drawing up of an acceptable dowry.

I have seen the faded and worn marriage contract that in formal and stilted language transferred to my father 2000 gold drachmas, an orchard of 37 olive trees, free and clear of debt, some adjoining orange and peach trees, and assorted household items, bedding, spreads, pots and pans, knives and forks. In addition he received my mother. They were married in the spring of 1908, and my father accepted ordainment shortly afterwards.

After my parents married they lived in the city of Rethymnon for the following seven years. The first children were born and, true to her pledge, my mother's cooking put meat on my father's lean frame. He served as priest to a small, prosperous parish where he was respected for his resoluteness and praised for his marvelous voice. Men and women came from outlying villages to hear him sing the *troparia* on Sunday mornings.

I never heard my father's magnificent voice. When I was less than six months old and we were living in St. Louis, he developed a nasal obstruction and had an operation. His voice was never the same. In the upper registers it lost its strength and became a kind of reedy wail (God punishing him for vanity, an old virago once wrote him vehemently).

In 1898, the Allied Powers, culminating decades of machinations and intrigues, forced the Turks to leave Crete and granted the island autonomous status. Finally, in 1913, Crete was united with Greece. But the blood-wounds of the abortive uprisings, the passions and the rivalries, had left the island poor and scarred. The first migrations of Greeks began settling in America, and the letters they wrote back to the towns and villages glowed with the marvels of the new land.

In 1916, Europe aflame with war, my father was offered a parish in Price, Utah, a coal-mining community with many young Greek immigrants working in the mines. My father might have been content to remain in Crete, but he knew that America would provide a better education for his children. He considered the offer carefully, discussed it with my mother, and finally, not without some apprehension and anguish, accepted. They made ready to leave for the long journey. He did not realize then that he would never return to Crete again.

The night of their arrival in America, they were detained on Ellis Island by the immigration authorities because the Greek church official from the community in Utah had not arrived. My father was embittered and angered at the separation of his family into the male and female compounds. In his fury he broke a chain bearing a gold coin from around his throat. Before the immigration officials he bit at the coin to confirm its purity and offered it to them as a bond for the admission of his family.

In later years he spoke of lying awake through that long unhappy night listening to the snores and mutterings of immigrants sleeping in cots around him. He would laugh wryly and assert that was his first pungent introduction to democracy, the first substantive lesson to his venerable, bearded, and cassocked old-country pride.

My family remained in Price for two years and were then transferred to a parish in Savannah, Georgia.

Three years after moving to Savannah, my father moved once again to St. Louis, Missouri. In 1923, the year I was born, he was assigned to a large parish in Chicago, the Sts. Constantine and Helen Church that he would serve until his death twenty-eight years later.

From this point in time, I begin. . . .

II

I seem to forever remember streets of matching brick three-story apartment buildings, all with cramped-as-kangaroo-pouch entrances, and the windows veiled by flimsy, gossamer curtains. Separating the buildings were narrow gangways the sun never touched, leading into grassless back yards littered with scraps of old newspapers. A maze of porches with paint peeling from the wood hung in tiers above the yards. At dawn, the milkmen jingled and clinked their bottles on the stairs, and in the twilight the janitors lumbered up and down carrying the huge containers strapped to their backs into which they emptied the waste from the garbage cans. Standing like ragged kings on the landings of the porches we surveyed the landscape of our domain, numerous identical porches and below them desolate, crumbling garages flanking the oil-soaked and turd-spattered alleys.

These were the reservations of the city where we lived wedged together, Poles and Lithuanians, Irish and German, Greeks and Jews. We had no common bond excepting that which we shared as the sons and daughters of parents who had forsaken their homelands and through successive years sought to retain what they might lose when they became the uprooted. For each of us, as children, the city existed only as a province of the land from which our parents journeyed.

My earliest memories, tangled and ambulatory, had to do with what was almost totally Greek. Greek parents, Greek language, Greek food, Greek school and Greek church. There were artifacts that belonged to the new land—candy and baseball, ice cream and movies. For the most part these existed as a kind of exotic bazaar outside the gates of the real city in which I lived.

Since we were a large family, my father, mother, Naka, who took care of us, and her son, five of my brothers and sisters and myself, the ten of us needed at least seven rooms, and even with that amount of space, we were cramped. The layout of the succession of flats we rented was invariably the same. The kitchen was at one end, and the living room at the other end. Connecting them was a long narrow hallway from which a series of doors opened into small dark bedrooms with a single window that looked out over the gangways at bedroom or bathroom windows across the way. In one or two of the half-dozen apartments we lived in over these years there were also sun parlors graced by windows on three sides.

The furniture that we moved from apartment to apartment consisted of certain indestructible items that never seemed to wear out. There was a ponderous bulky sofa that opened into a bed on which I slept for a number of years. When we had company in the evening, my older brothers and sisters entertaining their friends, I went to sleep in one of the bedrooms. After the guests had departed and the couch opened, I was wakened and walked sleepily from the bedroom to the living room. In the morning, after I was up, the bed was closed, the cushions replaced, and not a trace left of my nightly sojourn. This disappearing bed provided me the tenuous, uneasy status of a boarder.

There was a dining-room table, a sturdy monster of heavy walnut which opened to accept three additional leaves. On this table we ate our meals, did our homework, and played Ping-Pong. The edges of the wood became chipped and the surface scarred and stained, but with a clean tablecloth spread across its full length, the table assumed a majestic elegance.

There were six chairs that belonged to the table, one of them an armchair, which was always placed at the head of the table for my father. That chair had one of its arms broken for almost fifteen years. We tried to cement it many times, but wear would loosen the mucilage and a day always came when my father would sit down in the chair, bend his head to say grace, and afterwards sit back grasping the arms of the chair to pull himself closer to the table. The broken arm fell off to the floor. From my childhood into my adolescence I recall my father sighing with resignation as he looked grimly around the table at his silent sons and daughters.

"If one of you," he'd say slowly, making an effort to be patient, "if just one of you would give up planning to become millionaires or philosophers and study a little carpentry...."

He'd reach down and pick up the arm and replace it on the chair. He ate the balance of the meal leaning slightly to one side, while the rest of us pledged anew our determination to make a permanent repair.

We had an old upright player piano that was hauled from third-floor apartment to third-floor apartment accompanied by the groans and curses of the movers. There were dozens of rolls of music for the spindle. I loved to play the rolls, imagining I was a brilliant concert pianist, my feet pumping wildly, and my hands and fingers flashing along the keys. Over the holidays the piano played a more conventional role when one of my sisters, Barbara or Tasula, played her repertoire of old favorites and the family gathered about her to sing loudly if not well.

The day in our house began early, with my brothers and sisters snatching pieces of toast and gulping a few sips of coffee or milk before leaving for colleges or jobs. My sister Irene and I, both in elementary school, ate more leisurely. Because our time of departure generally coincided with that of my father, the three of us usually ate breakfast together. He had certain table requirements that Naka rigidly observed. Regardless of whether a tablecloth was already spread on the table, a clean linen napkin would be opened before his place. On the napkin would be his bowl of dry cornflakes, a pitcher of cream, knife and fork, a cup for coffee or tea, and, because he was a diabetic, a small container with saccharin. When he had finished his cereal, Naka would bring him his eggs, which had been boiled for exactly three minutes.

After breakfast, my sister and I walked beside my father clad in his black coat, black hat, white clerical collar glistening around his throat, down 61st Street towards Michigan Avenue where the parish church and school were located. The storekeepers (mostly Jewish immigrants) sweeping their walks and opening their stores would greet my father's tall, dark figure with respect, bowing in an old-country courtliness that overflowed across my stiff, proud shoulders as well.

On Sunday mornings our ritual was altered. My father would wake me early and I would dress in my best and only suit and the two of us would walk to church along the streets of the sleeping city. The windows of the stores were shaded and still, only the sound of our steps sharp and clear off the silent pavements. Now and then a prowling tomcat marked our passage with a baleful eye.

When we unlocked the door and entered the church, it would be cold and bleak with the dampness of the night. In a short while the sexton would begin to light the myriad candles before the icons of the white-bearded, fierce-eyed saints. I'd assist my brother Manuel as he helped my father into his vestments, the two of us binding the bright, bearded layers of cloth, cord, and ribbons. Afterwards I'd hurry to join the white-robed altar boys sitting with their arms folded and their lips tightly sealed under the ominous eye of my oldest brother, Dan. He was an athlete, strong, agile, and swift in baseball, basketball, and track. The sport at which he truly excelled, however, was the reverberant slapping of our heads at the slightest infraction of his rules. Hard as I tried to keep my conduct exemplary to avoid his swinging injunctions, I was slapped more than any boy at the altar. This action was necessary, he patiently explained to me at home, to prevent any possible accusation of favoritism. I felt ardently that such estimable fairness should be rewarded, and many nights I grimly pondered ways to properly repay him for his zeal.

As the time approached for the start of the liturgy, the church blazed with the warmth and flame of hundreds of candles. The black-gowned, white-collared girls of the choir clustered before the stately choirmaster, listening attentively to his final whispered instructions.

When I was young, I saw the parishioners who filled the church simply as a crowd of blurred faces, without separate identity. As I grew older I began to apportion differences to them. In the front pews, closest to the sanctuary, the oldest and most infirm men and women sat, regarding the ornaments of the liturgy somberly, without a fragment of pleasure or joy. Their attentive faces reflected the anguished questions in their minds. Would the balance sheet of their lives permit them entry into the city of God? Was it reasonable to take solace in piety and assurance in faith?

After them, the middle-aged men and women entered and took places in the pews. These were fathers and mothers who had lived more than half their lives, whose children were grown with scant patience for parental counsel any more. Strange longings and fitful pains assailed them, sometimes their nights were troubled and sleepless, and they were unable to dispel the dark awareness of time as a clock that never paused and never missed a beat.

The young married couples entered church with babies squirming in their arms, babies whose shrill voices cried out like flutes on scattered islands. In the intervals when they were not soothing the infants, the young parents would proffer their devotions a little impatiently while making plans for things to be done after church.

Finally, when the Sunday School classes marched into church for the last hour of the service, there would be added to the congregation young boys and girls, secured to their seats by the eyelocks of stern teachers. They radiated the arrogance of youth, the courage of innocence, and the security of good health.

At the end of the service, the girls of the choir, my sisters among them, would file past my father to receive a piece of the bread of the sacrament. Then, pew by pew, the congregation would rise, make two lines on each side of the church and walk slowly toward the altar to kiss my father's hand and receive the bread. By the time the last of the parishioners had passed, my father's cheeks were damp with perspiration, his brocaded vestments glittering with the reflection of the candles.

When we returned home after church on Sundays, we would have the main meal of our week, a festive dinner that often served, in addition to the family, visiting priests, theological students, young Talmudists, commercial travelers, all setting their feet with anticipation under my mother's table. For although Naka cooked many of the meals at our house during the week, it was understood that Sunday dinner belonged to my mother.

I, early in my life, accepted and understood the miracle of the multiplying loaves and fishes, since whether there were fifteen, twenty, or twenty-five visitors gathered at our table for that Sunday dinner, my mother fed us all a savory and abundant meal. She accomplished this despite the fact that her household budget could rarely afford more meat for the dinner than a pair of meager chickens. But, with rampant guile, she prepared great pans of pilaf, the succulent, steaming rice garnished with a redolent tomato sauce. We ate plate after plate of pilaf, until we were full to bursting. And we did not feel deprived, for within the mounds of rice, small slivers of chicken glittered, confirming that there had been meat on the menu as well.

After the meal, the men loosened their belts and lit cigars. My sisters served small cups of sweet "Turkish" coffee, the delicacy chauvinistic Greeks called "Greek" coffee. There were also tiny glasses of ouzo and cognac, and the syrupy honey-nut baklava. In the thick, spiraling columns of smoke and nectareous mist, the discussion and debate began. Philosophy, politics, and social revolution were all given free play, since these were the first years of the Franklin Roosevelt administration, the New Deal, and the N.R.A. There were manifold things with which to disagree.

When we moved from politics to religion, my brother and sister who were students at the University of Chicago sharpened their knives as if they were zealous apprentices in a butcher shop with a fresh shipment of beef on the block. My father, smiling in his chair at the head of the table, would finally let them loose.

The words and arguments flew up from the table like feathers being plucked from startled chickens. After a while a harried priest or theology student assaulted by my sister's and brother's cries for reason and scientific truth might turn to ask my father how he condoned heresy and agnosticism in his house.

"Democracy," my father would shrug with a wry smile. "That's the trouble here, democracy."

Our neighborhood was a city within a city bounded by the walls of our streets. We knew there was an area called "downtown," made infrequent trips there with one of our parents, knew there was a North Side (home of the ritzy Cub fans) and a West Side, but for all the relevance these sections had for us, they might have been cities in Europe.

There was a tangible smell to our neighborhood, a warmth and reassurance in recognizable faces and sociable friends. I walked delightedly along our street at twilight, watching the lights from the windows throw their misted gleam across the walks. I knew who lived in each of the apartments. There was a basement flat where the husky German janitor lived, a cur-tained sanctuary of bacchanalian revels with the janitor and his friends singing boisterous drinking songs. Late at night their voices grew low and husky with nostalgia for the Black Forest

and the Rhine. In a first-floor apartment a few doors from our
own building lived my friend Marvin Salant, our friendship
begun years before in an argument over our tricycles. In the
middle of the block was the two-flat where the Asher sisters
lived. Bernice and Florence, names that will forever connote for
me those dark-eyed and black-haired beauties who graced our
block with a basaltic elegance.

There was Belson's grocery, a neat, clean store with the fruits
and vegetables stacked in careful tiers. Max Belson himself came
to wait on my mother, the wife of the respected Greek priest.

"How much for this lettuce, Mr. Belson?" my mother would
ask. This question she accompanied by holding the lettuce
gingerly in her hand, involving it precariously on the scales of
her decision. Max Belson would look at her with the suffering
visage of a man who heard too many similar questions too many
times.

Whatever the daily price he quoted my mother, her response
was always the same. With the fervor of a tragic chorus she'd
emit a low moan and drop the lettuce back on the pile where it
seemed to shrivel in shame. Max Belson calmly smoothed the
ruffled leaf.

"Your price, Mrs. Petrakis, you tell me. You tell Belson what
you think it's worth."

But my mother would not be drawn into that artful game and
had already swept on to the tomatoes, to do battle over still
another patch of produce, until the fortifications were breached
by a dozen deployments and the defender so distracted he could
not be sure where or on what item the final major assault would
come.

There was a delicatessen run by a man with the euphonious
name of Morris Satin. I can remember the pungent kosher
scents when I stepped inside, the trays of glistening scarlet and
pearl corned beef, pepper-riddled pastrami, and great swarthy
pickles soaking in barrels of brine.

There was a magazine store with long racks of pulp magazines
(before the days of the pocket book and TV) and the tall, thin
dark-haired owner whose name escapes me now. At an early
age I sought to expand my libidinal horizons by purchasing an
occasional copy of *Spicy Western* stories. (That was the real
West.) When I had selected the magazine from one of his racks
and carried it to the register where he waited for me to pay him

the quarter, our dialogue never varied.

"Does your father know you're buying magazines like this?" he asked.

"They're for my older brother," I said, looking at the tip of my scuffed shoes. That was not true and he knew it, but the identical question and answer each time satisfied the moral proprieties and assuaged whatever slight proddings of conscience he felt.

Farther along the street was a tiny candy store, the narrow space inside the door filled by a counter of jelly beans, spice drops, and a few varieties of hand-made chocolates. Almost filling the area between the counter and the door was a popcorn and caramel corn stand. The owner, a gentle, mild-voiced little Greek who lavished as much courtesy on a penny customer as he did on the dollar purchaser of his chocolates, drew almost all his trade from people attending the small neighborhood show next door.

During the Depression the show was sold to a pair of enterprising men, strangers from the North Side, and they quickly installed a candy counter and popcorn machine of their own. After that, the candy store closed down. For a long time, when I passed the abandoned store, the Coke placard in the window faded more deeply into the dust.

But remorse did not prevent me from going to work for those same ruthless violators of small business. I joined fifteen other ten-and eleven-year-olds an hour after school, two afternoons a week, stuffing the show's prevue handbills into neighborhood mailboxes. Because the owners were suspicious men, we were regularly pursued by a half-dozen older boys, hired as finks, to assure we did not dump our handbills into the first convenient garbage can.

Our salary came in the form of one free admission apiece to a regular showing. On Saturday afternoons, pursuers and pursued would be grouped together in a roped-off area in the lobby of the theater, while the prosperous children who paid cash for their admission tickets walked briskly past us. Only after the film, a Tim Holt or Buck Jones Western, or a Laurel and Hardy comedy, had run about ten minutes were we allowed to file quietly to our assigned rows in the back of the theater. Those ten minutes that we waited after the picture started and we could hear the sounds from within the darkened theater were among the most agonizing moments of my childhood.

If one traveled west from our neighborhood, across Cottage Grove Avenue to the location of my father's church, the district was almost completely black, Cottage Grove being the dividing line. The church included our parish school, which taught English subjects from 9 to 12:30 and, after a break for lunch, Greek grammar and history from 1 until 3.

Our teachers were both Greek and American, and achieved a common ethnic denominator by their reliance upon the stick. Hardly a class passed without someone getting walloped. As a rule, the American teachers struck without any great conviction, but the Greek teachers struck with a rampant fervor.

We had boys in our class who, for continued infractions, received most of the punishment. There was one swift classmate of mine who when threatened with a beating would sprint to a rear window, open it, and leap through a second before the outraged teacher reached him. He was called "The Racer." We had another boy called, for obvious reasons, "The Howler." At the first blow, however light, he would begin to howl and shriek in unremitting agony, rolling his eyes, clutching his head. There was still another boy called "The Dodger," for his gymnastic ability. As supple as a snake, he would twist and coil his body, neatly evading most of the violent flailings of the stick. We watched these bouts with rapt admiration until the exhausted teacher gave up, having failed to land more than two or three blows out of thirty.

My own experience with the stick included a period when for some reason I was never struck. "You never get hit 'cause your father's the priest," classmates told me resentfully. There was another period when I suffered the cursed stick for the most trivial infraction. "You always get hit 'cause your father's the priest," classmates told me consolingly.

Across the street from our church and school was a Roman Catholic church and parish school. That was a foreign country ruled by long-black-skirted, white-cowled sisters with the awesome capacity to deliver bare-handed blows that equaled the force of the ones struck by our teachers with sticks. I once witnessed a boy pulled out of line by an irate sister who held him by the scruff of his jacket and then delivered a short, fierce blow to the side of his head. The boy landed crumpled against the fence, apparently out cold. It was a knockout Jack Dempsey would have envied.

Reflecting the neighborhood, most of the students in the Catholic school were blacks. We came as interlopers from the white neighborhood across Cottage Grove. Black and white, we were mortal enemies, constantly at war. Our assaults and forays against one another ranged from curses and stone-throwing to full-scale battles with fists and sticks. I cannot remember anyone getting killed, which was a wonder considering the number of broken teeth and bloody heads. After such encounters our teachers pulled us inside and beat us, much as the black boys were being beaten across the street. The punishment served only to intensify our fury

There was a black boy I will never forget, tall and strong, although he was no more than fourteen, with the speed and body of a superb athlete, who spread terror among us. The sight of his flashing eyes and great white teeth bared in a scream of battle struck us with panic. One ignominious day he hurtled the fence to enter our playground, and a hundred of us, boys and girls caught in some mob fear, fled frantically for the protection of our school buildings. The spectacle of that boy, all alone, chasing a hundred of us into the school remains with me to this day.

But our most disgraceful battles, organized and led by older boys, were reserved for Halloween. By twilight on that day we would have armed ourselves with overripe tomatoes, bottles, and sticks, and after dark, in gangs of fifty or more, we'd move into the alleys across Cottage Grove. Meanwhile, gangs of black youths would be foraging through our alleys, searching us out. Sometimes there were brief, preliminary skirmishes by patrols of a few boys, but ultimately the main forces were joined, the battle becoming a massive, tangled melee of bodies and missiles flying in the darkness. I was one of the younger boys, fighting in the rear ranks, and since it was impossible to distinguish friend or foe, we threw our tomatoes and bottles at random. We must have struck our own boys as often as we hit those of the other side. But this dereliction was equaled by the fact that our antagonists were doing the same thing.

In the basements afterwards where we retired to wash and dress our bruises before returning to our homes, a wound was a wound, whether inflicted by friend or foe. Shamefully, ignorantly, we felt a primal pride in the scars of battle.

Where are they now? The boys I played with, the girls I walked beside? Where are the young blacks we fought in the senseless, dupable bigotry of our youth? Where is the black Achilles who struck such terror in my heart? Where are "The Racer," "The Howler," "The Dodger"? Do they still meet the assaults of life as they once met the attacks of angry teachers?

Where is Belson, who suffered with patience and fortitude the daily assault of a hundred determined women? Where are the cruel men (invaders from the far North Side) who made us wait those frantic ten minutes on Saturday afternoons? Where are the storekeepers who greeted us each morning as my sister and I walked proudly beside my father on our way to school?

I know where my father is. He is dead now and lies straight and still beneath a flowered patch of cemetery sod. How many of the others must be dead, as well, their sons and daughters scattered across the country and the world, remembering even as I remember now?

If I could I would say to them, this is the way it was on those crisp mornings in autumn when we scuffed our sneakers through the brown, wrinkled leaves; those afternoons in early spring, the windows of our classrooms open to the scent of new buds; those twilights in the summer with the mothers calling plaintively as we crouched hidden in the shadows.

For we shared this kingdom of our childhood, lived there as sprinters and fools, first learned of joy and sorrow, played against time in games we always won, and felt no dread of age and death.

And thought the sun would remain young forever....

III

My father was an imposing figure to me as he moved about the sanctuary in church on Sunday mornings. The candles and the cross reflected on his vestments so that he radiated the majesty of a Byzantine king. Although he could be gentle and warm as well as stern and demanding, there was an irrevocable dignity about him. He was no ivory-tower cleric, but a man with a good deal of common sense. Few of his enemies in the councils of the parish made the error of underestimating him more than once. Even those who had felt the sting of his censure accorded him an unreserved respect.

Only my mother seemed to lag behind in the procession of adulation that followed my father. By her unwritten articles of dissent she implied that behind his revered presence, his imposing demeanor, his eloquence and gift for laughter, a man with foibles and intemperate pride existed, as well. He was, she said, for all of his epiphanies, a mortal, and she zealously reminded him of this simple fact.

Sometime in the early years of their marriage, for reasons which remain unknown to me, my father and mother began a resolute and unyielding struggle to impose their will upon one another. When this battle achieved only a stalemate, neither side able to assert any dominance, they divided their efforts and activities, doing what they wanted without consulting each other. Neither would compromise their position and for all the years I can remember they remained antipodal points on a compass.

Nowhere was this rivalry more clearly revealed than during the dinners we ate with guests assembled at our long dining-room table. My father sat at one end, his lambent brown eyes and fluent voice charming the guests about him with a story. He'd smile a crooked little curling of his lips, lower his voice to heighten suspense, gesture with his slender, mobile fingers, and then finish with animation. Men and women responded like a chorus of woodwinds and brasses. My father laughed delightedly with them until, as their appreciative mirth crested and declined, he picked up my mother's voice carrying an independent melody from within the circle of guests gathered at the other end of the table.

If my father was the orchestra conductor, my mother was the coloratura soprano, a defiant, talented, and persuasive artist in her own right. Because she was less than five feet tall, she'd always tilt her chair forward, sitting on the edge, so her toes could reach the floor. From this vantage point she cajoled her coterie of listeners, enchanting them with a pithy text of her own. She had a quick, lilting voice, full of ripples, breakers, and billows and flecked with a wry penetrating humor. As my father dominated one end of the table, my mother prevailed at the other end.

For a small woman, my mother had an incredible abundance of energy and strength. A certain rampant force of life within her drove her forward. She had no fear of the before and the after, of the above and the below, of this world or the world to come. Her faith was the wellspring from which she drew certainty.

She believed firmly that God held the earth in His eyes. Using her faith as a compass, she charted the undeviating course of her life. All roads led to service. She founded, directed, and helped sustain numerous organizations within the parish. Given blocks of tickets for a community raffle or picnic, she outsold everyone else, disposing of the pile with equanimity to willing and unwilling purchasers. Storekeepers fled out the rear doors when they saw her entering. They need not have bothered, because she would invariably return. A strong believer in the parity of religions, she did not solicit ads for a church program book from Christians alone, but adeptly canvassed Jews, Moslems, and agnostics as well. In the areas outside the church she worked like a zealot for the Red Cross, Community Fund, Interfaith group, and hospital auxiliaries.

Her more ingenious efforts involved helping individuals whose suffering and misfortunes had been overlooked by the church or social agencies. She developed a network of women across the city who brought these cases to her attention. For one crippled old man she gained admission into Oak Forest, the county home. For an ailing mother with young children she obtained regular delivery of free bread, eggs, butter, and milk. For an old woman without any means of support she obtained a pension. For another woman, whose son had been caught in an attempted robbery, she procured legal counsel for the boy and appeared herself as a witness on his behalf.

There were also times my mother was called upon to act as a marriage broker, a role she played with artful cunning and delight. She approached each connubial crucible as if the survival of the race depended upon her making the match. When she managed to bring a man and woman together, her only reward, usually, was the gratefulness of the parents and, sometimes, being asked to become godmother to the couple's first child. After many years of successful matchmaking, my mother had two score children calling her "Nouna."

Sometimes my mother's zeal prodded her into areas where her help was not solicited and not infrequently was resented. Hearing of a feud or quarrel between families in the parish, she'd wangle a meeting between the dissidents and earnestly seek to establish a common ground for reconciliation. My father conceded there had been a few reconciliations attributable to my mother's efforts. These came about, he said, because my mother's relentless quest for peace produced such distress in the dissidents that peace was the only method by which they could eliminate my mother's intervention.

My father, sometimes ruefully, acknowledged the benefits of my mother's labors. At the same time he wished fervently she would exercise certain restraints. She had slight patience with the evasive maneuverings of affluent parishioners she approached for help, or the ceremonial forms and courtesies practiced by the protocol-riddled vice presidents of parish organizations. Often when one of these men or women had been subjected to my mother's bold importunings, they'd complain angrily to my father. My father would bitterly accuse my mother of eroding the carefully wrought structure of diplomacy he had erected. He understood to a much greater degree than my mother the necessities of compromise and negotiation to achieve results. He'd try patiently to explain these things to her. But my mother could not be prevailed upon to operate by means of soporific courtesies or committees. She wished my father were less like Disraeli and more like Luther.

"When things need correction, an effort should be made to correct them at once," she said. "When people need help, they must be helped at once. Hunger doesn't wait for societies to take a vote. Illness doesn't wait for a formal delegation."

I came to understand that my father, like an assured and dedicated surgeon, sought to remain objective as he performed the ministrations of charity. My mother scorned detachment, involving herself with all kinds of people who pursued her, pleaded with her, plagued her. Deserving and undeserving, she made an effort to help them all. While my father solicited order in his life and harmony in his surroundings, my mother thrived on disorder. My father considered conventional channels of charity conserved energy and minimized the possibilities for abuses. My mother hastily assembled her own artifacts of assistance. If most people were repelled at the sight of stark suffering and decay, my mother fearlessly touched the festered sores of sickness and the wounds of anguish. Sometimes, it was true, as my father said, that she was duped and gulled. She simply could not ignore a cry for help.

During these Depression years of the 1930s, hardship existed in families all around us. My father's salary kept slipping until it barely managed to cover the basic food and housing needs of the ten people in our house. Gas, phone, and electric bills were outposts perpetually under siege.

My sisters and brothers worked at part-time jobs to help with school expenses. The most difficult task fell upon my mother. From the small household allowance given to her by my father, she had to perform an economic wizardry. In the neighborhood groceries and meat markets she was feared and respected as a ruthless bargainer. She stubbornly walked an additional three blocks to save ten cents on some item.

When she managed to cover our food needs for the week, there were still those emergencies when one of her children went to her with a desperate request for money to buy pants or a pair of silk stockings. We were reluctant to ask my father but, somehow, my mother scraped together what was needed. I think she accomplished those feats by paring her own personal expenses to the bone. She never went to a beauty shop in her life and wore her dresses and hats and coats until they were shabby and worn out.

Regardless of the thrift she practiced, my father felt somehow that my mother's whirl of activities outside the house added to our financial hardship. In addition he felt we were being deprived of a warm and maternal environment in our home. But although she was willing to make personal sacrifices, my mother refused to limit her role to consoling her children and balancing her household accounts. She was more vitally concerned with the accounting she would have to make someday to God.

In this way my parents continued for years to live and work divided. For better or worse this division fashioned their achievements and left unresolved whatever benefits might have accrued from a placid and unchallenged union. Sometimes they worked toward the same goal, but these truces never lasted for long. Some indefinable core of unyielding strength in each of them, some wellspring of identity they had to maintain, kept them alienated. When there were no longer new grievances to muster, they'd spend hours recounting the old complaints to their sons and daughters.

"If your mother had not been so stubborn," my father said.

"If your father had been more understanding," my mother said.

"She could have helped me in so many ways," my father said.

"He would not let me help him," my mother said.

In the last few years of my father's life, when illness had weakened him and enemies snapped at his heels, my mother joined her force to my father again. Like vigorous and tenacious roots of a single great tree that had existed apart for decades, their strengths were merged once more. But they were no longer young, the years had scarred and wearied them, and all they could do in the end was to suffer with and try to console one another.

When my father entered the hospital for the last three months of his life, my mother remained with him from early in the morning until late at night, tending to his needs, shielding him from overzealous friends. She read to him for hours, told him of events taking place in the community, endured his querulous complaints, his pain, and his resignation. As his strength declined, she made a mighty, futile effort to bind him to life. They grew closer, I think, in those days than they had been since the early years of their marriage. And, sometimes, as he silently watched her, or she stared at him while he lay asleep, there was a sense of remorse, a plea for forgiveness, the mute placing of a seal once more upon their hearts.

When his family and friends mourned prematurely, my mother spoke with conviction of my father's strength and will evidenced many times over the years. She accepted without our awe his capacity, time and time again, to fight back from the precipice of death.

"I know this man better than any of you," she said to us impatiently. "When he assembles his spirit, he has the strength of five men. He has given his years to God, and God will not forsake him."

But my father's strength and spirit, worn by illness and grief, finally drained away. He died late one night in his sleep less than an hour after my mother had left the hospital. When I returned with her to the hospital, a nurse took us into his room. My father lay still in death, his arms along his sides, a narrow band of cloth around his head holding his mouth closed. My mother's face was burned with a terrible grief, and she stood beside his bed in silence looking down at him. "Now he is at peace," she said softly. "Now he is at peace." She touched his hand gently with her fingers and bent and kissed his lips for the first time I can ever remember in all the years we had lived together.

To this day I am not sure if right or wrong can be equated between them. Perhaps, like the table in our house at which they sat, there are simply two ends, one end that belonged to my father and the other end to my mother.

IV

There was one storekeeper I remember above all others in my youth. It was shortly before I became ill, spending a good portion of my time with a motley group of varied ethnic ancestry. We contended with one another to deride the customs of the old country. On our Saturday forays into neighborhoods beyond own own, to prove we were really Americans we ate hot dogs and drank Cokes. If a boy didn't have ten cents for this repast he went hungry, for he dared not bring a sandwich from home made of the spiced meats our families ate.

One of our untamed games was to seek out the owner of a pushcart or a store, unmistakably an immigrant, and bedevil him with a chorus of insults and jeers. To prove allegiance to the gang it was necessary to reserve our fiercest malevolence for a storekeeper or peddler belonging to our own ethnic background.

For that reason I led a raid on the small, shabby grocery of old Barba Nikos, a short, sinewy Greek who walked with a slight limp and sported a flaring, handlebar mustache.

We stood outside his store and dared him to come out. When he emerged to do battle, we plucked a few plums and peaches from the baskets on the sidewalk and retreated across the street to eat them while he watched. He waved a fist and hurled epithets at us in ornamental Greek.

Aware that my mettle was being tested, I raised my arm and threw my half-eaten plum at the old man. My aim was accurate and the plum struck him on the cheek. He shuddered and put his hand to the stain. He stared at me across the street, and although I could not see his eyes, I felt them sear my flesh. He turned and walked silently back into the store. The boys slapped my shoulders in admiration, but it was a hollow victory that rested like a stone in the pit of my stomach.

At twilight when we disbanded, I passed the grocery alone on my way home. There was a small light burning in the store and the shadow of the old man's body outlined against the glass. Goaded by remorse, I walked to the door and entered.

The old man moved from behind the narrow wooden counter and stared at me. I wanted to turn and flee, but by then it was too late. As he motioned for me to come closer, I braced myself for a curse or a blow.

"You were the one," he said, finally, in a harsh voice.

I nodded mutely.

"Why did you come back?"

I stood there unable to answer.

"What's your name?"

"Haralambos," I said, speaking to him in Greek.

He looked at me in shock. "You are Greek!" he cried. "A Greek boy attacking a Greek grocer!" He stood appalled at the immensity of my crime. "All right," he said coldly. "You are here because you wish to make amends." His great mustache bristled in concentration. "Four plums, two peaches," he said. "That makes a total of 78 cents. Call it 75. Do you have 75 cents, boy?"

I shook my head.

"Then you will work it off," he said. "Fifteen cents an hour into 75 cents makes"—he paused—"five hours of work. Can you come here Saturday morning?"

"Yes," I said.

"Yes, Barba Nikos," he said sternly. "Show respect."

"Yes, Barba Nikos," I said.

"Saturday morning at eight o'clock," he said. "Now go home and say thanks in your prayers that I did not loosen your impudent head with a solid smack on the ear." I needed no further urging and fled.

Saturday morning, still apprehensive, I returned to the store. I began by sweeping, raising clouds of dust in dark and hidden corners. I washed the windows, whipping the squeegee swiftly up and down the glass in a fever of fear that some member of the gang would see me. When I finished I hurried back inside.

For the balance of the morning I stacked cans, washed the counter, and dusted bottles of yellow wine. A few customers entered, and Barba Nikos served them. A little after twelve o'clock he locked the door so he could eat lunch. He cut himself a few slices of sausage, tore a large chunk from a loaf of crisp-crusted bread, and filled a small cup with a dozen black shiny olives floating in brine. He offered me the cup. I could not help myself and grimaced.

"You are a stupid boy," the old man said. "You are not really Greek, are you?"

"Yes, I am."

"You might be," he admitted grudgingly. "But you do not act Greek. Wrinkling your nose at these fine olives. Look around this store for a minute. What do you see?"

"Fruits and vegetables," I said. "Cheese and olives and things like that."

He stared at me with a massive scorn. "That's what I mean," he said. "You are a bonehead. You don't understand that a whole nation and a people are in this store."

I looked uneasily toward the storeroom in the rear, almost expecting someone to emerge.

"What about olives?" he cut the air with a sweep of his arm. "There are olives of many shapes and colors. Pointed black ones from Kalamata, oval ones from Amphissa, pickled green olives and sharp tangy yellow ones. Achilles carried black olives to Troy and after a day of savage battle leading his Myrmidons, he'd rest and eat cheese and ripe black olives such as these right here. You have heard of Achilles, boy, haven't you?

"Yes," I said.

"Yes, Barba Nikos."

"Yes, Barba Nikos," I said.

He motioned at the row of jars filled with varied spices. "There is origanon there and basilikon and daphne and sesame and miantanos, all the marvelous flavorings that we have used in our food for thousands of years. The men of Marathon carried small packets of these spices into battle, and the scents reminded them of their homes, their families, and their children."

He rose and tugged his napkin free from around his throat. "Cheese, you said. Cheese! Come closer, boy, and I will educate your abysmal ignorance." He motioned toward a wooden container on the counter. "That glistening white delight is feta, made from goat's milk, packed in wooden buckets to retain the flavor. Alexander the Great demanded it on his table with casks of wine when he planned his campaigns."

He walked limping from the counter to the window where the

piles of tomatoes, celery, and green peppers clustered. "I suppose all you see here are some random vegetables?" He did not wait for me to answer. "You are dumb again. These are some of the ingredients that go to make up a Greek salad. Do you know what a Greek salad really is? A meal in itself, an experience, an emotional involvement. It is created deftly and with grace. First, you place large lettuce leaves in a big, deep bowl." He spread his fingers and moved them slowly, carefully, as if he were arranging the leaves. "The remainder of the lettuce is shredded and piled in a small mound," he said. "Then comes celery, cucumbers, tomatoes sliced lengthwise, green peppers, origanon, green olives, feta, avocado, and anchovies. At the end you dress it with lemon, vinegar, and pure olive oil, glinting golden in the light."

He finished with a heartfelt sigh and for a moment closed his eyes. Then he opened one eye to mark me with a baleful intensity. "The story goes that Zeus himself created the recipe and assembled and mixed the ingredients on Mount Olympus one night when he had invited some of the other gods to dinner."

He turned his back on me and walked slowly again across the store, dragging one foot slightly behind him. I looked uneasily at the clock, which showed that it was a few minutes past one. He turned quickly and startled me. "And everything else in here," he said loudly. "White beans, lentils, garlic, crisp bread, kokoretsi, meat balls, mussels and clams." He paused and drew a deep, long breath. "And the wine," he went on, "Wine from Samos, Santorini, and Crete, retsina and mavrodaphne, a taste almost as old as water...and then the fragrant melons, the pastries, yellow diples and golden loukoumades, the honey custard galatobouriko. Everything a part of our history, as much a part as the exquisite sculpture in marble, the bearded warriors, Pan and the oracles at Delphi, and the nymphs dancing in the shadowed groves under Homer's glittering moon." He paused, out of breath again, and coughed harshly. "Do you understand now, boy?"

He watched my face for some response and then grunted. We stood silent for a moment until he cocked his head and stared at the clock. "It is time for you to leave," he motioned brusquely toward the door. "We are square now. Keep it that way."

I decided the old man was crazy and reached behind the

counter for my jacket and cap and started for the door. He called me back. From a box he drew out several soft, yellow figs that he placed in a piece of paper. "A bonus because you worked well," he said. "Take them. When you taste them, maybe you will understand what I have been talking about."

I took the figs and he unlocked the door and I hurried from the store. I looked back once and saw him standing in the doorway, watching me, the swirling tendrils of food curling like mist above his head.

I ate the figs late that night. I forgot about them until I was in bed, and then I rose and took the package from my jacket. I nibbled at one, then ate them all. They broke apart between my teeth with a tangy nectar, a thick sweetness running like honey across my tongue and into the pockets of my cheeks. In the morning when I woke, I could still taste and inhale their fragrance.

I never again entered Barba Nikos's store. My spell of illness, which began some months later, lasted two years. When I returned to the streets I had forgotten the old man and the grocery. Shortly afterwards my family moved from the neighborhood.

Some twelve years later, after the war, I drove through the old neighborhood and passed the grocery. I stopped the car and for a moment stood before the store. The windows were stained with dust and grime, the interior bare and desolate, a store in a decrepit group of stores marked for razing so new structures could be built.

I have been in many Greek groceries since then and have often bought the feta and Kalamata olives. I have eaten countless Greek salads and have indeed found them a meal for the gods. On the holidays in our house, my wife and sons and I sit down to a dinner of steaming, buttered pilaf like my mother used to make and lemon-egg avgolemono and roast lamb richly seasoned with cloves of garlic. I drink the red and yellow wines, and for dessert I have come to relish the delicate pastries coated with honey and powdered sugar. Old Barba Nikos would have been pleased.

But I have never been able to recapture the halcyon flavor of those figs he gave me on that day so long ago, although I have bought figs many times. I have found them pleasant to my tongue, but there is something missing. And to this day I am not sure whether it was the figs or the vision and passion of the grocer that coated the fruit so sweetly I can recall their savor and fragrance after almost thirty years.

V

We called her Naka, the origin of that name lost somewhere in the garbled utterances of childhood. Her maiden name is lost, as well. She was of Swiss descent and had married a Greek-American named Joseph Angelos in Cairo, Egypt. He had been a chef in a resort hotel, and she tutored children in French and German. When they returned to St. Louis, Missouri, they became active in my father's church and good friends of our family.

In later years Naka would speak proudly of having seen me at the hospital, on the night I was born, before my mother did. She had no children of her own by her marriage to Angelos, but they had adopted a boy who was about twelve the year I was born.

Late that year my family moved to Chicago. Shortly afterwards Joseph Angelos died of a stroke. Naka wrote my parents a desperate letter, telling them she had been left penniless, without a relative to ask for help, asking if she could come with her son to stay with us for a while. My father warned my mother against the hazard and responsibility of taking another family into our house, but my mother's compassion won out. Naka arrived in Chicago a few days after receiving the letter from my mother. She remained with my family for twenty-five years.

In the beginning she came alone, her son remaining with friends in St. Louis. For a few months she slept on a pallet on the floor in the dining room because there wasn't a spare room or bed for her in our crowded house. When we moved in the spring to a larger apartment, there was an added bedroom for her. She wrote to St. Louis and her friends sent on to Chicago her son and her trunk.

I do not know what her son looked like when he first joined our family. By the time I was old enough to become aware of him, he had grown into a tall, slim, moody youth of nineteen or twenty, playing chess interminably with himself, while chewing relentlessly on the stem of a pipe.

The trunk I remember well as one of the marvels of my childhood. It was a cavernous metal receptacle, huge as the hold of a ship, the corners battered and dented, the surface smelling of oceans and distant cities, trussed with great strong belts and glistening buckles and lock. When it was placed in a corner of Naka's room, there wasn't enough space remaining to move freely from the dresser to the bed.

But Naka vehemently rejected all suggestions that the trunk be emptied of its contents and stored in the basement. The trunk was her sturdy link to the past, an essential and integral part of her life. Within it were stored the memorabilia of her childhood and maidenhood, postcards, albums, diplomas, photographs, packages of faded letters tied carefully in ribbon, her wedding dress, pressed flowers from her bridal bouquet, a lace-edged handkerchief, a fluted fan. There were Easter and Christmas cards, mementos and souvenirs, trinkets and knickknacks, all things she treasured and touched with reverence, nostalgia, and affection. There was the leather-bound Bible her father had given her, the Bible she read each morning and each night. And there were the first picture-storybooks she had known as a child. As I grew old enough to understand the words and pictures, she drew these books from the trunk and read the stories to me.

In the shifting struggles going on between my mother and my father, Naka became my father's ally. She fashioned this alliance despite her awareness that my mother's compassion was the reason she lived in our house. But I think Naka could not help resenting my mother, envying her the sons and daughters born of her flesh and blood, a living husband, a house to manage, and a mission and position respected in the community.

By unwritten agreement Naka and my mother divided the household responsibilities. Naka prepared breakfast for the family, cooked the dinners my mother planned, with the exception of Sunday dinner, and ironed and washed our clothing. Since my mother was gone a good part of the day and evening, Naka's main responsibility was caring for my younger sister and me. She was attached to both of us, but she unfairly favored me. She protected me and spoiled me. On a very few occasions through my childhood she made a pretense of punishing me.

It is almost impossible for me after all these years to recall Naka as she was when I was a child. I can only remember her as she looked in the last ten years of her life. She had heavy, shapeless legs, discolored and distended by varicose veins. On one leg, torn in an auto accident years before, the knee was a mangled, scarred knob of flesh. She had gray hair that she wore short, thin lips that could curve into a lovely smile, and even white false teeth that added luster to the smile. She had a prominent mole on one cheek, and she wore metal-rimmed eyeglasses that etched two perpetual red marks across the bridge of her nose.

All I remember of her physical appearance was related to age and decline, except for one memory, as a boy, when I saw her naked back, unblemished and curved with a strange and seductive loveliness. That was only once, for most of the time she wore shapeless, sleeveless housedresses that she bought in Woolworth's for less than a dollar. With these housedresses she wore cheap cotton stockings that she tied into a knot below the knee, and felt house slippers. Pair after pair of these slippers always looked the same, whether they were new or worn, because as soon as she bought them she slit them at the toe and heel to relieve the pressure on her callused and cornriddled feet.

In June of each year, as soon as school was over, one of my brothers would drive Naka, my sister, and me to a small cottage near a chain of lakes northwest of Chicago, where we spent the summer.

My father came out to stay with us whenever he could manage a day or two in the middle of the week. My mother rarely came to the cottage, because she accepted that abode as Naka's province. For two months out of each year Naka could be unquestioned mistress of a house, small and monastic as it was.

When I was about eleven, I was ordered to bed for a confinement that lasted almost two years. During my illness Naka cared for me with unflagging devotion and may well have saved my life.

After I had recovered, Naka sought to continue the same unyielding wardenship. We argued furiously over her efforts to choose my clothes, the meals I ate, the hours I came and went. If I stayed too late at a friend's house, Naka would phone the family and ask them to send me home. She was convinced that any girl who smiled at me was scheming to seduce me into premature and illegitimate parenthood. When my patience had been driven to its limits, I reminded her ragingly that she was not my mother, that we were not bound by ties of blood, that she had no legitimate authority over my life. That merciless blow drove to the indefensible core of her grief. She would begin to cry and I, stricken by remorse, sought desperately to reassure her of my filial devotion. For days afterwards I accepted in expiation the full spray of Naka's maternal pollinations.

I consoled myself vengefully by asking Naka for money, knowing she would not refuse me. In the beginning, the amounts I requested were small, less than a dollar, but as I grew older and my activities expanded, I asked for several dollars at a time. She would complain querulously she did not have the money or that she needed it for certain small purchases of her own. When I persisted, she would go into her room and close the door. I'd hear her unlocking the trunk, unbuckling the belts, the creaking of the hinges as the lid was raised. A few moments later she would emerge from the room and silently, morosely, hand me the money I had asked for.

I came to marvel at the bottomless, never-ending cache of dollars in her trunk. I knew her only income, beside the few dollars my father gave her each week, was an old-age pension she had obtained a few years before, which provided her twenty-two dollars a month. Since my monthly requests easily equaled the combined amounts, I secretly believed she had inherited money from a legacy or an insurance policy, a bequest from her husband or a relative in Switzerland. As a consequence I paid little heed to her recurrent laments that she was virtually penniless.

In the last year of the war I married and left my father's house. By that time my sisters and brothers had already gone their separate ways. Naka's son had also married and moved to another city. Since my parents came home only to sleep, Naka spent her long days and a part of her nights alone. I knew she suffered loneliness, and I made resolutions to visit her regularly. But often weeks passed without my getting up to see her. I was working varied shifts at the steelmills, struggling to put the first trembling words from my heart on paper, trying to meet the whirling responsibilities of being a husband, and there was scant time remaining to consider Naka's distress.

I cannot recall the day or the week it was, nor even the season of the year (it might have been spring), not the name of the horse I had been following that was scheduled to race at one of the tracks that afternoon. I had lost on him the last three times he had raced, and I was hungry to recoup. I had finished my shift at the mill, was broke (my usual condition), and decided to pass and see Naka for the first time in three weeks. I calculated an hour for the visit, ten minutes to get the loan, and I'd still reach the handbook in time for the race. With true fidelity to a sacred cause, I even planned to tell Naka I needed the ten dollars to purchase a toy I wanted for my newborn son.

When I arrived at my parents' building, I let myself in the lobby door with the key I still retained, and on the third floor inserted it into the lock of the door to the flat. The door opened only several inches before banging against the chain latched from inside. I shouted for Naka a few times, impatient at the unscheduled delay, but there wasn't any answer.

Thinking she might have gone down the back stairs and forgotten the chain on the front door, I went around through the yard and up the open stairs. The screen door of our flat was locked on the inside. I felt the first twinge of uneasiness and hurried around to the front door once more. After shouting and knocking loudly a few more times, I rammed my shoulder against the partly opened door, the weight of my body tearing the bracket of the chain loose from the wooden frame. I stepped inside and saw Naka lying on the floor in the hallway, still alive, but breathing harshly, her eyes staring at the ceiling as if she were blind.

Swept by panic and fear, I phoned for help. A few moments later a police ambulance arrived and the policemen came up with a stretcher. I rode with Naka in the ambulance to the hospital, where my father and mother joined me a short while later.

We kept a vigil at her bedside through the next two days. Still unconscious, she sucked breath hoarsely from the tubes of a tank of oxygen. I left the hospital from time to time, went home to my wife and son, returned to the hospital to sit beside her bed and wait. I cried a great deal during those two days remembering all the years we had lived together, knowing that for better or worse she had helped form my own clay. I came to life in my mother's womb, but Naka's fierce love made for me a matrix of her own. For her devotion I gave her a fragment of love, a little pleasure, but mostly ingratitude and abuse.

After a while I could not bear watching her fight for life any longer. I left to walk along the midway near the hospital, and when I returned a couple of hours later, my mother waited for me outside Naka's room with tears in her eyes.

"Where have you been?" she asked.

"Walking," I said. "Is she dead?"

"She is dead," my mother said.

I have forgotten what Naka looked like in death, although I remember my father's dead face in that same hospital a few years later very well. It was as if death had effaced with a quick stiff brush what life had already blurred and muted. Naka died in the way she had lived, causing little change in the lives of those around her.

There was a funeral service for her in a Lutheran church, a spare, aseptic house of worship. There was a dark-cassocked, young and handsome minister in the pulpit, a cluster of our family, and a few friends among the pews. In deference to my father the minister delivered a short eulogy about a "woman he had never known, but a woman who had been, from all reports, good and true and faithful to her Christian trust and love."

We buried her in my father's plot, the first of the six family graves to be filled, her grave the one closest to the gravel road. Later, mostly because of my mother's urging and efforts, a small tablet of stone was placed at her head, recording simply her name, beneath it NAKA, and the dates of her birth and of her death.

A few days after the funeral, alone in my father's apartment, I sat in Naka's small bedroom. The room retained the thin musty scents of lavender water and sachet powder, and the pungence of the Mentholatum ointment she used for her arthritis. That was all that remained, besides her dresser, lamp, bed, Bible, and trunk.

In the small box on top of her dresser I found the key to her trunk and got down on my knees beside it. I wanted to separate the things I would keep and give to my sister and mother. But there was also a strange flutter of excitement in me, the feeling of an heir nearing the revelatory moment of his inheritance. I recalled the endless times over the years I had asked her for money and the way the trunk never failed my need. I unlocked the lock, unbuckled the straps, and raised the creaking lid.

When the last postcard, diploma, photograph, packages of faded letters tied carefully in ribbon, fan, lace-edged handkerchief, pressed flowers, memento and souvenir, trinket and knickknack she treasured had been spread upon the bed and the floor, I discovered her fortune, my inheritance, a total of eleven dollars stuck within the pages of an album that contained snapshots of me taken when I was a child.

So, I came finally to understand that the miracle of the trunk had not been money, but love, for which Naka hoarded her meager dollars, never failing the amount I asked for, and, in the end, leaving just enough reserve to settle the sum I wanted on the day I found her dying.

VI

The cottage where Naka, my sister, and I spent the summers was frame-built, a single large room partitioned into several smaller rooms by thin plasterboard panels. As if it were some lavish country house or manor, we painted the name STELMARK in decorative black letters over the front screen door. We formed this appelation by joining the first syllable of my mother's name, Stella, with my father's name, Mark.

The cottage stood on a dozen concrete posts (they had been wooden posts until an onslaught of termites required a recasting of the foundation). There was no electricity or indoor plumbing, and water for drinking and washing was obtained by violently flailing a long-handled pump in the yard. Afterwards we carried the filled buckets inside.

The trips we trudged to that small outdoor shack made infamous in cartoon and story were always traumatic. The odor was miasmic, there were webs spun in the shadowed corners with spiders poised for swift descent, while outside in the brush nameless creatures slithered through the weeds waiting for us to emerge. Sometimes, if a hornet or bee entered by way of the unscreened vents, we huddled in terror while the assassins droned ominously about our heads. These visits gained an added discomfort in September when the first chill of autumn came at twilight, and the wooden board with the cut-out seat was woefully cold

But the summer days were long and golden and sometimes in the evening we sat on the porch with the kerosene lamps reflecting their quivering flames across the screens. Insects were drawn to the wire mesh, and large-winged dragonflies and moths beat vainly against the barrier. Outside in the darkness the crickets trilled their clamor, and in the distance on the stark, unplumaged branches of an old elm we called the ''ghost-tree'' an owl whooped its querulous cry.

The cottage was situated on a slight rise of hill above a pasture, woods around us, and a lake about a mile away. The hill was thick with trees—leafy maples, hardy oaks, and venerable catalpas and elms. Sometimes, in the frenzied winds that howled across the earth at night, the trees bent low, their branches scraping the roof and battering the eaves until it seemed the cottage would be crushed under their poundings. But we survived and in the morning the earth was cool, clean, and fresh, the trees purged of their weak boughs and frail leaves, the bushes and flowers glittering with drops of dew.

My father loved the cottage, the woods, and the lake. When he was able to escape his duties in the city, he'd catch a train late Wednesday or Thursday night to bring him into the depot of the small town, about six miles away, a little before midnight.

On the nights that we knew he was coming, my sister and I would lie awake in bed waiting for him. We fought sleep desperately until, just before midnight, we'd hear the clear, haunting wail of the train whistle as it passed Grant's Crossing before entering the town. We waited impatiently then, staring out the windows toward the pitch-black road. After about a half-hour we'd spot the lights of his taxi flaring across the upper foliage of the trees.

Naka, my sister, and I would hurry from our beds to wait for him at the door. There'd be a brief delay while he paid the driver, and then as the taxi backed and turned to leave, we'd see my father's tall figure striding through the yard. At the last moment, to discourage the mosquitoes, Naka would open the screen door with one hand and swipe at the air with the other. When my father entered, he kissed us, and I could smell the Aqua Velva lotion he used on his cheeks after shaving.

In the main room of the cottage that contained a table and cots for my sister and me, we'd watch with delight as my father emptied his suitcase. There'd be a round loaf of church bread, fragrance of yeast and sanctity, a tall bottle of red wine, a box of candy and fruit...fine oranges and pears and clusters of glistening dark grapes swollen with sweetness and juice.

"We will rise to go fishing at five," my father told me, and then he'd somberly ask, "How many worms?"

"A hundred," I answered. "Maybe more."

That was always an extravagant lie, which I justified by the knowledge that he rarely used more than fifty worms in a day's fishing. But he apparently endured nightmarish visions of being out in the middle of the lake, his boat anchored in a school of rampant fish, and discovering the big can of black earth devoid of any worms with which to bait his hook.

"Better dig some more in the morning," he said, because he understood my derelictions, and he'd kiss me goodnight. Naka went to her bedroom, and I'd slip into my cot on one side of the room, my sister already asleep in her cot on the opposite side.

My father entered the small bedroom, separated from our room by a drape, carrying the kerosene lamp. He'd put the lamp down on the small table and pull the drape across the doorway. Because the drape ended several inches from the floor, I followed the shadow of his movements as he undressed. Finally, I'd hear the springs in the mattress of the old metal-postered bed creaking as he slipped beneath the blanket. He'd read for a while, the newspaper rustling as he turned the pages. Then he'd lower the wick of the lamp and blow out the flame so the cottage sprang evenly into darkness. I'd finally turn to sleep, feeling the darkness warm and consoling because he was near.

It was still night when he shook me firmly awake. I'd stumble sleepily from bed, staring enviously at my undisturbed sister sleeping soundly. I'd wash, shivering, in cold water at the pump while Naka fried bacon and eggs. We'd eat breakfast on the porch as the first faint traces of dawn broke the rim of the night sky. Then, while my father assembled the gear, I'd unhappily dig out a dozen more worms. We started down the gravel road to the lake, laden with the worm can, a bucket for any fish we might catch, a thermos of water, the oars for the boat, and the long bamboo fishing poles.

There were elegant homes astride the edge of the lake, green sloping lawns that swept down to the water, and whitewashed docks to which sleek motorboats were moored. The owners of those boats and their friends, I lamented to myself, did not have to trudge a mile loaded like mules with gear. They skimmed across the lakes like gulls, and when they paused to fish, they cast with gleaming rods and reels, after selecting a fly from a colorful assortment of snares.

I stared longingly at the motorboats as my father and I launched the shabby little rowboat we kept tied to the residents' pier. While I sat in the stern, my father rowed us slowly to the center of the lake. The tranquil stillness of early morning hung across the water, and the shoreline around the lake was still cloaked in mist. The only sounds were the echo of our oars clumping in and out of the water, and a frog croaking on a lily pad, its mottled back awaiting the rising warmth of the sun.

Now and then my father paused, his forehead furrowed in concentration, until, as if he were suddenly in receipt of revelation from an unseen power, he'd boat his oars and wave his hand.

"Drop the anchor here," he said.

I'd peer skeptically over the side of the boat, seeing only the slimy tendrils of seaweed like wriggling serpents just beneath the surface of the water.

"Doesn't look to me like there's any fish here, Pa," I said.

"Here!" he spoke with conviction. "Right here!"

I'd lower the anchor and we'd unfurl the lines of the poles, bait our hooks with the worms, and then cast them into the water, where the tiny buoyant corks bobbed slowly in the slight ripples.

Sometimes we'd catch a few fish, small sunfish hardly the size of a man's hand, but my father pulled them in with the pride and delight of a man who had landed a marlin. He'd look at me with a gleam of triumph in his eyes as if his selection of place had been overwhelmingly vindicated. More often, however, we'd sit for hours without catching a fish, our corks and hooks undisturbed by the slightest nibble. And I'd become as desperate as a sailor, in the middle of an interminable voyage, for a return to port.

My father did not mind the hours of waiting. He sat slumped over his pole, humming under his breath, now and then brushing away a vagrant fly. I was awed and yet irritated, as well, at how much he seemed to enjoy doing nothing while I suffered. Once, only once, did the clamps of my patience shatter, and I cried out resentfully.

"What are you thinking of, Pa, sitting there for hour after hour, watching a cork that never moves?"

He raised his head and looked at me, suddenly understanding my impatience and distress. He nodded in a rueful apology and stared wistfully across the lake toward the pier where we tied our boat.

"I am thinking how quickly the time is passing," he said, "and how soon I must leave."

I never asked him again. After that day, by unspoken agree-ment, I stopped going fishing with him. He'd rise before dawn and get ready to leave without waking me. He'd start down to the lake burdened with oars, buckets, and his poles. I was remorseful when I considered how much he enjoyed having me with him, but I was grateful I did not have to spend the endless, monotonous hours in the boat. And by the time he returned in the late afternoon, only a few small fish in his bucket, he walked with the vigor of a man who had spent a fruitful day.

When the time came for him to return to the city, my sister and I accompanied him in the taxi to the town where he caught his train. Sometimes we ate dinner together in one of the town restaurants, or made a visit into the general store, where I replenished the week's supply of pulp magazines. When his train with the single coach pulled slowly puffing into the station, we crossed with him to the depot. He gave us each a quarter, paid the taxi driver to drive us back home, and kissed us goodby.

He boarded the train and stood smiling down at us from the top of the steps, tall and sturdy in his black suit and white shirt and straw hat. He'd wave to us and we'd run a short distance beside the slowly moving train and stop as we reached the end of the depot platform to shout a final goodby.

After my illness, when we stopped going to the cottage each summer, my father ceased going as well. He often made plans to spend a few days fishing there again. The plans never materialized. In the next few years he replaced the kerosene lamps at the cottage with electric lights, whether as an induce-ment for us or for himself I don't know. He visited the cottage once or twice more and then stopped pretending he was ever going again. There simply wasn't any pleasure for him in the empty rooms, eating alone, and going out to fish alone.

The cottage stood vacant for almost twelve years until my father's death. To the end he could not bring himself to sell the place, although he often needed the couple of thousand dollars the sale would have realized. But knowing he still owned the cottage provided him with a consolation. After his death we sold it, and I do not remember mourning about its disposal.

Yet, when I look back from this vantage point in my life to the summers we spent in the cottage, I recall serene and contented hours lying beneath the crabapple tree, the sun speckling through the branches and leaves across my body. I remember standing beside the pump in the clear summer night, marveling at the chandelier of stars above my head. And I cannot hear the distant whistle of a train in the night without a tremor in my heart, remembering the trains that brought my father to me.

Perhaps my homesickness comes because my father is dead and my youth has passed. I am ensnared in the details and rituals that burden us, the dilemmas of work, family, society that we all yearn, at times, to flee.

Now, as my sons stir restlessly in my presence, impatient to return to their own pursuits, memories of the summers of long ago return. The words of a question I put to one of the boys are muted; instead I hear myself ask, "How many worms?"

The boys' lips move nimbly in answer, but instead of the tangled, evasive explanations about school, studies, or chores, I hear him respond.

"A hundred," he tells me. "Maybe more."

I am besieged then by a multitude of feelings...melancholia, amusement, awe at the way in which generations replay the endless games of the heart.

And I cannot help thinking how quickly the time is passing and how soon I will have to leave.

VII

My illness came as quietly and unassumingly as twilight. A family friend, a doctor, was having dinner at our house one night, and my brother and sister teased me about being lazy. My mother mentioned my listlessness. An arrangement was made to phone the doctor for an appointment, and the following week Naka took me to his office.

He was a gentle and humorous man who prodded and tested me, bantering all the while to keep me at ease. In the course of an X-ray he discovered lesions on my lungs. The prescription was that I remain quiet in bed for a month.

My first reaction was pride at being able to return home to my brothers and sisters and boast of lesions, an ailment I did not fully comprehend but one sufficiently grave to require a month in bed. My second reaction, following quickly, was delight at the prospect of a month's vacation from school. I thought that a mistake had been made, that I couldn't feel as well as I did and be seriously ill. I even began to gloat that in some sly and canny way I had deceived the doctor, had pulled off a brilliant ruse.

Returning home from the doctor's office on that afternoon, I undressed and went cheerfully to bed thinking the whole affair a lark. I remained in bed, except for bimonthly visits to the doctor's office, for almost two years.

Those two years were a strange, intense period for me, weeks and months of boredom, excitement, discovery, despair, and terror. They affected my life, I am certain, more than any other interlude of my childhood and youth.

The small sun parlor in which I spent my days and nights was margined on three sides by rows of windows, and on the fourth side by two doors, one leading to the parlor and the other into the bedroom of my two older sisters. The room was just large enough for a bed, a couple of chairs, an end table, and a lamp.

Through the abundant encirclement of glass I watched and

marked the coming and passing of the seasons. I went to bed in the autumn still indifferent to the gravity of my illness. Instead of rising hastily in the mornings as I had always done, I could idle the hours away, listening to the noises of activity in the house, until the last of my family, excepting Naka, were gone. I looked then toward the windows, enjoying the smells of the turning earth, the scent of burning leaves seeping into my nostrils. I felt like a warm, lethargic animal preparing to hibernate for the winter.

The birds assembled that autumn as they must have done every year, but I had never paid attention to them before. Now as they paused resting on the sill of my window, staring at me through the glass, I felt a latent kinship with them. Later, as the days grew shorter, I saw a flock of starlings, soaring and free, passing in synchronous flight over the roofs of the buildings across the street.

The autumn passed into the gray, bleak days of winter. Restless by then in bed, the cold wind pawing at my windows, the season reflected the desolation in my own body. Conscious of my illness for the first time, I lay for hours with my arms folded across my chest in a kind of senseless propitiation of the disease within me. Only when snow fell in the night, the first snow of the winter, and I woke in the morning to see the fine flakes piled on my window sills, did I feel a redeeming in my heart. I rose from my bed and opened a window and dipped my fingers into the cold, moist snow, relishing the shivers that swept my body.

The spring came suddenly, abruptly, long after I'd given up hope that the relentless winter would ever end. It came in a bird's song, a strange, jubilant sound, because I had not heard a bird for months. Spring was evidenced, as well, in the tree across the street, a solitary maple dying year by year in the cincture of the arid city, yet still erupting a few buds on the branches that remained alive.

My mother brought me a small cluster of early blooming April flowers, given to her from a neighbor's garden, and set them in a pitcher of water beside my bed. The scent of their blossoms rendered the air about me cloying and sweet, making me feel a disquieting nostalgia for something in the past to which I yearned to return.

The summer pounced like a cat, the terrible, scorching heat, discomfort, and sweat twisting sheets and pajamas about my body. The clamor of the city burst into my room through the open windows, trucks and horns and cries of peddlers. Only in the occasional brief summer rain was there a momentary relief. The clouds that clustered to herald a storm, a rumble of thunder vibrating the frames of the windows, a sudden change in the wind. Naka hurried into my room to close and lock each window and draw the shades. I heard the first, heavy drops pelting the glass. And afterwards, I opened the windows to a fresh, clean, for a moment almost cool, scent of earth.

In the beginning of my confinement, to help pass the time, I read the pulp magazines I had been reading for years. The ones I loved best were those recounting the exploits of World War I flying aces. Eddie Rickenbacker, Frank Luke, the Red Baron (Charlie Brown has him now), the Lafayette Escadrille, the Spads, Sopwith Camels, and Fokkers, all swooped and dived through my fantasies. I flew at the point of my squadron, a scarf billowing from my helmeted, goggled head. I dived endlessly, unfailingly, to the rescue of companions fighting off hordes of black-crossed Fokkers. These dogfights were always climaxed by my engaging the Fokker triplane of the Red Baron, a savage and brilliant duel between two masters, ending in a draw, so we could return to fight again. We dipped our wings to one another to acknowledge that we were foemen worthy of each other's skill. In the evening in the mess, we toasted our companions who had gone down in flames and drank and sang our heroic songs.

But in the middle hours of the dark and lonely night, when uneasiness and fear prevented sleep, I drew upon a swarm of heroes that belonged more distinctly to me. Achilles and Hector, Agamemnon and Odysseus entered my room carrying their great war swords. Brawny, bearded, and fearless men, they clustered about my bed, counseling and protecting me, hardening my resolve to grow well and strong so I might join them in the storming of enemy citadels.

As the months passed I moved from the sky above Flanders and from the battlements of Troy into a carnivorous assault upon a tattered set of the *Book of Knowledge* that we had in our house. Without program or direction I informed myself about the Suez Canal, Byzantium, Siam, the effect of the moon on the tides, the Sistine Chapel, the Pre-Cambrian period, Rembrandt, "The Charge of the Light Brigade," "Ode on a Grecian Urn," Why Grass Is Green, Mars and Venus, Merlin and Excalibur, Troilus and Cressida....

From the *Book of Knowledge*, which I finished completely in less than two months, stirred by the phantasmagorias of fiction, I moved to novels. My brothers and sisters began buying them for me in used-book stores or bringing them home from libraries. Quickly bored by the colonic Hardy boys and the humbug of Tom Swift, I began and discovered Irving, Hawthorne, Poe, Melville, Balzac, Maupassant. Gorki and Chekhov moved me to tears. But of all the books I read in this period, the one that touched me the most was *Martin Eden* by Jack London. I identified my own hunger for knowledge with Martin Eden's hunger, the obstacle of his ignorance equated by the obstacle of my illness, both impediments to be overcome. In the end, even while savoring his triumph, I felt the chilling and indefinable truth of his disillusionment and death.

During those interludes when my weary brain and aching eyes prevented my reading, I lay motionless in the bed listening to the sounds of the street. The stillness in the morning after the children were in school, a stillness broken only by the shrill squeaking of a housewife's cart, now and then the petulant voice of one of the women arguing with a janitor about garbage or heat.

The hardest parts of the day for me to endure were the afternoons when the children returned from school and invaded the street beneath my windows. I'd listen to their delighted shrieks as they played baseball and tag, kick-the-can and hide-and-go-seek. Their play lasted until twilight, when their mothers called them in for supper, and only a few stragglers remained calling to one another longingly across the shadows.

Late at night, the streets quiet once more, I studied the reflections of the headlights of passing cars flashing across my ceiling. When the street grew still again, I'd listen intently for the sound of footsteps on the pavements. It was easy to distinguish the hard, heavy tread of a man opposed to the staccato tapping of a woman's heels. I listened to their footsteps coming nearer, for an instant rapping directly beneath my windows, and afterwards receding until the faint, final echoes merged into the murmurs of the city night.

I am not sure of just how it began, perhaps an erotic dream that caused a startling ejaculation, but in this period of visions and daydreams I discovered the sizzling pleasure that could be derived from rubbing the erogenous zones of my body. These new sensations, conveniently suited to pajamas and bed, delighted me, and I practiced them with zeal.

Most of the time I indulged myself when I was alone, but as a variant excitement, I became adept at masturbating in the presence of others, one hand concealed beneath my sheets, the other hand holding a book or magazine, strategically placed, to cover my throbbing erection. I took lightning-like advantage of any opportunity. When the twelve-year-old girl who lived upstairs came down to visit me, she leaned out my window to call to a friend in the street below, her dress hiking up her slender, glistening bare legs. I leaped to my quarry and in the space of time it took her to call out several words, close the window, and turn around, I had achieved my fevered release.

When there were no nubile young girls leaning out my windows, I utilized photos of girls in bathing suits from magazines, or the sleek, lovely girls in the underwear ads of the Sears Roebuck catalogues. Somehow none of these visual aids motivated my libido as effectively as words. Words were the prongs to skewer my excitement for the real feast. I remember a phrase from a story in one of the racier pulp magazines, a phrase I whispered as I masturbated:

"Relentless he thrust his rod between her golden thighs...."

I used pictures, images and fantasies, and once, God help me, barely avoiding what might have been permanent injury, the wrapped beaters of a Mixmaster, but none of these artifacts could match the ardor of those words:

"Relentless he thrust his rod between her golden thighs...."

Yet, ancient as the story of Creation and the aborted sojourn in Eden, my innocence and joy were darkened by the knowledge that I had sinned, and kept sinning. The serpents of guilt and remorse joined me in my moist bed. I anticipated in terror the consequences of my aberration—blindness, madness, the rotting and withering away of my limbs.

A more severe crisis of illness lay ahead of me, and my terror aggravated the condition. One night I coughed up specks of blood, and the doctor came grim and foreboding. After he had examined me I heard him gravely discussing with my parents the possibility of sending me to a sanitarium.

I became reluctant to sleep, in fear that death would come and snatch me away. I fought sleep, and when my burdened eyes finally closed and I dozed, demons and wild-beaked monsters ripped and dismembered my body. I woke screaming and did not dare close my eyes again. Sometimes my mother sat with me, or one of my brothers and sisters, but mostly the task fell to Naka. She sat for hours in a chair beside my bed while I watched tensely so that she did not leave me alone.

On those nights I slept fitfully for a few hours and woke in the darkness, the rooms about me silent as a grave, I'd hurry from bed and go to one of the bathrooms and lock the door to wait out the night. As a result of these excursions I first began to play the role of voyeur.

The bathroom was narrow, with a single frosted window facing the window of a furnished housekeeping room across the gangway. By sitting on the rim of the tub in the dark bathroom and opening our window an inch, I could peer directly into the room across the way, see the small icebox, stove, table, chairs, and foot of the bed.

Three different tenants occupied that room over the following four to five months. The first one was a woman, possibly around fifty, who came home at the same time each evening. She changed into a silk Chinese dressing gown adorned with dragons and scrolls. She turned on the radio, fixed her dinner, and sat down to eat it alone. After dinner she'd wash the few dishes, read a newspaper or a magazine, and then polish her nails. Finally, she'd brush her hair, leave the room to go to the bathroom next door, and return to go to bed.

In the beginning I watched her, titillated at the prospect of seeing her undress. After a while I watched in wonder, marveling at the weary, unchanging tedium of her routine. And then, one night, I saw her put down the emery board with which she was smoothing her nails. For a moment she sat rigid, and then she put her head down into her hands. After an instant I understood she was crying, a silent, desperate unleashing of tears. I felt witness to some revelation of loneliness and grief that belonged in the domain of God. I fled the bathroom, and for a while I dared not look across the gangway.

That was in the early spring. One night a few weeks later when I entered the bathroom, the window open several inches, I saw the light of the window across the way and heard the sound of husky, male laughter. Apprehensive but curious as to whether the woman had found a friend, I went to peer through the narrow opening.

There was a strange woman in the room. She wore a slip, was lean and dark with a coarse, unlovely face. The man who had laughed was bald-headed, with beefy, hairy arms, wearing underwear shorts and top. At that moment he grabbed the woman, pulling her hard against him, clawing at her breasts, dragging her toward the bed. They fell across the bed, and although I could not see their sexual union, the foot of the mattress rocked violently.

Each night after that, he had another woman. Sometimes one looked familiar, but for the most part they resembled one another in being hard-featured, misshapen, with sagging, blemished breasts. They were graceless and unredeemed for me by any vestige of beauty. Yet the bald-headed man embraced them and dragged them to his bed. After the union, he swaggered and strutted naked around the room, his belly hanging, and what seemed to me to be a huge penis and testicles dangling in a clump of dark tangled hair. In a little while he'd make a motion with his organ toward the woman, a gross gesture that appeared to excite her and delight him. Then he'd be on her again like an animal seeking something to ravage and tear apart.

I wondered many absurd and terrible things, if that confrontation between man and woman comprised the romantic world of adult love I had read about in poetry and novels. Were all the words merely a mask for that graceless assault of bodies, that savage tearing of flesh against flesh?

Then the big-cocked, bald-headed devourer of hideous women moved away. A young couple rented the room. The girl was blonde, with silky, glistening hair and a radiant face. The man was handsome and vigorous. They pranced and played together as if they were children, smacking and pinching, teasing and giggling, laughing and shrieking. Sitting across from one another at the small table, eating their dinner, he might jump up and take her into his arms for a buoyant little dance. And one twilight when she was alone, waiting for him, I saw her sweeping the room, completely naked. She sang softly as she swept, her bare feet gliding across the floor in a kind of lithe, glowing grace, her exquisite golden-nippled breasts trembling in the enchantment of her joy.

Strangely, then I grew better, the lesions healing, my confinement drawing to an end. I know that my recuperation did not come about for any reason except the long months in bed. Yet, over the years that have passed since then, I have also come to accept and believe in the therapeutic benefits I received from the young couple across the way.

They were young and, I think, poor, their housing confined to a single wretched room, but they radiated love and joy in being alive. The light of their happiness filtered even into the dark, guilt-ridden world of my nightmares and terrors. And I believe with all my heart that they strengthened my bond to life and my desire to live.

VIII

When I emerged from the bilious and morose solitude of my two years' illness, I fell like a newborn babe into a startling world. The tranquil mornings, lingering afternoons, evenings creeping from twilight into darkness, were blown apart by the smacking winds of scramble and haste.

Naka woke me at dawn. I hurried to dress, gulped a few swallows of milk, chewed a piece of toast, rushed to school, moved rapidly from class to class. Lunchtime in the midst of hundreds of boys and girls passed with bewildering swiftness. The afternoon vanished into dinner and the homework to be done until bedtime. Although my years of reading had made me proficient in words and stories, I had fallen behind in science and mathematics. I had to work furiously merely not to fall further behind.

I was once again conscripted into household service, no longer spared my share of family tasks, or running errands to the store. Before I knew it the time had come for me to fall wearily into bed and after some hours of sleep rise for another belabored day. Time, so long an indolent friend, became a relentless taskmaster.

Adding to my confusion was the detonating nearness of all the lovely girls I had only dreamed and schemed about during the past two years. Upon the barren soil of my graceless reentry into the world burst all the seedlings of girlhood, shrill, shrieking hordes of peahens, ewes, does, and tigresses.

I moved precariously between high little breasts, round undulating bottoms and bare glistening legs, stammering and mumbling, faltering and longing. In a group of students walking up the stairs I stumbled a number of times when the golden legs of girls flashing above me caused me to ignore my own gait.

I was racked by formless agonies, loving first one beauty and then another, bestially desiring all, tormented lest my lust be revealed in scarlet letters on my face.

At fourteen I had grown taller and stronger, but also more ungainly and awkward. My ears, which had always been long-lobed, hung like the appendages of a retriever from my lopsided head. The constant reading during my illness had strained my eyes and I wore metal-rimmed eyeglasses (how fashionable they are now) that rested on the bridge of my substantial nose giving me the brooding appearance of a myopic hawk. I was hardly concocted to bring a flutter to any young girl's heart, but that did not keep me from loving them.

By the time I was fifteen I had mustered enough tatters of confidence to ask a few girls out. Our dates were generally hand-holding marathons along the lake or in the park, Coke and sandwich excursions into a sweetshop, sometimes—dependent upon my tenuous finances—even a movie.

I began to write love lyrics, sad, melancholy hymns of unrequited desire. A girl praised my voice, and in a delirium of delight I composed and sang a song for her in the basement of her building while a crowd of scoffers hooted and howled in the backyard. I wrote another poem about the lovely teenage daughter of a neighborhood butcher and sent it to her house via Special Delivery mail. The butcher intercepted my ode, opened the letter (violating the privacy of the U.S. mails) and carried it angrily to my father for translation. My father pondered the poem a few moments and then explained courteously to the butcher that it was not written in Greek.

My father warned me gently of misusing the mails, and the butcher, wary of the syntax of my passion, banished me from crossing the steps of his porch forever. Remembering the dismembered sides of beef that hung in his icebox, I religiously obeyed. If my darling had been a princess waiting for me to rescue her from the tower of the evil butcher's castle, she must be languishing there yet.

There was a girl named Betty with a sweet and tuneful laugh, a girl named Greta with hair the citreous shade of the honey that my mother used to gild her pastries, and a girl named Irma with a shapely contrapuntal behind that bedazzled the eyes. Once, from a window of our third-floor apartment, seeing her passing on the street below, I leaned out so far I knocked off the screen and nearly fell out myself.

For a few fervid weeks I was enamored of a black-eyed girlfriend of my sisters who visited often in our house. I admired the reckless and insouciant way she lounged upon the floor, her skirt up almost to her waist, exposing a stunning acreage of leg and thigh. She walked in on me once while I was sitting on the stool in the bathroom, my trousers crumpled around my ankles, and I avoided her after that. Good breeding suggested a knock on the closed door first, and there are certain events even love may not survive.

I was sixteen, nearly seventeen by then, a somber and serious youth, withdrawn and grave as a pallbearer, with a pedant's vocabulary and a face that considered it an affliction to laugh.

The panzers of Adolph Hitler had just invaded Poland, and there was little reason for a young man approaching draft age to laugh, anyway. In sudden rejection of brainless, insipid girls I directed my libidinal arrows toward a teacher of twenty-five who consented to picnic and play tennis with me a few times. We spent some lovely afternoons on the grassy banks of the lagoon in Jackson Park while I read her the poetry of Swinburne and Yeats. When I grew more serious and ardent about her, she gently disengaged herself. Her affection seemed genuine and her remorse at our separation unrehearsed. That consoled me even as I sorely missed the hours we had spent together.

There were a few other girls during my first years in high school, a random assemblage of dates, some improvident fumbling on shadowed park benches, and then there was Marina.

She was about five years older than my seventeen, a junior at the University of Chicago while I was a junior in high school. We met at a gathering of our families, related to one another through my sister's marriage to a relative of Marina's. She was an attractive, articulate girl with exquisite almond-shaped eyes and comely full lips. She was pensive and serious with a quality of melancholy that drew me to her.

I did not have the courage in the beginning to ask her to go out with me. Instead, when I got out of school in the afternoon, I hurried to the University library where she studied and sat at an empty desk close to her. I studied myself, sometimes, since it was the supposed reason for my presence. Much more often I spent the time watching the radiance of her face as she pondered over a book. I came to know each small gesture of her hands, the way she tapped her pen impatiently at a page whose thesis displeased her, or the way she flung back the strands of taffy-colored hair that fell forward across her cheek. Sometimes she'd look up and catch me watching her. She'd shake her head reprovingly and motion me back to my books. Then, relenting, she would console me with a warming little smile.

Afterwards we walked in the twilight across the campus arguing heatedly about books. She often humiliated me by exposing my intellectual inconsistencies and pretensions. I felt like a scolded child even as I was forced to accept the truth of her observations. Still, there were a few times she was moved to admit she gained some insight from me, an emotional intuition her severe rationalism prevented her comprehending.

We walked to the Illinois Central train station that ran trains to the far southern city suburb in which she lived. I waited on the platform with her until the train arrived. After she boarded the train, for a final, fleeting moment I'd catch a glimpse of her arm raised in a brief farewell through the glass of the door. Then she would be lost to me in a surging blur of train windows. I would stand on the platform staring wistfully after the train until the two small red lights on the rear of the last car were lost in the darkness.

For several months we spent afternoons like that, studying, walking, and talking. All that time I never even dared take her hand. There was a wariness and dignity about Marina that discouraged any liberties. In addition, there was the difference in our ages. This fact bothered her a great deal, and she berated herself for keeping me from girls my own age, ignoring my protests that I couldn't stand the silly adolescents. The difference in our ages also caused her to become, at times, insufferably maternal, advising and admonishing me on matters of growing up until my teeth were set on edge.

I tried desperately to grow up as fast as I could. I shaved twice a day to stimulate the growth of my beard and brushed my hair in various ways to appear older. I practiced before the mirror with a pipe in imitation of the suave Ronald Colman. I even bought a pair of elevator lifts to wear in my shoes so I might stand taller beside her. She discovered the deception when we sat together on the grass and she noticed my heels rising out of my shoes. She did not mock or laugh at me, but gently consoled my distress by reassuring me that I was older than my years.

When our families discovered the amount of time we were spending together, they became fearful. Marina had to finish college, and I was still in high school. The pressures made her peevish, and she suggested we stop seeing one another for a while. I argued bitterly with her but she firmly prevailed.

We did not see each other for several months after that. I missed her poignantly, but pride prevented my telephoning her or making an effort to see her against her wishes. I passed a desolate and lonely summer.

One night, in the beginning of September, Marina telephoned me at home and asked if I could meet her on campus. I was surprised and grateful and I hurried to the Midway. We walked for hours on that night and for the first time I sensed the violent confusions and uncertainties that beset her, the people and events she felt helpless to control. Convinced that her destiny would be a significant one, she still possessed a strong apprehension that her capacities were limited, her talents frail. The brutal war that was killing young men her own age demanded she take a part, fashion a contribution that would help toward peace. Yet she lacked any sense of the direction these efforts should take. Above all else she felt the haunting mystery of life, the predicament between having been made in God's image, and the incrimination of being descended from fallen Adam.

We walked from the park to the edge of the lake, sitting on the ledge of the rocks along the water. South of us the red flaring flames of the mills reflected into a sky that she said made her think of the burning of a bombed city in Europe. We sat huddled close together, our fingers tightly clasped.

Swept by the memory of the misery and loneliness I had felt during the months of our separation, I confessed to Marina that I loved her, poured out to her the brimming fullness of my heart. For the first time, that night we kissed.

I wonder now if time has not ornamented that kiss, if the years have not made of the memory more than it was. Yet, I remember, too, a strange intense bonding of our hearts, a union of spirits under the burning sky, and the sadness of the passing summer. And I understand now her terror, as well. Because even then she must have felt herself drifting, slipping away from the moorings that held her to life.

She could not tell me she loved me because it would not have been true. She told me she cared for me very much, had missed me, too, wanted us to remain close together. Perhaps time would provide us an answer.

For a few weeks after that night I journeyed exultantly to the library once again. We walked on campus as we had done months before. There was, for the first time, a greater measure of equality between us, the distress because of the difference in our ages muted and diffused by her fear and need. For the first time, as well, I took a train to the suburb where she lived and we spent the day together, walking, talking, visiting with her family. Her father was a steelworker, a good and taciturn man. Her mother was a quiet, kind, and somber woman. Neither of them, like so many immigrant parents, was able to understand their daughter, born and reared in the new land.

There was an afternoon at the beginning of October. I went to meet Marina at the library, carrying a small tissue-wrapped cluster of violets I had bought from a flower vendor on the street. She told me gravely she wanted to talk to me, and we sat in a deserted corner of the library. She told me we could not see one another again. She liked me, enjoyed being with me, but neither of these compensated for the guilt she felt because of my age, her fear that she was distracting me from my studies. She advised me to forget her, concentrate on my studies, develop my talents as a writer or as a priest.

I grew angry, called her fickle and a fool, accused her of caring for someone else. I threw the violets bitterly at her feet and left.

Almost a year passed before I saw Marina again. It was at the end of the summer of 1941. She had graduated from the University in June and had enrolled for graduate study beginning in the fall. I was eighteen, had finished high school, and had just registered for the draft.

We met one afternoon by chance at my sister's house, and I walked Marina to the train she was taking home. She appeared lovelier to me than ever before, endowed with the same fragile grace I remembered. But there was a further change in her, a curious sadness and withdrawal, a quiet resignation that permeated her words and feelings. All the agitation and distress she had revealed the year before, about her life and the war, was gone, leavened into a passive and unconcerned calm.

The year's separation had cooled some of my ardor and my bitterness. I was pleased when she said I seemed older, more mature. We talked quietly of a few books and of remaining good friends always.

We walked up the steps to the station platform, and a moment later the train pulled in, stopped, and the doors slid open. Marina boarded one of the cars and turned as she had done so many times on those nights we walked from the library and waved a fleeting farewell to me through the glass of the door. Even that gesture seemed somehow changed, an action performed by memory without significance or purpose. Yet I had no sense of foreboding, nothing beyond a feeling of strangeness about her.

A few weeks later Marina killed herself. She took a gun her father kept in the house as a precaution against thieves and put the gun to her heart and pulled the trigger. She died without leaving a note or speaking a final word to anyone.

There have been many times over the years since then when I have felt Marina's destiny was decided, her death foreshadowed when she first opened her eyes to life. It is a lighter burden to carry than to consider that if I had been older, less filled with the vanity and passion of my youth, I might have comprehended her terror, the spindles of the loom on which she wove her decision to die. I don't know. I have learned since then that we can live beside those we love and not really discern the measure of their longings and their loneliness. In the midst of multitudes we exist like barricaded islands, fearful or unwilling to reveal ourselves or to discover the meaning of others. Even had I loved Marina more, I am not sure I could have held her to a life she no longer desired to live.

I know that within my stories, the fragments of her that I loved will forever endure even as they wear the masks of other faces and speak words from other mouths. For she has left within me, as long as I live, the image of a fragile and melancholy spirit who died in her blooming twenty-fourth year because her soul, like that of a wild bird, could no longer endure the cages of man and the caverns of earth.

IX

The first exposure I had to gambling came when I entered a bookie's with a friend who had come to collect on a bet. I looked around with wonder and amusement at the large room crowded with men and women, faces raw and stark with excitement and longing.

I returned alone after a few days, as much to observe as to bet. Little by little I began arriving earlier, making a few small bets on various races, and staying around to see how they fared. I started cutting one class at school and then two and three. After about a month, the static, monotonous routine of school could not equal the ebullient curriculum of the races, and I stopped going to class completely. I deceived my parents and Naka by leaving for school in the morning at my usual time. I'd walk down to the bookie behind the Illinois Central station on 63rd Street, under the tangled arabesque of the elevated tracks. I'd pass the scrutiny of a hooligan at the door and then walk up a dimly lit flight of stairs to enter a large, unadorned, and brightly illuminated room.

At that time of morning, before any of the day's races had begun, the room would be sparsely occupied. Aside from the cluster of employees preparing for the day's activity, there were a few early arrivals like myself, earnestly studying the long sheets tacked to the walls that listed the horses running at tracks across the country.

I'd find a chair along the wall and spread my scratch sheet and racing form across my knees. I'd diligently ponder the past performances of the horses running that day, their assigned weights, the jockeys riding them, the distances they would run. Each time I raised my head there would be a few more people in the room, a rising mutter of voices, a musty odor of shabby, worn clothing.

When the wire service announcer came on at eleven o'clock to record the first changes in the line posted the night before, the room was about half-full, suffused with cheerfulness and buoyant spirits. Men and women called gaily to one another, their voices sparked by anticipation. The disruptive defeats of the day before had been forgotten in the luminous dawning of a new day.

By noon the room was rumbling and crowded. There were grillmen from nearby lunchrooms, gravy and soup stains like badges on their soiled jackets; waiters who wouldn't start serving food until later in the day; ebony-faced redcaps from the railroad station; housewives with grocery money clutched tightly in their fingers; girls with bleached hair and rouged cheeks looking as if they had bounced all night and were exhausted; pensioners, sports, shopkeepers, the dispossessed and the unemployed, fleeing flophouse cot and soup kitchen coffee and roll, and pimpled, jittery youths with the first fuzz of beards sprouting on their pale cheeks.

As post time neared at the first of the tracks to begin racing, I'd rise and merge with the crowd, joining its fetid and yet compelling affability. We shoved in ragged, amiable lines toward the impassive ticket-writers sitting in a row behind the long table. After getting down our bets we'd straggle to form a tight, worshipful cluster of bodies and pale, vigilant faces beneath the loudspeaker. We'd stare up at the disk of wire netting as if it were a venerable idol from which we might conjure, by sheer force of our faith and longing, the benediction we yearned to hear.

When the loudspeaker cried, *"They're off!"* we answered with a constricted and explosive gasp followed by silence. With each call we swayed, prayed, groaned, or cursed. Some could not remain rooted in one place and shuffled like graceless dancers within the tight circles of space in which each of us was confined. As the horses entered the stretch, a fervent murmuring of hope and despair began, fading into the most unremittingly tense silence I have ever known. When the godhead announced its final verdict, we answered with a roar.

If we had won, we'd wave our tickets over our heads, informing all the others that we had triumphed, that sagacity and virtue had been rewarded. We'd push jubilantly toward the small line forming before the cashier, our tongues loose in the babble of gleeful children.

When we lost, we'd throw our tickets fitfully away, twisting in frustration because we had ignored all the pertinent data that pointed to the obvious winner. With each defeat we'd struggle harder to salvage the glow of our early ardor.

But we were given scant time to mourn or cheer. Other tracks began their races, the loudspeaker droning steadily of last-minute changes in odds, weights, and jockeys, horses at the post, races beginning. We rushed to place bets before the first call shut us out, waited, listened, whirled like dervishes before the confusion of several races starting at the same time.

And through the hours of the day, our pores exuded bile and sweat, hope and fear. Our cramped bowels hissed, a burning in our kidneys erupted sometimes out of control. But we accepted these debilities in others and in ourselves without disgust or reproach. We understood that the canonized purgings of these poisons evoked a catharsis that would leave us clean and guiltless once again.

By late afternoon only the final races at a few of the tracks remained to be run. The crowd was small again, the ones who had gone broke driven out. A few winners, very few, quitting while they were still ahead. Other winners still played, casual and loose in their victory. The losers with a little money left played desperately in the final hours to redeem the day. For until the very end, until the last horse had run the last course, a dream of tagging a longshot on which to finish triumphant was always possible.

When the loudspeaker had finally gone mute, those of us who still remained stood uncertainly in the large, nearly deserted room, our feet treading the carpet of shredded, discarded tickets that littered the floor. Finally, slowly and reluctantly, we'd move toward the door, looking back one final wistful moment at the room darkening under the silence and shadows.

Often, unwilling to relinquish the warm bonds of the day, we'd gather in bars and restaurants along the street, recounting endlessly to whoever would listen how narrowly victory had evaded us. A photo finish, the blocking or bumping of our horse around a turn, a jockey's poor ride, these were the broken records of our lament. On and on we performed our indignant autopsies until it was time to go out to the newsstand and meet the evening delivery of the racing form with the index and past performances of the horses running the following day.

Sometimes, pondering those capricious days, I remember old Gero Kambana. He was a white-haired old man with turbid and creviced cheeks dark as the bark of an ancient tree. For seventy-five of his ninety years on earth, he had been abstemious in all facets of his life but gambling. He had never married, never given any woman more than the embers from the fire of his true love. When I met him for the first time, he was almost blind and nearly deaf. But he sat for hours in a corner of the gambling room, absorbing the tension and excitement, now and then crying out at something he imagined he saw or heard.

I would place a bet for him and return to sit beside him while the race was run. He would stare from his bright almost sightless eyes at the sheets where the marker chalked the changes in odds, his ears pendent toward the loudspeaker over which the wire service announcer made his calls. All through the race, unable to distinguish the name of one horse from another, Gero Kambana sat trembling in his chair, his cheeks shaken in suspense. At the finish of the race I'd tug at his sleeve and make a sign close to his eyes letting him know whether he had won or lost. He hissed exultantly when he won and grunted a curse when he lost. I came to understand he didn't really care. The old man lived only for the ritual of suspense, the frenzy of gambling. The mystery was not in the beginning or in the end, but in the moment of play.

Was there ever a time, I have often wondered, when the old man could still have made a choice about his life? At what point were the patterns of his days and his nights set unalterably?

For a while I was certain that unlike Gero Kambana I could cease gambling whenever I wished. That facile boast reassured me even though the hours I wasn't gambling hung over me like a pall. I'd wake at night yearning for daylight. If I could not fall asleep again, I'd rise and study the racing form, trying to elicit shamanic vibrations as I murmured the names of different horses. Now and then, with a premonitory uneasiness, I swore if I made a killing, I'd quit gambling. I did not realize how ancient and benighted an oath that was.

Since I lost more often than I won, money to play with remained an incessant problem. I wheedled a few dollars at a time from Naka, made out false receipts for items supposedly purchased for school which I gave to my father, explaining that I had borrowed the money from a friend. I begged money from relatives and friends without the slightest comprehension how I would repay them. I sold my books and the books I borrowed from others. (The *Dialogues* of Plato was lost on a maiden named Marty's Choice, and Oswald Spengler's *Decline of the West* was lost on a filly named Carmela.)

Every item and artifact in our house I recurrently appraised in terms of the amount of money it might bring. Once I even sold a suit belonging to one of my brothers and suffered a stricken remorse as he searched desperately to find it. In this untamed period I came to understand the brutal dimensions of my obsession.

I had been dating Diana, a girl I had known from childhood, for a year and a half. Soon after the war we decided to marry. She knew of my gambling, but we were both convinced of the reforming zeal of love, anticipating that marital responsibility might be the raft on which I'd flee the whirlpool.

We rented a third-floor kitchenette apartment that had three windows looking out on a huge shadowed court of similar apartments. Diana found a job as a salesgirl in a downtown department store. I had an evening job in a neighborhood liquor store. We decided I'd look for full-time employment and meanwhile could spend my days reading and writing.

Following this program, we rose early in the morning and had breakfast together, and then I'd walk Diana to the 47th Street station where she'd catch the train going downtown. After leaving her I'd walk on to the Blackstone Library, a high-ceilinged and cavernous building. I'd locate a table in a corner of one of the reading rooms and assemble my books, pencils, and pads.

For a little while, in a flurry of eagerness, I read and made copious notes. An hour would pass swiftly. After it seemed to me I had been working through lunch, I'd catch a glimpse of the clock on the wall and be surprised to find it was only eleven o'clock. My attention began wandering. When I sought to concentrate, the words in the book blurred slightly before my eyes. I envisioned the gambling room, the early patrons and my cronies preparing for the zestful day. The first New York track began racing at about one o'clock and as the time dragged interminably toward that hour, I grew more restless. I pushed aside my books and leafed through a series of magazines and newspapers hoping they'd provide a halter for harnessing my interest. But in the oppressive silence of the library, a librarian's cough erupting like a minor explosion, I couldn't evade the ticking of the clock that swept like wind into the remotest corners of every room. I felt a constricting in my chest, a mounting panic that if I did not flee the library, I would somehow cease to breathe.

The first time I abandoned the library, the first of what would be countless times, I hurried along the street with my head down, guilt and shame burning my body. But when I entered that great, warm womb and lost myself within the tribe, my grief was aborted and spirit and joy merged once more in my heart.

The following year a good friend of mine and I purchased a small, dingy lunchroom in a factory and railroad district. As my share of the down payment I used the $1200 my wife had saved in three years of working before our marriage. In some cave of the winds I had heard that all any Greek (even one born in America) needed to grow wealthy in a restaurant was to possess a facility for rapidly opening and closing a cash register. After about a month, the long, tedious hours of labor an abrasive prison, I relinquished that sacrosanct mirage.

My parole began when I discovered a bookie operating in the railroad yards a few blocks away, his base of operations a small, shabby carpenter's shanty with hand-scrawled placards warning patrons not to urinate in the corners. Five or six times a day I'd slip down to the shanty to make a few bets and check the outcome of the earlier races.

The man who had sold us the lunchroom had been in the restaurant business for thirty years. My friend and I could not match his canny experience in buying or in salvaging the scraps. When we began to lose money each week, the long hours we were forced to work became unbearable. We decided one man should remain to salvage, if possible, the floundering wreck. We flipped a coin and I lost.

I managed to hang on a few precarious months by firing the cook and waitress and taking over their duties myself. I still retained a dishwasher, and when I wanted a fast jaunt to the bookie's shanty, easing my despair in the fashioning of parlays and daily doubles, I left him in charge of the lunchroom, an assignment hardly calculated to improve my business.

In the early autumn of that year we discovered my wife was pregnant. She worked a few more weeks and then had to stop. Without her salary to aid us in meeting our expenses, we edged closer to calamity. The crisis came in the first week of November when I lacked the money for the rent on my apartment and for the payment of the mortgage on the lunchroom.

On a few occasions in the past, to pay an overdue gas or electric bill, I had borrowed small sums of money from my father, money I knew he wasn't really able to afford. Since there was no place else to turn, I went to him again in November. Diana looked after the lunchroom while I rode a bus to my father's church. In his office, subduing my shame, I asked him for $150. That was a huge amount for him then, almost half a month's salary, and I could sense his distress. But he did not refuse me and had his secretary prepare an advance on his following month's salary so he could give me the money.

On the way from the church to the restaurant, the bus passed the gambling room on 63rd Street. Driven by an impulse, I got off at the next corner. I had about ten dollars of my own and if I could win $150 betting that amount, I might return the money at once to my father. Before entering the bookie's I sealed the envelope that contained my father's money and put it safely away in my pocket.

The first race I bet on seemed to confirm my anticipation of good fortune. I won $27. Another race was going off in a few moments with a sharp horse I had been following. Overlooked in the mutual betting, he was a tantalizing 10 to 1. I bet $30 on his nose to win. When he lost in a heart-wounding photo finish, raging at the taunting closeness of victory, I bet the remander of my own money on a horse that ran third.

Unwilling to believe that I could have come so close if there were not favorable portents swirling about my head, I went into the small, reeking washroom and took out my father's envelope. I opened it carefully and took out a ten-dollar bill, making a futile effort to seal the envelope again. My parched mouth could not infuse the saliva to moisten the flap. I hurried to make my bet as the race was going off.

When I lost that race, fearful of having to explain to my wife the discrepancy between the $150 my father had given me and the $140 remaining, I made another trip to the washroom and emerged to make another bet. When I lost once more, I abandoned all reason and restraint in a frenzied scramble to regain the money he had given me.

I remember that afternoon as one of the most deranged and fevered days of my life. My father's money, half his salary for the following month, slipped away until with less than five dollars remaining of his $150, I stumbled out into the cold twilight. It had begun to snow, a light film of white flakes settling across the city. I stood in the alley, under the elevated tracks, and cried then for the waste and debris of my life.

When I finally returned to the lunchroom, I found the door locked and my wife waiting in the shadowed interior. I knocked on the glass and she opened the door, her cheeks frightened and pale.

In the darkened lunchroom, sitting beside one another on the stools, I told her what I had done. That too was an anguish I will never forget, that confession of shameful infirmity to my wife carrying our first child.

Somehow we managed to keep from telling my father. We borrowed some money from my wife's sister and sold several of the appliances we had received as wedding presents.

In the days that followed I thought often of the old gambler, Gero Kambana, almost blind and nearly deaf, haunting the rooms where gamblers played. I saw the long terrible span of his life. In the brazier of his heart all other loves had grown pale and vanished under the brightness of a single consuming flame. In the end, hollowed and burned out, he was left without warmth, without love or hope, only loneliness and the savage riddle of thirty thousand days and nights.

Months would pass before I was free of my longings, months of small failures and tremulous fears. But in looking back I see that time as a kind of beginning, a renewal of my spirit when I understood I had to break free, because the alternative was for me to remain in a dark and corrosive bondage for as long as I lived.

X

The small, shabby lunchroom that I owned with a partner for a while and finally retained by myself had once been a barn in the younger days of the city. At certain dismal moments one could still smell the residue of horses that had somehow endured through a thousand scourings. In this porcine kingdom of four tables and twenty-three stools, a grease-blackened, coal-burning stove, and an octogenarian icebox built before the Civil War, I began a year of astringent unveilings.

My trade came mostly from the factories and railroads. There were also some hobos and drifters off the freights. Entering Chicago or stopping a while before moving on, they found my lunchroom a convenient spot for a cup of coffee and a bowl of soup. (This combination seemed to be the most filling and least expensive.)

They would wash the dust of a dozen states from their hands and faces in my battered kitchen sinks. Some were rascals and some were thieves and some were men made restless by their secret furies. It was hard to tell them apart, and in the beginning, they skewered me on the prongs of my own gullibility. I rapidly lost my innocence and became hardened to the endless tales of hardship, the interminable laments. I became less inclined to believe their stories, which were often graced with a bright versatility. Perhaps, like the wanderers of medieval times, they created a balladry of their own.

The man called Ed (I cannot recall the name he gave me then) came in on a Saturday afternoon. He was about fifty, of medium height, dressed in the drifter's shabby pants and worn jacket, neater than many others but unmistakably marked as a man down on his luck. He had thinning hair, a pale, tight-fleshed face, and eyes that glinted with the harried appeal of the wino. He managed the price of a bowl of soup, and I threw in a cup of coffee. It was a quiet part of the day, and in conversation he told me he was a chef, had been working at a hotel in Denver, had come to Chicago for a job.

I had a part-time cook, a taciturn Swede who prepared the few dinners I sold. I told Ed I could not use him. He lingered over his coffee, his manner growing more distraught, until during another lull he motioned me urgently back to his stool. He produced a baggage check from the freight department of the depot nearby, covering a suitcase he had sent on ahead a week before. In the suitcase were clothing, some books, and his chef's knives. There was a dollar and half due in storage charges, and Ed asked me to lend him the money and he would bring me the knives as security for repayment.

I wavered for a moment and then refused. My own situation was tenuous, the lunchroom business declining every day. I had heard some artful stories before and a number of times had been drawn into their nefarious web. A man gets tired of playing the fool.

I did not see Ed again for several days until an evening when he returned looking more harried and desperate than before. My dishwasher had left early that day, and there were some soiled dishes remaining in the sinks. Ed agreed to wash them. For a couple of hours he worked vigorously in the suds, afterwards swept the floor, growing more nervous as he sobered. I gave him the dollar and a half we had agreed upon for the two hours' work. I asked if he had redeemed his suitcase. When he told me he hadn't, I gave him another dollar and a half. He thanked me and left.

Several days later, early in the morning, when I opened the lunchroom, I found an envelope inserted under the door. The envelope contained Ed's baggage check, still unredeemed, an offering to compensate in some way for his violation of my trust.

I kept the baggage check in a compartment of my register for another two weeks, expecting him to return. When he did not appear, irritated at aiding his duplicity, I sent the dishwasher to the depot to retrieve the suitcase so it wouldn't be lost for storage charges. He returned with a shabby canvas bag, the lock broken and the clasps held together by a metal buckled belt.

For almost three months the bag remained in a storage alcove off the kitchen. Finally, one evening after closing when I was alone, I decided Ed wasn't ever coming back. I opened the suitcase.

There were pieces of drab clothing, a pair of pants, a jacket, and a sweater—a lot that would bring fifty cents from one of the used-clothing stores along the nearby Skid Row. There were half a dozen books, including copies of Emerson's essays and Longfellow's poems, a few dog-eared menus from restaurants where he had apparently worked, and a half-dozen butcher knives of fair quality. There was also a slim packet containing some letters addressed to him at a restaurant in Denver. Because I had a sudden, strange foreboding, I thought of burning the letters unread. But I opened them because curiosity overcame my apprehension.

The first letter, dated about six months before, contained a black-and-white snapshot of an attractive light-haired woman and a girl of about ten. They stood frozen in the solemn rigidity of snapshots. The woman was Ed's wife and the girl his daughter and the letters were from them.

I read them and then, swept by sadness, read them again, fitting them together like fragments of a puzzle. Ed was an alcoholic, and all his anguished efforts to overcome his illness had failed. In a desperate effort to battle it out alone he had left his home in Los Angeles, taken the job in Denver, keeping his home and family a treasure that he had to earn by curing himself.

Yet, each of his wife's letters grew more frantic, scrawled appeals and pleas, reminding him of their love, asking him to return; they wanted him home under whatever shadow there might be rather than go on living without him.

The last letter of the four was dated about a week before he turned up in Chicago. His route suggested he was not going home but running farther away.

For weeks after that night I considered things I might do to help them. I talked to a policeman who ate on occasion in my lunchroom, and he took Ed's name and description and passed it around to some of the men who patrolled the bars and flophouses of Skid Row. But I never heard anything from their search. Several times I walked the streets of Skid Row myself, staring into the faces I passed, the men huddled in doorways for warmth. After a while I wasn't even sure I could have recognized him any more.

I tried to reassure myself that he might have made it somehow, that the love of his family had drawn him back from the brink of his hell, but I did not really believe that was true. I thought, finally, of writing his wife and then had to accept the burdened truth that I could write her nothing to console her. Perhaps she'd even condemn me for not having made a greater effort to save him.

I can never be certain, but perhaps the final glimpse I was given of Ed might well have been the last time he was recognized on this earth.

It took about a year of the long weary lunchroom hours and the floundering for a slim margin of profit among the scraps of food to batter me into wretched defeat. Desperate to get out from under the load and assisted by the ministrations of a disreputable real estate broker named Pericles (how the mighty have fallen), I sold the lunchroom to a pair of old Greeks out of Halsted Street.

Zakinthakis was a chef, a creator of dishes in the tradition of elegant cuisine. His treasures included a set of venerable knives and menus from a dozen major hotels and restaurants he had graced with his skill. Having grown old and slightly deaf, he could no longer work in their gleaming kitchens, but he had lost none of his pride.

His partner, Pappas, was a small bald man with skin the shade and texture of hardened grease. Although he had never been more than a counterman in lunchrooms as shabby as my own, his wife's death had left him a modest sum of insurance.

Pericles, the broker, convinced the two men who were strangers to one another that an alliance of talent and money would be fruitful. He accomplished the miracle of my liberation by driving a hard bargain. There was a small down payment and the remainder of the purchase price (much less than my partner and I had paid for the place) to be paid to me over a period of three years. I also had to agree to work with the partners for the first couple of weeks. Pericles fled counting his commission.

From the beginning, the partners were ardent in their hatred for one another. Zakinthakis, contemptuous of the untalented lout fate had pushed upon him, took undisputed charge of the kitchen. He scrubbed and polished the old blackened stove until a surface emerged that had not been visible in years. He installed new rubber lining on the icebox doors. He discarded my mundane and uninspired menu and began creating delicious specialties of his own. The freight handlers and factory workers continued to order hamburgers and cheeseburgers and, despite the availability of some lovely raisin and sherry puddings, continued to request with implacable curiosity, "W'at kind of pie ya got?"

Pappas shrieked in fury as he paid the bills. Since Zakinthakis had threatened to sever both his ears if he stepped foot into the kitchen, he cried out his threats and imprecations safely outside the kitchen door.

I tried to talk to the chef several times and make him understand that perhaps the neighborhood was not yet ready for his cuisine. He listened politely but remained adamant. He would open new vistas of culinary pleasure for our customers. He admonished me against losing faith.

That was in the middle of December, and when word was passed to us that the factories would work full shifts on Christmas Day, Zakinthakis conceived a bold plan to prepare a Christmas dinner worthy of Maxim's or the Waldorf and offer it to our customers at the price they would pay for an ordinary dinner. In this way they would become ardent converts to the efficacy of our menu. Zakinthakis, out of his own pocket, paid for the printing of a thousand handbills announcing the sumptuous treat, and, ignoring the vehement outrage of Pappas, he set about preparing for the great day.

It was an astonishing experience to see the chef at work. He moved as if he were a Renoir or Degas among the cabbages and tomatoes, oranges and pears. Drab clusters of vegetables and fruit gained luster and beauty as they emerged from his hands. Driven by his faith into expecting a miracle, I washed the counters and tables and even polished some of the tarnished and battered silver.

In the last furious hours of preparation on Christmas Eve, an enigmatic and baleful quiet had descended upon Pappas. He seemed to sense that Zakinthakis had challenged destiny and he was content to watch and wait.

Christmas Day began slowly with a trickle of business involving no more than coffee and rolls. Several times, as the morning wore on, I noticed Zakinthakis in his clean white chef's hat peering through the partition from the kitchen. A few groups of customers entered for lunch, perhaps a dozen altogether, but as hard as I tried, I could not prevail upon more than one to order the special. That man ate the five courses quickly while reading his newspaper and paid without saying a word. We spent the remainder of the afternoon in a dreadful solitude. I sat at one of the tables while Pappas leaned on the cash register, his lips curled in a glittering smile. There wasn't a sound from the kitchen.

A little past eight o'clock, when we finally closed, I entered the kitchen for the first time since early afternoon. Zakinthakis was sitting in the corner beside the stove he had scrubbed and polished, his white hat folded in his lap. All about him were the untouched splendors of his dishes: the kettle of lemon soup, the trays of creamed and garnished potatoes, and the great garlanded ribs of meat. The look on his face was one of the most indescribable despair I had ever seen. Mute before his anguish, I took my coat and fled. Before I was even out the front door, Pappas had boldly entered the kitchen. I did not stay to hear his scornful shrieks, but I knew somehow, for the first time, Zakinthakis would not answer.

A day or so later they abandoned the lunchroom and I returned to salvage what I could. I sold off the battered fixtures to a restaurant supply house, and locked the door on the old barn for good.

For many years after that, particularly during the holidays, I remembered Zakinthakis. I reproached myself for a long time because I had not offered him a word of reassurance or comfort. But young as I was then, and not nearly wise enough in the ways of the artist and the world, what could I have said to console him?

XI

From Michigan Avenue and 61st Street, where my father's parish church was located, to the Woodlawn Hospital on Drexel Avenue is a span of about thirteen city blocks. My father passed the hospital on his way to church almost every day for twenty-six years. He died in the hospital after three months of confinement, on Memorial Day, 1951. I was in my twenties at the time, had been married five years with one son, my wife shortly to become pregnant with our second child.

For some years prior to my father's death, there had been dissension and bickering in the parish. Part of the turmoil was simply parish politics, one crafty faction seeking to impose their will upon another group equally as cunning. But there was also concern about the changing racial patterns of the neighborhood. Over the years, as the blacks slowly broke free from the rigid environs that imprisoned them in ghettos, the church became an island in a black neighborhood. Many parishioners, including prominent members of the Board of Trustees, felt the parish buildings should be sold and a new church and school built elsewhere.

In the beginning my father opposed any sale and move. He knew the painful efforts required in building a new church. He had been through that experience years before when the original church had burned down. While conducting services in a nearby small Episcopalian church, my father and a group of parishioners pursued elusive mortgages and loans to finance the building of a new church. Many years were to pass before the last of the oppressive encumbrances had been paid off.

In addition, my father did not share the apprehension of some parishioners at the complexion of the neighborhood surrounding the church. When the first black families crossed South Park, for years a dividing line between white and black residences and apartments, a group of agitated white landlords brought my father a petition to sign, asking property owners to resist the invasion by refusing to rent or sell to blacks. They explained that although my father was not a property owner himself, his position as priest of the large Greek parish would add luster and force to the catalogue of signatures. My father listened courteously and then told them if they obtained his boss's signature, he would be permitted to sign.

"Your Bishop?" they asked.

"The Big Boss," my father said. "Jesus Christ."

Despite my father's objections, the church was sold. Plans were drawn envisaging the construction of a million-dollar church-school complex, a proposal my father felt was extravagant and unrealistic. For more than a year the parish was without a church, the various liturgies and services being held in borrowed churches, until a foundation and basement were constructed on the new site. When the basement had been roofed, an altar and icon station were set up at one end, and services were held there. After the projected construction ran into financing and contract difficulties, for a while it appeared they might never rise above the basement.

There were members of the Board of Trustees who complained that my father was not fund-raising for the new church with sufficient energy and dedication. My father responded that the years of labor had taken their toll, he suffered from diabetes and hypertension. The arguments, constant importunings for money from parishioners and banks, as well as the fetid and damp basement, did not improve his health. Finally, he took a month's leave of absence that year and a few weeks off in the one following. When he was reproved by the Board for these absences, he reminded them in a letter that for the first twenty-three years spent as a priest of the parish, he had never taken a vacation. Now, his health and general physical weariness required he do so. Disregarding their continued grumblings, at the end of the year, with services still being held in the chilled and comfortless basement, my father requested permission from the Archbishop and the Board of Trustees of the church for a year's leave of absence so he could "regain my health." He felt that the parish duties could be, for the most part, performed in his absence by the assistant Rector. He also admitted his fervent hope that by the time of his return, they would have emerged from the "catacombs, where Christianity began more than 2000 years ago."

The Board of Trustees called a general meeting to consider my father's request. After voting, the membership approved my father's request for a leave. They also authorized a payment to him for the year of $200 a month. This amount rankled those who would have preferred not to pay him anything, despite the common knowledge that my father had no savings and no other source of income except his salary to provide for my mother and himself. My father was also warned by friends that a small but powerful faction hoped the leave of absence might become a wedge to prevent him from returning to his parish. He could not believe that so harsh and ungrateful a tactic could be successful. He felt that twenty-six years of devoted service to his church would weigh overwhelmingly in his favor.

A little over a year earlier, Naka dead, my other brothers and sisters living away from home, my father had suggested that my wife, my son, and I move in with him. We would save the expense of separate rents, and if he were able to go away to rest, he would not leave my mother and younger sister alone. From this agreement came our purchase of a small, old house about a mile from the church for $16,500.

Since I had nothing to contribute to the down payment but enthusiasm, my father cashed in the $4000 he had managed to save in U.S. Savings Bonds during the war. This amount, added to his slim equity in the cottage, comprised his total savings and estate.

In December of 1949, when he had been granted his leave of absence, and after we had been living together for less than a year, he wrote a letter of farewell to the members of the parish asking them "to pray for our parish and for me in your prayers," promising that he would return to them at the end of the year, strengthened and refreshed. He left for California shortly after Christmas and soon afterwards began writing us warm and glowing letters from the desert community where he stayed.

"In all my life I have never experienced a lovelier and healthier climate. The sun burns as if it were the middle of July instead of March. The sky is as blue as the sky over Greece I have not seen for so many years but can still remember. We are 3000 feet above sea level and surrounded by mountains. There are no flies, no dust, no clouds or storms. Only a clean breeze that blows into the spirit and purifies me. O I cannot tell you how lovely it is here and how much better it makes me feel."

When he left the desert for the ocean community of Huntington Beach, he sent back snapshots showing himself clad in a mackintosh jacket and a floppy-brimmed hat, proudly holding aloft a string of slim, meager-fleshed fish. They were slightly larger fish than he used to catch in the lake near the cottage. He had purchased a rod and reel since those days, but he never really mastered or enjoyed the intricacies of casting. He remained a quiescent fisherman all his life, a bamboo pole and worm-on-the-hook man who realized as much pleasure from sitting in a boat and contemplating the cork bobbing gently in the water as he did in pulling up his catch.

But his idyllic sojourn in those early months of rest were shadowed by letters from friends who told him of plans to prevent his returning as Rector of the parish. There were rumors that another priest was being brought from Greece to replace him.

My father wrote letters to his supporters pledging that with his health regained he would return and lead the fight against those who sought to oust him, to divide the community and besmirch the parish. In his letters to our family, he continued to write warmly of his surroundings, and yet he could not conceal his apprehension and his outrage.

> "I thank God that he has brought me here to cleanse me of the poisons I have had to absorb from these men," he wrote us in April. "I feel myself growing stronger every day. When I am well again I promise you that I will return and kick some of the empty cans that clutter up the church."

His determination to retain his parish and his position as Rector was not simply a matter or pride. If he were forced to retire, there was no social security for priests at that time and no provision for any kind of pension.

As the weeks passed and it became irrevocably true that a priest was being brought from Greece to replace him as Rector, retiring my father on the mythical fortune he had acquired during the years he had served the parish, he wrote us indignantly:

> "Write me!" he demanded of my mother. "Write me the names of those people who claim I am wealthy, that I own acres of land, farms and apartment buildings. Write me so I can write them and ask the exact location of all this wealth I am supposed to have!"

As his bitterness mounted, he pungently assailed the men he felt were betraying him.

"I know the leader well. He composes the letters that others sign. He is a man without love in him, without any emotional understanding of human beings. And the duck, the monkey, the parrot, the weasel, and the nanny-goat do his bidding. God will punish them!"

A few paragraphs beyond he would ask:

"Why are they doing this terrible thing? What have I done to them that now that I am sick, they want to throw me out? Why, why, I ask myself over and over, why, why, and I cannot find the answer."

A week later he was in the hospital with a cold grown harsh and menacing in his chest. He wrote to reassure us that the confinement was precautionary and not serious. In a line near the end of that letter, he wrote:

"Sometimes I feel so heavy a resignation I don't know what to do."

In October of that year he returned from California to Chicago to plan and, as he said, "take charge of my program to return to my church." He knew the priest from Greece had arrived and had been installed in the parish, and was conducting services. But there had been no formal notification to my father about the replacement. My father could not believe that when the year's leave of absence was over, he would not be allowed to return to his church. Meanwhile he waited, wrote endless letters, attended conferences with friends, sought support, argued and pleaded. He alternated between spells of brooding and of confidence, between fits of indignation and of helplessness.

On those nights when restlessness would prevent his sleeping, I'd come off the midnight-to-dawn shift at the steel mill where I had been working for some months and find him at the dining-room table in our house. There was his small black attache case on the chair beside him, and numerous letters and carbons of letters spread out before him. He assembled all the memos and correspondence concerning his leave of absence and his return to his church in the attache case. He carried the case up and down the stairs endlessly, from his bedroom to the dining room, even keeping it beside him at the small telephone stand when he made a call.

There was an evening when several family friends, one of them a young attorney, came to our house to discuss the situation with my father. My father once again recited his position and his complaint, his voice trembling as he read passages from the various letters, the evasive sentences from members of the

Board of Trustees, the noncommittal syntax from the Archbishop in New York.

At the end, the attorney, who was genuinely fond of my father, and who had become agitated through the recital, burst out.

"You want to know what legal position you got, Father?" the attorney cried. "You got shit! That's what you got, Father, shit! No contract, no guarantee they'll allow you to go back to your church, no pension or money of any kind if they don't want to give it to you! All you got is shit!"

My father understood English well enough to comprehend the miasmic composition of shit, and he nodded mutely and sadly. And the attorney, remorseful after his outburst, advised my father to write a letter to the Board of Trustees, informing them officially that he had returned from his leave of absence and was fully prepared to assume his duties as spiritual leader of his parish on January 1 of the New Year.

On the 18th of December my father notified the Board of Trustees of his desire to resume his duties at the beginning of the New Year as Rector of the Church that, he reminded them, he had served faithfully for twenty-six years.

Through the holidays that year, my father somehow managed to retain faith that things would work out all right, that duplicity and cunning would be vanquished. The Archibishop in New York would intervene on his behalf. The Bishop in Chicago would help him. Above all else, he relied upon the spiritual covenants he had formed with the members of his congregation. For more than a quarter of a century he had listened to their confessions, married their sons and daughters, baptized their grandchildren, spoken final words over their dead. He had shared the dark burden of their despair. If he were older, not as well as he had been, he needed their solace and support as they had so often needed his prayers and service. He knew they would not willingly forsake him, even as he ruefully understood that a group of wealthy and determined men were directing and leading the affairs of the parish.

"I am not asking for charity," he said over and over. "I want my justice. If I do not have the strength or the health I had once, neither am I worthless. I served my church for twenty-six years and they have no right to throw me out, unconcerned with how I live and care for my family. I want my justice."

In early January, the Board of Trustees met to consider the matter of my father's return. Two days later the mail brought the certified letter with their decision.

"The Board of Trustees carefully considered your request for reappointment as Rector of the Church, and carefully weighed the fine and loyal service which you rendered to the congregation over the past years, also your present state of health and your present ability to adequately serve the community. It was the resolution of the Board of Trustees that it would not be to the best interest of your health or to the best interest of the community to reappoint you as Rector of St. Constantine Church. The feeling of the members of the Board was that the requirements, duties and responsibilities of the position would impose too great a demand upon your physical stamina. The Board further resolved that as of December 31, 1950, your duties and responsibilities as Rector and your leave of absence would be terminated."

In thee, O Lord, do I put my trust: let me never be put to confusion.

"The members of the Board further considered your own financial requirements and resolved that you were to be paid the sum of $200.00 per month from January 1, 1951 to December 31, 1951, and that before December 31, 1951, the Church would again consider the financial condition of the church and your financial requirements and determine whether or not any further contribution would be paid to you. The Board of Trustees, as further recognition of your long, faithful and excellent service to the Congregation, resolved that you be designated as Rector Emeritus of the St. Constantine Hellenic Orthodox Church, and that your name appear as Rector Emeritus on all the stationery of the Community."

Deliver me in thy righteousness, O Lord, and cause me to escape: incline thine ear unto me and save me . . . for mine enemies speak against me; and they that lay wait for my soul take counsel together.

"The Board of Trustees further resolved that the foregoing provisions, pension payment and title were granted on the condition that you find them agreeable and acceptable, and were willing to abide by them, and that you would cooperate with the Board of Trustees and the Rector to the best interest of the Church and the Community."

Deliver me, O my God, out of the hand of the wicked, out of the hand of the unrighteous and cruel man.

"In order to conclude the matter and commence the payment of your pension at the earliest possible date, we would appreciate your acknowledging receipt of the original of this letter and indicating your acceptance hereof in the space provided therefor on the copy of the letter which is enclosed herewith, and returning the copy to the office of the Church in the enclosed envelope."

Cast me not off in the time of old age; forsake me not when my strength faileth.

"On behalf of the members of the Congregation and the Board of Trustees, I extend to you our deepest and sincerest appreciation and gratitude for the fine and excellent service which you have rendered to our Community in the past, and we hope and pray you will soon be restored to full health.

O God, be not far from me: O my God, make haste for my help.... Save me, O God, for the waters are come in unto my soul....

How many times my father read that letter, slowly and with effort, or had us read it to him, I do not know in numbers. But those first days after it arrived, we came to memorize each word and line as if they were a catechism. "What does that word mean?" he'd ask. "What does the line explain?" "Read that sentence to me again."

As we read and explained the sentences again, his pride and dignity suffered fresh wounds. He'd go alone to another room, to sit in the darkness for a while. We walked softly and gravely about the house, feeling the waves of his despair.

I was grateful to go to work, to leave the house for a few hours. When I returned home we'd be back at the letter once more. He'd ask me to read it to him again, trying in futile, whirling repetition to understand why he was being driven from the house of his Lord.

"What does that word mean?" "What does the line explain?" "Read that sentence to me again."

Through the remainder of January and into the early part of February, my father would not sign and return the letter. As a result he received no salary from the first of the year. He worried about the expenses of the house that he knew could not be sustained on my wages alone, or even on my wages and the tenuously renewable pension they offered him. He continued to solicit support, addressing urgent letters to the Archbishop in New York asking "for my justice."

In a final, canonized encyclical, the Archibishop wrote my father that settlement of the matter hinged on the question of whether or not my father was able to function, fully and completely, as Rector, performing all, not simply part, of his duties with unflagging energy and constant activity. He could not waver or lapse in servicing the economic, educational, spiritual, intellectual, and moral needs of the community. He must visit the sick in the hospitals, visit the homes and stores of the Christians for the purpose of preaching and teaching the faith and to offer his congratulations on their holy name days. If my father deemed himself able to meet this demanding schedule, the Archibishop first required the sworn affidavits of two competent doctors (to be selected by the Board of Trustees) who would examine my father and attest to his unqualified fitness to resume his duties (that would exhaust the strength of even a young, strong priest). The letter ended with the Archbishop's paternal and affectionate blessings.

A little more spirit was driven from my father's body, and he went through his days and nights in a kind of numbed and querulous wonder. Still he could not bring himself to sign and return the letter.

There was an afternoon in the middle of February when I sat watching television, my son playing at my feet, and my father came home. He had gotten a haircut and he took off his black hat and his shorn scalp made his head look stripped and misshapen. He sat down for a moment to play with my son, and I brought him his slippers and untied and removed his shoes.

"Is there any wrestling on the television now?" he asked.

I told him no, and he rose and walked upstairs slowly, to go to bed, he said, because he was not feeling well. He remained in bed for several days and then, feeling better, came downstairs for a few hours at a time in his robe and slippers. He'd sit quietly staring out the windows at the cold, bleak February day.

During this period of my father's confinement, the Archbishop from New York arrived to visit him. His Eminence had been informed his brother in Christ was ailing, and he swept into our house, robed and bearded, a benign and solicitous apostle of mercy. For almost four hours he and my father were locked behind the closed parlor doors. Afterwards the Archbishop emerged, invoking his blessings upon our house and upon us before he departed.

A few days later the last of the letters written by the Board of Trustees to my father arrived in the mail. The Archbishop had hastened to them with the joyous tidings. Expressing the Board's gratitude and sincere appreciation for my father's pledge of cooperation to the Archbishop, they were delighted to agree to certain modifications in their original letter. In return for my father's acceptance of the new priest as undisputed Rector of the parish, they would allow my father to officiate at Mass once a month, if he were able and so desired, also to perform baptisms, weddings, and funerals when the involved parties requested him. He would be, as they had promised, designated Rector Emeritus, his name appearing as such on the church stationery, and as evidence of their good faith, they enclosed the check of the church in the amount of $200.

My father went back to bed for almost a week. The doctors worried about pneumonia and made plans to move him to the Woodlawn Hospital. The last afternoon he was home, as we waited for the ambulance, a group of old women from the parish came to visit him. They sat in a row of chairs at the foot of his bed, the only light in the room a faint glow from a small lamp. When I entered the bedroom to bring my father one of his medicines and a glass of water and bent over him, I saw him watching the silent, dark-garbed women with a curious intensity. I realized then how much they resembled dark crows or ravens, drawn together in some ancient, premonitory ritual of a death-watch about his bed.

My father lived in the hospital for three months. They were months in which he endured unremitting pain, needles taped into his veins and iridescent bottles and coils strung like plumes about his bed. The flesh melted from his body until all that remained was transparent skin stretched tightly over a network of his bones. Yet, his anger and bitterness burned away, as well, until by the end he radiated an awesome tranquillity and calm acceptance at the imminence of death.

My mother absorbed the brunt of my father's confinement, spending the entire day, every day, with him. My sisters and I visited him at odd times during the day to sit with him for a while.

He had always enjoyed reclining in bed and talking. During the years we lived together, on those nights he was in bed and he'd hear me coming in the front door, he'd call me into his room. My mother might be up late baking in the kitchen and I'd slump wearily on the edge of her bed. Across from me in the other twin bed my father would read me a passage from a newspaper or book. Since he always regretted not having mastered English, there were English vocabulary and grammar books on the table beside his bed. Sometimes he'd ask me to listen as he read one of the lessons so I might correct his errors.

We made plans to work regularly at these lessons. He remained eager and willing, but I think he understood that I felt it was a chore, so we stopped after a session or two. But one of the books he carried to the hospital was an English vocabulary text. As if to make up for all the times I had avoided the lessons, I asked him to read from the text so I might correct him. He would try for a few moments, until weariness made him stop.

He talked, often, of California, his voice shaken with nostalgia for the sun and the desert, the clear, serene passage of days. I promised him that after he was well, we'd take my mother, my wife and son and move the family to California. The prospect of that seemed to please him.

There were many times, especially as the weeks went on, when drugs and pain rendered him inert and silent, I'd sit beside his bed, trying to find something to say to reassure him and myself, yearning to leave so I would not have to see his veins, swollen and purple along his wrists, the pulse that wriggled like a small dark worm in his forehead. Worst of all was the smell of decay like a rank mist from his body. I couldn't understand how my mother endured the endless hours she spent with him. After sitting with him a while, I'd lie to him about an appointment or an errand that prevented my staying longer. He never complained about my departures, never tried to detain me, but urged me to go and meet my obligations.

Sometimes I grew angry at the measure of his suffering, resenting his acceptance of the cathartic qualities of pain. When I lamented what he was being forced to endure, he reproached me softly.

"I have done things, harbored thoughts, spoken words for which I am ashamed," he told me. "Now God gives me a chance to clean myself of these poisons."

In accordance with that conviction he sent for men from the parish, men he had denounced as his enemies. He forgave them and asked each one of them to forgive him.

Still, incredibly, he clung to life. His body became a pale and pearly filament of flesh that the thrust of a finger might rupture. Through it all his eyes remained warm and alive, glowing with what he must have known were his final days of life. There were nights when the doctors called the family to the hospital, telling us gravely they did not expect him to survive the night. All of us believed them, except my mother, who knew my father best of all. We'd gather silently in the shadowed corridor outside his room, seeking to console one another through the long hours of the night. In the morning my father was, somehow, miraculously alive.

On those days he felt a little stronger, he enjoyed sitting by the window in his room, looking across the roofs of the buildings toward the faintly visible spire and belltower of the old church that had been sold. Since he no longer had the strength to walk, on these occasions I lifted him from the bed and carried him to the armchair by the window. His wasted body seemed to float in my arms.

On such a day, alone with him in the room, as I carried him the few feet from his bed to the armchair, he rested his cheek against my cheek. "As I once carried you in my arms," he said softly, "now you carry me."

He died a few days later, quietly in his sleep, a short while after my mother had left the hospital to come home.

For three days my father's body, attired in the gilded, colorful robes of his vestments, lay in state in a casket sealed under glass. For three days several thousand people passed through the catacombs, the damp basement of the church, circling his casket, crossing themselves, kissing the glass above his heart. Many of them were the parishioners whose confessions he had heard for more than a quarter of a century, whose sons and daughters he had married, whose grandchildren he had baptized, and over whose dead he had spoken final words. He had often shared the dark burden of their despair, and they came now in solemn, grieving lines to offer him their solace and support.

And like an awed and silent menagerie, the man without love in him, the parrot, the duck, the monkey, the weasel, and the nanny-goat took turns standing about his bier. I was swept with bitterness and fury at the sight of them, and for a while I thought of crying out against them, driving them away. I remained silent during those long days because I realized that if my father had made his peace with life, I had no sanction to carry hatred over into his death. I kept silent, also, because I knew nothing they had done to him surpassed what I had done to him because he loved me and was vulnerable before that love in a way he could never have been with strangers.

But I am grateful for those months of my father's dying, for those hours with him that I twisted to avoid, for they bequeathed me a compact of recognition. Nothing I had experienced in my life to the time of my father's death had grieved me more, no loss more severe for me than the pain of losing him. Yet, long after his death, I can clearly remember his pale face, his slender-fingered hands, his warm eyes, and the gentle whisper of his voice as he spoke longingly of the sun in the desert.

I have come to understand that in those anguished moments when we are torn by love and loss, a part of us stands aside, absorbing words, sounds, movements, the firmament of joy and grief, so it is never forgotten. And for a writer, this divisible yet indivisible bond between memory and the writing of stories makes a requiem of death and provides those who have died with a legacy that lives on.

To the very end and beyond, the old man paid me far more than he ever received from me, leaving the ledger of our lives together imbalanced in my favor.

And with each of my stories and books, I try again to make an entry and an adjustment on his page.

XII

I began writing casually, almost indifferently, when I was still a child, impressed by the rythms of words and by their effect on adults. During Thanksgiving and Christmas and Easter holidays, I scribbled quick, effortless poems that my father delighted in having me read before the captive guests assembled at our table. The verses were simple and artless, unsuspicious of any discordance beneath the surface of life. The first two lines (all I can remember, fortunately) of one such poem began:

Here we sit drinking wine at the table
From a bottle with a bright red label.

Barely literate, but from the applause my passionate recitation drew from my father and the guests, one would suppose my creation ranked beside the hallowed poetry of Longfellow and Tennyson.

The two years of my illness gave me the chance to read voraciously, garlanding my vocabulary with numerous words I could not pronounce, enabling me to accumulate a swarm of facts, events, and theories, all unmoored in the puddles of my imagination but there, someday, to be trickled into the stream.

I took for granted that I was going to be a writer. After my illness, confirming my expectation, I was designated storyteller laureate of my seventh-grade class at our parochial school. I was often called upon to read my stories before the class, and my teacher, with uncommon consideration for the literary sensibilities of my classmates, retained my readings for last.

When my turn came to walk to the podium at the front of the room, an unmistakable flutter of anticipation swept from the desks of the eager students. I would wait until the room was absolutely silent, meanwhile savoring the warm, admiring smile of a dark-eyed lovely plum of a girl sitting at a desk in the first row.

I'd begin to read my story, pitching my sentences slowly and carefully into the attentive stillness that gripped the room. At the end of the reading I'd steal a quick, longing glance at the plum of a girl in the first row, feeling my heart washed in the radiance of her cheeks. I'd walk back to my seat through waves of applause, affecting a demeanor of modesty even as one of my eyes, slitted and baleful, glared at some lout more restrained in his clapping than the rest.

These balmy and delirious triumphs were midnight snacks I retasted in the last few moments before falling asleep, my ears ringing again with the echoes of that heady approval. What joy, I thought, what jolly happiness was a writer's life!

Despite the fact that I had read enough of the old Greek tragedies, I could not divine that the relentless gods might punish hubris in Chicago as well as in Thebes. My retribution came one day at the beginning of the noon hour when my teacher asked me why I had no lunch. I was suddenly appalled at the banal flatness of having to answer, "I forgot it at home." My imagination took flight like a gull. I began explaining that on my way to school that morning I noticed a forlorn old man sitting in the gutter. Moved by his obvious misery, I asked him what was wrong. When he told me he had not eaten in two days, I gave him my lunch.

My teacher was so impressed by my unselfish charity she sent for the principal and had me repeat the story for him and the class. With a storyteller's fertile conjurings I added a number of flourishes. I detailed the man's wretchedness, his ragged, torn clothing, the broken seams of his shoes. I described his fingers trembling with gratitude as he accepted the bag of lunch, the tears in his eyes as he made an effort to thank me.

When I had finished the story, the class was so overwhelmed and awed that they neglected to applaud. The principal shook my hand firmly. The dark-eyed, lovely plum of a girl in the first row cried. I returned to a desk crammed with liverwurst, salami, and cheese sandwiches, chocolate chip cookies and Lorna Doones, gleaming apples, oranges, and one juice-glutted peach. I gazed upon the bountiful harvest and for a few moments believed the rewards were deserved, if not for the morality of my pretended action, at least for the versatility of my imagination.

I had no premonition of disaster when the classroom door

opened a few moments later and my mother entered. I was not surprised to see her, because she came to church often for a meeting or to visit my father. My teacher rose and greeted her warmly. And my mother handed her the bag of lunch I had forgotten at home that morning.

I have blocked the horror of the next few moments so effectively from my memory, I cannot honestly recall what took place. Perhaps it is best that way. Even in Greek tragedy, Medea murders her children offstage. I do recall, however, that the sheer immensity of my deception gilded my chastised head for months. In the schoolyard, hallways, and classrooms, I was pointed out with awe as "the biggest liar in the world." And for a long time after that fateful day, if I entered my classroom dripping wet, holding a drenched umbrella, and remarked that it was pouring down rain, everybody turned to look out the windows and make sure.

As I graduated from elementary school and entered high school, I continued in a euphoric assurance that if I never raised another pencil, or struck another typewriter key, publication and literary success would come whining like puppies at my heels, begging for the savory biscuits of my prose.

At about the age of eighteen, when my obsession with gambling began, my writing and dreams of literary success were submerged in more immediate excitements. This exile lasted until the second year of my marriage, after the abortive venture into the lunchroom.

I am not sure why I started to write again. Perhaps it came about as a clumsy, desperate effort to relieve the terror I felt about my life that seemed out of control. I started putting stories down on paper almost as a kind of religious ritual to exorcize my devils. For whatever the reasons, taunted with vague longings and frail memories, I tried for several dismal months to refurbish the confidence I once felt about writing. But I had lost the ability to bridge the chasm between reality and make-believe. The years of gambling had rooted me to the earth; the indulgent, undisciplined years when I fashioned parlays in place of sentences had scooped me out, left me hollow and homesick.

I also came, grimly, to learn the difference in the reactions to a child's composing of stories and similar endeavors by an adult.

In the steel mills, during the occasional night shift when the plate mill was down, I sat in the corner of the scheduling office and tried to scribble fragments of a story.

"What you doing?" a burly stoker asked me one night.

"Writing."

"Letter?" he asked.

"A story," I said, perhaps recalling the approbation the act had received from my classmates and family.

His big, open-palmed hand slapped my papers to the floor.

"What the hell are you?" he said harshly. "A goddam queer!"

I retrieved my papers silently, accepting his condemnation as containing a shame I could not perceive. After that night I learned to conceal my writing, and when questioned, to evade answering the truth.

I moved from the steel mills to work in the consumer complaint department of a firm that manufactured floor waxes and furniture polishes. In this environment I was encouraged to write.

> Dear Madam:
>   We received your letter of March 16 and were sincerely dismayed to read of your unhappy experience with our furniture polish. We cannot understand why the stains should not have been removed, but we want to assure you that we stand behind our money-back guarantee, therefore....

Sometimes on those afternoons when I pushed my baby son in his buggy along the lake, I stared across the haze above the water and wondered fitfully what legacy I might someday have to leave him. The task of writing seemed overwhelming, every small beginning fraught with inexorable labor and despair, my hands and heart useless, bungling tools. Since I could never succeed at writing, despite some pain, I relinquished my fool's dream by simply ceasing to write.

In an effort to rediscover a new direction, I resumed my schooling. I enrolled in evening courses at various downtown schools, studying history, philosophy, and the guitar. Because I had a fairly resonant voice, I considered the field of radio and television and signed up for courses at a school for broadcasting. I had classes in news editing, sports announcing, and dramatic writing. In the seventh or eighth week of the fall semester, one of the assignments in the writing class was a 1500-word story on a theme related in some way to Christmas.

For the first time in almost a year, I wrote a story again, composing it one evening at home and desultorily revising it the following night. I wrote of a waiter returning home from work on Christmas Eve, carrying a small pine tree and a few presents for his wife. Finding his apartment dark and deserted, he conducts a familiar search in the taverns along the street and finds his wife drunk with another man. He takes her back to their apartment and slaps her without any real fervor. Afterwards, remorseful, he carries her to bed, undresses and washes her, and sits beside her until she has fallen asleep. Then he decorates the tree he had brought home, spreads the presents he had bought for her beneath it, and goes to bed anticipating the few hours of warmth and pleasure they would share in the morning.

Several manuscripts, including mine, were selected at random to be read. When my turn came and I walked to the front of the classroom, I could not help remembering the buoyant journeys of my youth, my confidence and excitement. But the dark-eyed, lovely plum of a girl who once smiled at me from the front row was gone, in her place an austere-lipped, middle-aged man with tufts of hair sprouting like the stems of radishes from his ears. In that mournful moment, a century away from the playgrounds of my childhood, I read my story.

There was a long, tight silence after I had finished. I wondered, anxious and fearful, if the class so disliked my story that they had been rendered mute. As they slowly began describing their reactions, I understood with bewilderment and a massive relief that my teacher and the class had been intemperately moved.

In the excited discussion that followed, many of the students argued that the story must have been true, written from the anguish of personal experience, the only reason they could have been so affected. When I insisted the story was fiction, they simply assumed I was trying to conceal my shame and protect my afflicted wife.

After the class that night I walked the deserted winter paths of the park across from the school, staring at the street lamps that glittered frostily in the sluggish air. That night, the trees, and the cold formed a curious harmony in my body, a reconciliation between who I was and what I wanted to be. The years of digressions, impediments, and confusions were suddenly cleared away. I swore my soul and my hands to writing once again.

I was about twenty-four years old when I resumed the struggle to cast and fashion stories from words that creaked and strained like hinges and bolts rusted on a door sealed for years. Through a number of fitful and abortive spasms I managed to finish a story that I typed carefully and sent away to a magazine whose address and editor's name I had obtained from a writer's magazine. When it came back three weeks later, there was a small printed rejection slip clipped to the title page. "We are sorry...."

I wrote a second story, and then a third. By that time the first story had been rejected several more times and I retyped the frayed pages and sent them out again. I discovered the cursed expense of postage when an amount equal to that on the outside of the envelope had to be affixed to the self-addressed envelope enclosed within. As fast as a story was returned, I'd get it back into the mail again, hoping by sheer quantity to improve my chances of acceptance. But all that happened was that six stories returned as quickly as one. Besides the inevitable rejection slips, there were other indignities. One magazine took the first-class postage off my return envelope and replaced it with third-class postage. I imagined the vultures growing wealthy making similar substitutions on the thousands of manuscripts they received each week. When the magazine folded a few years later, I felt their punishment was deserved.

Over the months the printed rejection slips stretched out like the pages of a calendar. After about a year of futile submissions I was forced to accept the grim truth that my stories, singly or together, could not assess the value of a dozen empty pop bottles that littered the garbage, since the bottles could, if redeemed, at least bring a few pennies.

During this time, in order to live and support my wife and son, I stumbled through a procession of dreary jobs. I labored on the baggage platforms of the Railway Express, unloading mail cars with mufflers wrapped double around my ears and nose, a visor of wool futile against the stinging wind and bitter cold. After I quit, in an effort to melt the glaciers that rooted in the marrow of my bones, I went to work in the small, nest-warm shop of a tailor with yellow eyes and lopsided ears who taught me the rudiments of pressing clothes. That lasted until I nearly

expired inhaling the stink of steam floating up through dried
excrement and urine on men's pants. (You got a heavy foot, the
tailor told me when I resigned. Try castor oil and barley water.)

There was a brief stint in a drugstore, and then I answered an
ad for training as a typewriter repariman. Feeling that occupation suggested affinity with my desire to write, I went to the
factory where a cleark took me to see the plant foreman. We
walked through a massive shop containing several hundred
workbenches where men labored over the dismembered spleen
and glands of typewriters while others tested assembled
machines in an ear-piercing roar. The place seemed the
heartland of bedlam, the occupants a horde of madmen. The
foreman wasn't in his office, and the clerk went to find him. The
moment he disappeared among the benches, I turned and fled
back the route we had come.

That was one job I escaped, but there were others I caught and
lasted at only a few months. Part of the problem was simply that
I didn't want to work. The moment I landed a job I began
scheming for ways to justify quitting so I could salvage a few
weeks of writing full-time before going back to another job. The
irony was that when I finally quit or was fired, the insecurity
and pressing bills battered me into a morose immobility. I wrote
no more during these periods than I had written while
employed. And every time I returned to work I had to renew a
sardonic ritual of confession. On the application for new
employees, under the listing *Previous Positions*, I had to fill in:

Hired April 1946—left June 1946
Hired August 1946—Left December 1946
Hired February 1947—Left June 1947
Hired June 1947—Left September 1947
Hired December 1947—Left April 1948
hired June 1948—Left October 1948

Since there were rarely spaces for more than three or four
previous jobs, I kept running off the bottom of the application.
One personnel manager, after examining my record, looked
across the desk at me with a kind of awe. "Jesus Christ!" he
said fervently. "What's wrong with you?"

He was prudent to ask, since it was a question I often asked
myself. Looking around at friends and casual cronies, I could
not discern any pattern of employment remotely resembling my
own erratic flip from job to job. One of the fellows I knew had

gone to prison for stealing several adding machines from the offices where he worked, but even he had been employed with the company for five years before commiting the crime.

My family suffered through these reversals. My wife became adept at keeping the gas, electric, and telephone companies from discontinuing our services by telling them, "We have a sick child at home." She might have been referring to me.

And when my mother went to a tea or luncheon and met the mothers of other boys I had gone to school with, she'd have to listen to them expound on the achievements of their offspring. Eventually the conversation came around to me.

"Where is Harry working now?"

My mother would struggle to classify my current position in the best possible light.

"He's employed for a big company on Cicero Avenue," my mother said.

"Someone was telling me he's working for a brewery."

My mother nodded in resignation.

"In the office?" the friend might press relentlessly.

My mother accepted the fact that her position in the community as the wife of the priest consigned her to the truth.

"On a truck," she said.

If there is scant social approval for the aspiring writer, a greater dilemma exists because it is almost impossible for the usual creative writing teachers to teach the new writer to write. They can tutor him in grammar and direct his reading to the books of good writers, but they cannot teach him to construct a valid character or create a cogent story. He has to find his way through that twisting labyrinth alone by long and hard work.

I learned these grim truths, with one exception, when I signed up for courses in writing. The teachers were well-intentioned, haphazardly qualified men and women who had never written themselves (although they had degrees in literature and English) or were the authors of inspirational articles, obscure essays, memorabilia, gossamer poetry, and the history of lakes and mountains, towns and rivers. One adulated Virginia Woolf and scorned Ernest Hemingway. Another lavished inordinate praise on Henry James and sought to have us model our writing on his meticulous obfuscations. Still another teacher sought to funnel our diverse styles into a smooth, cloying farrago that would somehow adhere to the palates of the editors of *Woman's Home Companion*. I never completed any of the writing courses I began, and if there are benefits I somehow garnished from the time spent in those classes, they remain concealed from me to this day.

The exception I mentioned was a private teacher of writing whose office was in her home on the South Side of Chicago. Marjorie Peters, a writer and agent, was a slender, sensitive woman with a generous spirit who really cared for words and loved writing. For a number of months one winter I walked across the vacant lot that separated our apartments in Hyde Park to sit beside her on a couch spread with numerous pillows. An electric heater glowed at our feet to combat the chill of the rooms after the heat had been turned down. Weary from her own long day of teaching and writing, she donated several hours of her night, on many nights, gently endeavoring to impress upon me the need for discipline and self-criticism. Despite the relevant fact that I had no money to pay for these instructions, she helped me anyway.

The most difficult part of writing for me then, as it remains the most arduous to this day, was revising, the careful reworking of a story after the emotional explosion that produces a first draft. Writing in the heat of feeling was hard enough, but to return to the pages after the heat had cooled and see the words one thought diamonds and pearls become gimcracks and baubles is a somber and demoralizing experience.

To drill myself in these painful overhaulings, I borrowed or devised a series of exercises. Using photographs of men and women, country and city scenes, I'd begin by describing each photo in a paragraph of prose. I'd keep paragraph and photo in a folder. From time to time I'd select of the folders and rework that particular paragraph, expanding the visual description and introducing smells and sounds not visible in the photo but inherent in the scene. I'd also try to create an aura of the mood the scene suggested to me, whether of sadness or of joy. Then I'd grapple with the arduous problem of cutting, of reworking what I wanted to say in fewer, sharper words.

Yet, despite all my truncating and ripening skills, I could not sell a story. I continued to write them and mailed them off to the magazines. They kept coming back in the envelopes I enclosed with each submission. Most of the time the rejections were the impersonal, printed comments, but from time to time a reader or an editor penned a notation suggesting there was someone alive on the staff of the magazine.

Partisan Review said, "Sorry." *The Antioch Review* said, "Well told." *Redbook* Magazine said, "Nicely done." *The Sewanee Review* said, "My sincere apologies for my very long delay in reporting; I've been recalled to duty in the Navy and am finding it difficult to keep up with my reading." *Harper's Magazine*, with a printed rejection slip that included the sentence, "...the volume of manuscipts received is so great that we are obliged, for lack of editorial space, to decline many which are ably written and publishable," once returned such a slip rejecting a story with the words "ably written and publishable" underlined. In the margin someone had written, "Sorry we haven't time to help you. Good luck elsewhere." I treasured that rejection slip and for weeks carried it folded in my wallet.

As months went by and my submissions continued, certain editors began responding to my work with personally written comments. These letters and notes did not merely warm me by substituting a human being in place of the asphyxiating anonymity of the printed rejections, but by their clear, pointed observations helped uncover weaknesses I could not discern in my own work. I will never forget some of these editors: George Wiswell of *Esquire*, Esther Shiverick and Edward Weeks of *The Atlantic*, Eleanor Rawson of *Collier's*, Ray Russell and Pat Papangelis of *Playboy*, Paul Bixler of *The Antioch Review*. On a few occasions one of these editors suggested I revise my story and try them again. I set furiously to work, altering and reshaping as if my life depended upon the outcome. The revisions must have shown my desperation, because all were turned down.

Besides my wife, no one suffered as much with my labors as my father. Unable to fully understand my stories, his love mustered complete faith in my eventual success. He kept some of my manuscripts in the desk of his office at church. When visitors entered his office, he'd take the stories from the drawer as if, published or unpublished, they proved the existence of a mighty talent. "My son has written these stories," he'd say with obvious pride. "He's going to be a great writer someday. Out of respect for my father, the visitors discreetly kept their considerable skepticism about my future to themselves.

When my father died, he left a meager sum of insurance, less than $3000, plus the $200 a month his church had voted to continue paying to my mother until the end of the year. That sum and the insurance money dried up at about the same time, and the responsibility of house and family landed on my improvident head. Deprived of the bulwark of my father's presence, his soft, wry humor, his love and faith in me, I was a brawny and man-sized child suddenly thrust into the world alone. For the next five years I sought to replace my father as the mainstay of a house we were perpetually on the brink of losing, while continuing to write stories I could not sell.

If numerous frustrations stuck like the quills of porcupines in my craggy flesh during these years, few afforded me the sheer matchless misery I derived from our family business, begun by my mother after my father's death. Although the return was nominal, an average of about $150 a month, this amount paid the light and gas bills on the house and allowed my mother to send a few dollars each month to poor relatives and friends in Greece.

The business, which began modestly and thrived, was the preparing of large trays of Koliva, the boiled, dried, and sugar-garnished wheat used in the Greek Orthodox Church as part of the memorial services for the dead. As the wheat, when planted, sprouts from the earth, the Koliva symbolized the souls of the dead that would rise from their graves for rebirth and salvation. Through her capable and energetic labors in obtaining orders and making the Koliva, my mother helped numerous old friends rest in peace. If Death never took a holiday, neither did my mother.

Like a secret rite of some aboriginal tribe, preparing the Koliva required that the dried kernels of wheat be boiled in great kettles of water all day Saturday. The starch from the wheat formed a pungent, bubbling crust on the surface of the water which had to be skimmed off. The brew had to be stirred frequently with a long wooden spoon to keep the kernels from adhering to the bottom of the kettle. After the kernels had become tender, the kettle was lugged to the sink or a laundry tub, the viscid, sticky water drained off, the kernels rinsed a number of times, and then spread on large cloths to dry. That completed Saturday's labor.

Early Sunday morning my wife and mother began again. My mother browned sesame seed and flour in a shallow baking pan while my wife lined a large silver tray with wax and paper doilies. The sesame seed was mixed into the wheat, and then chopped walnuts, cinnamon, shredded parsley, and sweet white seedless currants were added. This mixture was then piled into a mound on the doilies of the tray. A half-dozen boxes of confectioner's powdered sugar were sprinkled over the mound and pressed down gently with wax paper to make a smooth and compact frosting of sugar. A cross and the initials of the deceased were outlined in the sugar and then slowly and painstakingly decorated with tiny silver dragées, each one placed gently to avoid marring the smoothness of the sugar surface. That completed the labor except for the delivery of the tray or trays to church early Sunday morning in time for the service.

That delivery was my assignment, an errand I performed sullenly, unwillingly, and resentfully, fearful of gusts of winds, squalls of rain, a hole in the street, a reckless driver in another car blithely unaware that a sudden stop could inundate and strangle me in a blizzard of sugar, nuts, parsley, sweet white seedless currants, and silver dragées.

To reduce the chances of such a calamity, my wife rode beside me, the tray of Koliva balanced carefully across her knees. When we had a second tray, she rode in the back seat, one tray on her knees while holding the rim of the second tray on the seat beside her. A third tray required us to make two trips until my son was old enough to join us. While driving the burdened mile from our house to the church, I evangelized zealously to my family on the sins of false pride.

When we parked before the church, I carried the trays, one at a time, up the stone steps. Other families arriving to attend church walked up the steps around me. Even as they greeted me pleasantly I envisioned mockery and laughter dragooning me from their eyes because my mother made and I delivered Koliva for the dead. Our occupation made of my family a cabal of vultures, a covey of ghouls. And I marveled that in all the journals and notebooks of writers I had read, none of them ever mentioned Koliva, which made the bloody wheat a rare and dreadful disease that belonged to me alone.

Through those years I came to hate the goddam trays of Koliva with a virulent passion. I despised every detail of the preparation. The boiling kettles filling the house with rank steam as if from a witch's cauldron. The tables aspread with the drying wheat. The mute, resigned labor of my wife on Sunday morning. Finally, the humiliating delivery of the trays to the church where my father had served with honor as the priest, where our family was known to everyone.

Sometimes, in a petulant revolt, I refused to deliver the trays. Then my mother engaged in a frantic last-minute effort to find other means of delivery. She phoned customers that I had taken sick, that my car had broken down, and asked them to pick up the trays themselves. The lies and the confusion, added to the complaints of customers whose clothing had been sprayed by sugar, were painful enough so that the following Sunday I returned, like Sisyphus, to the eternal task.

I tried many times to console myself that my wife and mother had the worst of it, that their labor was much more stringent and demanding than the brief time required for delivery. There was even a beneficial lesson in humility, I told my pride, if I only had the courage to absorb it. But all my rationalizations fled as I hurried with bent head up the steps of the church to deliver the glistening, ornamented trays.

I became so desperate that the death of a parishioner I barely knew caused me to mourn as if I were a member of his family. And one dreadful week when three members of the parish died, I was outraged at the lengths people were willing to go to embroider my humiliation.

In between the trays of Koliva I continued working at various jobs, and continued the writing of my stories. I made small, fitful advances. The critiques from editors on my rejected stories grew longer. I was encouraged and advised, but still not published. Over a two-year period I began, suffered with, and completed a novel. That bulky appendage joined my stories in the mail at a considerable increase in the cost of postage.

Publishing-house editors wrote me brief memos praising the novel's power, but clearly dismayed by the excesses, the lurid language and incident, the lack of discipline and control. I revenged myself by writing notes back to them, questioning their ability to distinguish poetry from prunes, suggesting they become plumbers in a colony of leeches. Fortunately, I retained enough reason so that I never mailed any of these letters. Finally, two editors whose opinions I valued and whose criticism I respected, Nancy Reynolds of the Atlantic Monthly Press and Dudley Strassberg of World Publishing Company, wrote me long, detailed letters defining with relentless clarity the glaring faults of the novel, advising me against any effort to salvage the book. Even as I unhappily accepted that what they wrote me must be true, I felt like a father with a deformed child, advised by well-meaning friends to strangle the baby and try again. In the end I put the book away forever, and consoled myself that I may have learned something about writing from the discarded 75,000 words.

On several occasions, wearying of the endless frustration, the ironic queries, "Are you *still* writing?" "You haven't sold anything *yet?*" I resolved to quit. I managed to maintain my decision for a couple of weeks, but the emptiness of my days gouged me more harshly than the disappointment of the rejections. I always began writing again, determined to make a fresh beginning, planning to destroy work I had done before that time. On one such night I entered our kitchen with a dozen stories in my hands and announced melodramatically to my wife and mother that I was going to burn them. Relishing my wife's distraught pleas for me to reconsider my awesome decision, I stamped down to the basement and flung open the furnace door. At the first terrible glimpse of the roaring fire, my resolve howled cravenly and fled. I quickly closed the furnace door. Then, unable to muster the courage to walk back through the kitchen clutching the unburned stinkpots of my prose, I hid the manuscripts in the basement to retrieve them after everyone else was asleep. Before my wife and mother I played the role of a strong and determined surgeon who had just amputated his own gangrenous right arm.

I do not believe that one story is suddenly good enough to publish and all the stories that preceded that one, worthless. More likely there is a gradual evolvement, a slow improvement, an absorbing and digesting of small skills learned through the process of writing.

I had gradually been turning away from the contrived sagas of pimps, whores, gunmen, and thieves, from the bloody and clumsy parodies of Greek tragedies. Little by little I had moved back into the experiences I was familiar with, the experiences growing up in my father's parish, the Greek immigrants tenuously suspended between the harshness of the acerbic city and the verdant memory of the land they had left behind them.

Slowly, painfully, and reluctantly, I think I had begun to understand and to accept that writing had to be approached as a profession. One does not expect to practice medicine, law, or architecture without years of study. Why should anyone suppose that the art of writing well can be achieved through some capsulated and abridged route? Mastering a blueprint, arguing a case in law, performing a delicate operation, might even be less of a herculean task than encompassing the schemata of pleasure and folly, misfortune and love, vice and elegance, perfidy, betrayal, vengeance, devotion. It is an undertaking as hazardous as seeking to capture the old man of the sea, the mythical Proteus who constantly eludes the grasp and forever changes shape and form.

For if the riddle of the player's art is how a man can so project himself into a play that he weeps for the anguish of the king, there is a greater mystery in how a writer reshapes into stories the dreams, joys, and terrors that have shaped him. As he works building this strange and haunting life within his life, the panic, fury, and desperation are driven out of him. Finally, he writes, as I began to write, with a curious calmness and resignation, no longer hopeful of anything, but content in those rare, matchless hours when my heart seemed a honeycomb of joy.

One of the last stories of this calmer period was one titled "Pericles on 31st Street." The story told of an old Greek vendor with a pushcart of hot dogs and peanuts, a defiant old man burning with pride in his heritage who teaches that pride to a group of storekeepers exploited by a landlord they were fearful of challenging.

In the early fall of 1956 I sent "Pericles" to *The Atlantic Monthly*. I had become, I thought, inured to the weeks and often months required for an answer. But as time went on I could not avoid inflating my hopes. I did so in spite of having learned from bitter experience that someone in the editorial department could be on vacation, an editor recalled into the Navy, or, the hardest blow of all, a manuscript had been lost.

I was selling real estate in Hyde Park that year, an occupation that allowed me greater freedom of movement but no more income than I was accustomed to earning. As the weeks passed after the submission of the story to *The Atlantic* and I received no answer, I could not prevent an occasional twinge of expectation, a sudden surge of hope I believed I had given up. By the end of the second month without an answer, I began bagging the days like peaches, taking a small, sweet bite from each one.

On the 17th of December, with the prospect of a bleak and lean Christmas before us, three months after I had submitted "Pericles," I wired Edward Weeks. I apologized for my impatience and pleaded with him to put my anxiety to rest. Were they seriously considering my story?

His answer arrived the following day, a telegram delivered to me at the real estate office, a telegram I could hardly open because my hands were shaking so violently:

YES. WITH SOME CUTS, WE BELIEVE YOUR PERICLES WILL QUALIFY AS A VERY AMUSING ATLANTIC FIRST. CONGRATULATIONS AND MERRY CHRISTMAS.
EDWARD WEEKS.

There are events like volcanic eruptions in the common filament of our months and our years, upheavals that leave us forever changed. Often they are clock-setting moments having to do with life and death. The radiance of my wife's face as she held our first son in her arms in the hospital bed. The ageless face of my father, moments after he died. And that instant in the real estate office holding the telegram notifying me that I had sold a story after almost ten years of writing and submitting stories remains an unmatched memory I will remember as long as I live.

I drove home to show the telegram to my wife and mother. My wife laughed and cried as she read the telegram over and over, sometimes aloud, sometimes to herself. My mother embraced me, told me to pray in thanks to God. My young sons, confused and a little frightened in the beginning at our shouts and cries, soon laughed at our laughter.

While my wife began the jubilant phoning of relatives and friends, calling my sister in Kansas and my brother in California, I started back for work. On the way I parked before the Rockefeller Chapel on the University of Chicago campus and walked into the silent and shadowed cathedral. I sat down in a pew near the back of the church.

I had struggled long enough to know that the sale of one story was only a beginning, that I would have to write harder than before, that for a long time I would not be spared the trays of Koliva.

But nothing could spoil that moment. I sat there alone and cried wild and grateful tears for the redeeming of my life, for, like Lazarus, the miracle of being reborn once again.

Journal of a Novel

Foreword

W e continued to live in our dune house through the period of the 1970s. Our son John attended and finished high school and our son Dean completed elementary school in Chesterton, Indiana. Early in that decade we had built a study above the garage of our house, easily the grandest working area I had ever owned. The room was high-ceilinged, the walls wood-paneled with broad beams and rows of tall windows. The vista of pine trees, sand dunes and water was so stunning I had to draw the blinds in order to work. But in that marvelous room which no other human being but me had occupied, I finished another novel, titled *In the Land of Morning*, that was published in 1973.

After completing that novel I formed a new publishing affiliation with Doubleday & Company through the efforts of a good editor there named Sandy Richardson, who had strongly supported my work. On the evening that Richardson flew from New York to Chicago to discuss what would be the first novel of the three books I had agreed to do for Doubleday, a bolt of lightning rattled the tail of his plane. When we finally huddled in the bar of a Chicago hotel, both of us solemnly agreed that the lightning bolt was an auspicious, Zeus-devised augury for our association.

During that salubrious evening we discussed a series of novels I had contemplated writing. Among them I spoke of a book I had been interested in writing for years and that I kept delaying, a novel on the Greek War of Independence. As with most other people who were not historians or of Greek ancestry, Sandy knew little about that epic struggle that took place from 1821 to 1830 and that freed Greece from 400 years of bondage to the Turks. He remembered vaguely the involvement of Lord Byron with the Greek cause. Lord Byron had indeed traveled to Missolonghi in Northern Greece and had died there during the struggle. But years before his journey, his poems had been stirring the conscience of Europe about the plight and suffering of enslaved Greece. Every Greek child in our parochial school had memorized lines from his poems that included the stirring stanza:

> *The mountains look on Marathon—*
> *And Marathon looks on the sea;*
> *And musing there an hour alone,*
> *I dream'd that Greece might still be free;*
> *For standing on the Persian's grave,*
> *I could not deem myself a slave.*

In addition to the poems of Byron and Shelley, there were other heroic poems about the nobility of the Greek struggle for freedom by Greek poets like Dionysios Solomos, who had penned the lines, ''Better a single year of freedom than forty years of slavery.''

March 25, 1821, was presumably the date the revolt started in Greece, and on the anniversary of that day for almost 150 years, in Greek communities and Greek parochial schools across the world, the children dressed in native costumes, danced and recited the heroic poems.

I had participated in these celebrations as a child, dressed in the white pleated highland skirt and beaded vest worn at Greek festivals, hoarsely shouting those stanzas before adoring parents and weeping patriots. In later years when I recalled the fervor of those events, I could never remember anything being recited about the brutality and cruelty exhibited on both sides. All that was stressed in the heroic poems was Greek valor and Turkish villainy. But by the time of my meeting with Sandy Richardson, I had lived long enough to understand that a darkness as well as a divinity existed in all human beings irrespective of nationality or race. I suspected that any effort to write a novel about the conflict would produce revelations for me that might scar the gilded, untarnished legends of childhood. Perhaps that apprehension had been among the reasons for the delay. No one longs to lose his myths.

Without underestimating the imposing challenge of the book, I had slowly and warily been preparing for the effort to write that epic. I had made my first trip to Greece and Crete in 1968 and had returned several times. Since then, traveling across the stunning Greek landscape of mountains, sky and water, I felt springing to life the legends and stories transmitted to me in my childhood. On Crete, the island where my father and my mother had been born, I journeyed to both their villages. I slept in my father's house, in the bed he had been born in, hearing the rain that night on the roof like the sighing of ghosts. In the dawn I stood on the terrace of the house looking up at the snow-crowned mountains he must have gazed upon as a boy, never dreaming of the long, hazardous journey he would someday make to America as a young priest with a wife and four small children.

Everywhere I traveled across Greece, I felt its mystery and magic. At Delphi I vowed I could hear the haunting voices of old oracles in the wind wailing from the ravines. My visit to Mycenae was on an overcast gloom-darkened day such as the one that might have shrouded Agammemnon when he returned from the war in Troy to be murdered by his wife and her lover. At Epidaurus, I sat entranced in the great theater and watched the *Oresteia* being performed by torchlight, that eerie, talismanic scene somehow unchanged from the play staged a couple of thousand years earlier.

Rilke, in one of his letters to a young poet, wrote:

> *Being an artist means, not reckoning and counting, but ripening like the tree which does not force its sap and stands confident in the storms of spring without the fear that after them may come no summer. It does come. But it comes only to the patient, who are there as though eternity lay before them.*

I felt that sense of ripening in Greece, renourished by a place I had never seen, but always felt existed in my memory and in my blood. Sandy Richardson, perhaps buoyed by the memory of Zeus' lightning and anxiously considering his return flight home, agreed with enthusiasm that was the book I should write.

I began my research on that revolution, entering what the wonderful anthropologist-poet, Loren Eiseley, had called "the necromantic centuries," that obsession with the dead of some legendary, heroic past. I understood the Greek lived to a greater extent in that hallowed past than many other nationalities. The grandeur of that tradition inspired them, and, in the case of modern Greek poets and novelists, burdened them by the need to articulate their own visions and voices in a landscape where even the stones of the ruins seemed to speak.

In my research I was aided immeasurably by modern Greek writers like Pandelis Prevelakis, Yannis Ritsos, George Seferis, Constantine Cavafy, Odysseus Elytis and others. But the writer who became my eyes and heart in understanding Greece was that greatest of the modern Greeks, Nikos Kazantzakis. In the brilliant translations of his work by Kimon Friar and others and in the stunning biography of his life and letters compiled by his beloved wife, Eleni Kazantzakis, his masterful books written despite adversity, poverty, famine and loneliness were an inspiration to me. Standing beside his grave in Herakleion, Crete, the stark stones and unadorned cross reflecting both the simplicity and yet the majesty of his life, I prayed for a fragment of his faith and strength.

Finally, on the matter of the use of a journal. Although I had read and admired the journals of many other writers, I had never attempted one of my own before. I assembled pages of copious notes that I returned to while writing. Now, starting what I suspected might be the most ambitious venture for me so far, the journal suddenly seemed a plausible tool to help me organize my research. In the beginning I planned it as a working chronicle, in which to make my notes, exploring viewpoint and voice, defining the focus of characters through what Eliot called "the lighthouse eye." If the writing of any novel is a series of probings, ponderings and apparently irreconcilable dilemmas, then the journal might be the place to write them down and thrash them out.

What I had not considered doing in the beginning and what consequently took place was that the journal also became a repository for my life and my family's life, with our own joys and sorrows, celebrations and journeys, illnesses and deaths. When the journal was finished three years later, the final entry in its pages was made on the day I completed the novel. Rereading it later I was astonished and awed myself at the ways the life of the writer and the life of the book had woven their fabric together.

I don't think I should say any more about it now. Like all writing, the journal of the novel that was published as *The Hour of the Bell* must, in the end, stand for itself. Perhaps, and that thought pleases me, it may make a new reader wish to read the novel, or one who has read it before wish to read it again.

1972

December 9, 1972
The ground outside my study is covered with frozen snow, the branches of fir and pine trees glazed with ice. Winter has begun as I make the first entry in this journal.

I have now completed three months of reading and research on the revolutionary novel, and have become so much more aware of the immensity of the work before me. While I was writing *In the Land of Morning*, this new book remained a vague, indefinable project somewhere in the future. There were flutters of excitement when I considered what the book might turn out to be, but there was no cohesive sense of where or how to begin.

This last summer in Greece changed that vagueness for me into something firmer. Leaving America so quickly after finishing *Morning*, talking with others about research on the revolution novel, I found myself in condition only to walk, sit, swim and soak up the stunning sun. But as with the earlier visits to Greece, so much I absorbed found its inexplicable way into plans for the book: the exquisite girl, Voula, who was apprentice to the Cretan sculptor; the grim shadows of Sugure Woods, where the massacre of Athenians by the Nazis had taken place; the courtesy of the taxi driver, John, on the island of Corfu; the ebulience of Mihali in Nauplion and the man's love for his son; the monolithic majesty of Deno's height and his strong, chiseled face which appeared to belong to an ancient Greek; the calm, resigned labor of people in the fields around the villages. All of these images have returned to me now as I plan the beginning of the work.

Then there was the day I visited the Historical Museum in Athens. I had stood in the high-ceilinged room that holds a score of large paintings of the great men who fought and died in the 1821 revolt. For a few moments I was alone in the room with them. Gazing up at their stern faces, swept suddenly by an eerie murmuring and whispering, I had a mystical feeling that they had been waiting for me. Across thousands of miles and nearly 150 years, over journeys and emigrations, through stirrings in the blood of my father and my father's father, we had come together, finally, in a configuration of our destinies so that I might save them. That may sound like a presumptious, inflated concept of my own talent. I don't mean it that way.

Kimon Friar, who worked with Nikos Kazantzakis on the sequel to the *Odyssey*, recently sent me a reprint of some notes and letters about his collaboration. Time and again Kazantzakis spoke in his letters of Kimon having saved him. He even offered up a prayer for Kimon's well being. "If the *Odyssey* is ever to be saved, I shall owe it to you," Kazantzakis wrote to Kimon, "because it would be unjustly lost if it remained in Greece. May you keep well that you may help me not to die."

That is something of the way I feel about those myth-laden giants who dwell in ornate frames on the walls of the museum. I remember their names from the March 25 holiday programs of my childhood: Kolokotronis, Botzaris, Diakos, Kanaris.... We recited the epic poems without understanding what we were saying. But that poetry must have left a resonance inside me then, for I have the task to save them now by returning them to life in a book about that savage ten-year struggle that ended four hundred years of slavery for most of Greece. Few people besides the Greeks know anything about that struggle. Some vaguely recall that Lord Byron died in Greece during that war, but the only records remain the histories and the commentaries that reveal Greece as a pawn of men like Metternich, who could ask contemptuously, "What is Greece?"

To my knowledge there has never been a major novel in English written on that conflict. Certainly the epic does not lack drama. As the good historian, Woodhouse, points out, in a single battle pitting a handful of Greeks against a band of Turks, everything is contained that exists in larger wars. There is the fanaticism, the cruelty and the chivalry, the small scale of action enlarged to heroic dimensions by the rage and devotion of simple, often unlettered men who became leaders of the people. They fight their battles against a landscape of mountains and passes that felt the tread of Persian armies and Roman legions thousands of years earlier. The fabric of jealousies and betrayals, of treacheries and vendettas remains the same.

I am challenged and frightened, sometimes overwhelmed by the immense canvas that must be filled. A part of me wants to hurry and a part of me warns to go slowly. I have had moments in these past months when I cannot believe I will have the strength, discipline and ability to finish this work. Yet I have other moments when deep in my soul I feel as if all the years I have lived have been moving me toward this book.

Like a novitiate about to enter a monastic order, I yearn to temper my spirit and discipline all the excesses that plague me, the resignation and the melancholy, the self-destructiveness and the drifting. I know that before I am through I will work as I have never worked before and suffer as I have never suffered before. But I am sustained by remembering the marvelous moments I have had in the past, when deep in the life of a book, I entered a domain of joy, a rhythm that borrows from all those who live and create.

I have begun this journal to set down a record of my progress. These are not to be daily entries, which may have me making up words about the work that are not needed, but they will be the steps of the journey, the exploration and the search, the ways a book is born. Perhaps, then, this journal may someday become a book with a life of its own. Even if I am unable to complete the work, this record of a journey toward failure may have some value.

Having begun, I will have to wait and see what role the journal plays.

December 10
A magnificent day! The earth is covered with snow that sparkles on the evergreens and on the boughs of the trees. From my windows I can see the caps of the waves breaking in across the beach along Lake Michigan.

I woke this morning feeling energetic and garlanded with enthusiasm. I wish there was some way to nurture or store these emotions for those dismal days when the work seems overwhelming and every effort is a burden.

Steinbeck wrote of proceeding slowly, a step at a time, one hour and one day at a time. That is how it must be done or the immensity of what I am attempting to do will render me immobile.

I have written a few random pages, some fragments of scenes, but they read like the drivel of an emotionally disturbed novice. I discard them into a meager little pile on the corner of my desk. When I finished *Morning* I had three-thousand pages stacked up beneath the bronze sculpture of the priest on my desk. From those efforts the final 300 pages had emerged. God, how many pages will join this small pile before the work is through?

I have decided to begin with a priest, in a village whose location remains uncertain at this time. Perhaps the town will be in a region that feels the first stirrings of war. The character of the priest will assist me in making the transition back in time and across the ocean to a land that still remains, in so many ways, strange to me. Suddenly that seems a logical step. I have always felt an affinity to priests because of my own father's occupation. I have a sense of how the lives of priests embody in sharper extremes the lives of most men. They have the same feelings and suffer the same dilemmas, but because of their role as shepherds of their flocks, they are under more intense pressures. In moving to Greece for my novel, I am taking my priest along as a companion and a guide. Even if I may not be familiar with the village where he lives, the parish he serves or the parishioners who are his flock, I am aware of his soul, his burdens and his anguish. That fate of a priest has not changed.

Shall I begin today? The fact that I have broken away from the work to write these notes suggests I am soliciting delay. A stack of blank paper sits on the right side of my desk. I have cleaned my typewriter keys and roller and have put in a new ribbon. The old one wasn't really worn but I have the feeling that the darker the print on the paper, the more impact I feel in the words.

I went downstairs for another cup of coffee and to make a couple of phone calls. Back to my desk to stare at the typewriter again. A beginning becomes less probable as the day wears on.

December 11
This morning I heard the news that Mark Van Doren had died. Although I had been with him only a few times and exchanged no more than half a dozen letters with him, I felt he was a generous and considerate friend. He had done a splendid review of *Pericles on 31st Street* when that book of stories was published. He had been gracious and encouraging in each of his letters to me. Last week, not knowing he was ill, I had written to wish him a good holiday season and to send him our love.

When we first met him at dinner in the Chicago home of his son Charles, he had struck me as a man radiating a great serenity, a poet who had discovered peace of soul and accepted gracefully the coming of age. He was a delight to hear and to be with. We were not close enough for me to know what physical or emotional debilities he suffered in these last years of his life, but his death fills me with a pervasive loss.

The death of someone close brings us to an awareness of our own end. I am a few months from fifty now. There are times when I consider that milestone with apprehension, as if that suddenly will push me into some front-line province where death is more active. I have written of death and age often. I think I understand something of that writ of dismissal, but who can say with what rage or resignation or fear one meets finally with death? Mock-heroics will be of little use then.

As I grow older, the shadow of what Kazantzakis called "the god in the black helmet" grows longer about me. His mobility increases as my own lessens.

December 12
One of the main problems in any historical novel is authenticating the setting. When I locate a character like Matsoukas or Father Naoum along Halsted Street in Chicago, I am so familiar with the street and the city, the sights, smells and sounds, shops, billboards and traffic, that I need not pause to think about them.

But when I move a village priest down a dusty path in Greece in December of 1820, I have to familiarize myself with all the unknowns of his surroundings. What do the houses look like? What are the materials of which they are made? What are the habits of the villagers and the patterns of their work? What do they plant and what are the seasons of the year for sowing and reaping? How does their day begin? What food do they prepare? What are the Greek and Turkish customs of the period? All these questions must be answered.

I am not writing a sociological tract, but in order to concentrate on my story, on the relationship of my characters to one another and to their community, I have to know all the details of their lives. I must absorb their environment well enough so that it flows through their movement, posture and speech.

Another essential problem in these early stages is the matter of control: keeping a flexible but firm rein on characters until they develop a life and force of their own. Later on they will become real enough to guide me with those marvelous flashes of character that are part of the creative process. Then they will begin to demonstrate feelings and to act in ways I had not planned but which are plausible for them.

One letter of good news today. Doubleday has extended my advance through next year, beyond the period called for in our contract. It is a generous action which will help relieve me of some of the perpetual burden of the assorted bills.

December 15
I awoke this morning to another heavy snowfall, the earth and pines obscured in a swirling of heavy flakes. From my study I have a sense of being confined in some lofty cloister, my room suspended in a world of tumbling white snow.

I began the novel, finally, on the 12th—a faltering, rudimentary start that is no more than a skeleton of what I hope the section or first chapter will hold. The priest is in his village and through him I set the scene and the time. I am working along tenuously now, trying a paragraph like a slim, fragile bridge to determine if it has the strength to carry me forward. When I stop after several hours to consider what I have written, I am disheartened. Yet I know from the writing of my previous books that this is the process.

Characters are like strangers who become dear friends. I see the priest vaguely, his face and figure not yet clearly defined, moving in a maze of shadows. As he responds to other characters I will grow closer to him. Even as I labor to fashion him, I draw on the other characters I have created to reassure myself that I can do it. I am consoled by Angelo and Tony in *Lion at my Heart*, Kostas and Katerina in *The Odyssey of Kostas Volakis*, Matsoukas in *A Dream of Kings*, Gallos and Asmene *In the Land of Morning*, all the men and women I have brought to life answer my entreaty when I call on them now.

I am faced with the problem of recreating a world and of populating it with people. That's all.

Oh, God....

December 18
One more week until Christmas. I feel curiously lethargic about the prospect this year and am not certain why. On Christmas Day all the vast segments of the family will gather here and we will eat, drink and laugh, the children running about and screaming in a bedlam. Even with the rampant disorder, I always enjoy the day. Except for this year. Perhaps I resent the interruption now that I have begun, weakly and hesitantly, to write.

Yesterday I finished the patchworking of the first section or first chapter on the priest and the village. There are almost forty rough pages. The transitions are awkward, but I think it is undeniably a foundation.

With the work on the section fresh in my mind, I can reflect on my working methods. I keep returning to a patchwork quilt, arranging the patches in patterns without sewing them into place, so they might be moved around to make a better design.

I wrote the opening pages, then jumped to the end of the section to do the final pages, the priest in the village cemetery gazing up at the mountain and seeing the signal fires. Then I returned to the middle scene where the priest goes to bless the men who are leaving in the night to join the mountain fighters. Finally, I wrote the scene where the priest visits his Turkish friend, the farmer Ahmed Bajaki, whose young son, Hassan, enters the room.

Having finished these fragments I had a sense of the cycle of the section. Afterwards I realized I had omitted the introduction to the renegade monk, Papalikos, important because later he plays a principal role in the intrigue at the monastery of Aghia Lavra.

I finish the day by writing an eight-page section in which the monk appears in the small village church at the end of a service on Sunday morning. Afterwards he sits and drinks with the priest before resuming his journey. It is potentially a good scene, with the demonic and licentious character of the monk becoming evident. Much more work will be needed to sharpen and define the complexity of his feelings towards the impending revolt and towards violence, blood and death.

December 19
I am at my desk again this morning. I clean my typewriter keys and roller again, insert a new ribbon, choose a different color paper than I used for the first drafts. Although I count this a second draft, certain scenes have already been written and rewritten five or six times. But I am moving through the whole section again.

The analogy of the patchwork quilt comes back. I do scenes or patches and then set them in a particular order, switching them around, hopeful that some pattern of continuity and design will help me along. I feel my way along in this stage, unable to grasp the section as a whole, but continuing to shuffle and alternate the scenes. Perhaps the quilt is not the best analogy:

"labyrinth" might be more apt. It is an inextricable maze that I stumble through slowly, seeking a glimmer of light that will bring me to some magic central chamber where the meaning of the maze becomes clear.

December 23
Two days before Christmas and a difficult time to work. Yesterday afternoon Dean and John and I went to do some shopping and ate together. We had a good time and there is that curious joy I receive from looking at my dark-eyed, and black-haired sons. Is it simply a sense of pride and love, or the continuity of generations, the feeling they represent parts of me that will live on after I am dead?

The war overshadows everything these days. Work and holidays are darkened by the madness of the Christmas bombing of North Vietnam on a scale that dwarfs any bombing in any war in history—saturation bombing that must be killing hundreds if not thousands of children, women and men. The barbarism of the action defies explanation. Just before the election the administration claimed that peace was "at hand." Kissinger said an agreement was 99 per cent complete. How brazen and hypocritical that statement seems now!

Even if one grants an honest anguish to Nixon at what he feels must be done, how can we live with any victory based on such destruction? We must pay for it someday.

I am driven by a need to write about it, to shout a protest with all those others who are protesting, to rush out and join them in the streets. Yet I also have the feeling that I must stay with my work. The book is what is most important in the long run. Passions and events will flow into the tide of what becomes history. Nixon and the generals will die and even the dead will be forgotten. But the book may live on, making its point on the inhumanity of man to other men. The war today makes me understand something of the pain of war.

The lake below my windows and the dunes has begun to freeze. Small peninsulas of ice extend into the water from the shore. With the partial freezing a stillness settles across the beach. It is as if the water, so turbulent and rough these last weeks, has grown slumberous and yearns to sleep.

I will try to work for a while longer, adding some details and transitions to the chapter. Later today a young man will come to see me whose work I have seen and commented on. He had his first story published last month in *Mademoiselle*. He is a talented, energetic young man who visits me with the veneration reserved for an elder statesman in his golden years.

December 29
Christmas has come and gone. The bombings in Vietnam continue making a mockery of the season we celebrate. Harry Truman died and was buried in Independence, Missouri. There were eulogies on the fact that he was a "People's President." I think he was probably a fairly good President, but I wonder if history may not record him simply as the man who ordered the dropping of the first atom bomb.

I have been working along slowly, arduously, on the opening chapter. The pace at the beginning is painstaking, yet it is necessary to write and rewrite these opening pages before I can move on. It is like the foundation for a building. If that isn't sturdy, the building will fail.

On Christmas Day our nephews and nieces, their children, my sisters and their children came. Diana served dinner for almost forty. In the midst of the pandemonium I remember how many years we have joined in this way on the holidays. My good nephews grow a little more expansive and affluent each year. The children get bigger. At the end of the day we have all enjoyed ourselves even if we are exhausted. I have come to understand over the years that it is in these family relationships that I have often found my material. Kostas Volakis, Matsoukas, Angelo Varinakis, their wives and children...all have in some way been drawn upon our families.

Yesterday I worked part of the day and in the afternoon Diana came up to my study and we made love. How drained yet fulfilled I feel afterwards. We lay together on the couch and I thought of the death of Harry Truman and the pages of my book in the first stumbling stages and my body warmed by love. The tides of love, work and death: in the end that is the Trinity of a man's life.

1973

January 1, 1973
It is the morning of a new day at the beginning of a new year. I am swept with resolutions and expectations. Nearing fifty, I remain hopeful of overcoming my frailties and my foolishness.

I have set down my resolutions once again, many of them unchanged from the resolutions I made last year: losing weight, exercising every day, working harder and longer, practicing the guitar, ignoring the arrival of the mail until dinner so I do not work with one ear cocked for the rumble of the truck. Over the years my hearing has become so attuned to that sound I swear I feel the vibrations when the truck is still a mile away.

All the resolutions are like a proclamation of excellence. Yet I know that many will fall by the wayside without even a respectable period of observance. I will worry about my failures later; meanwhile, this morning, things look good. The water is blue—the waves surging in against the frozen columns of ice along the beach—the sun is shining, the air is clear, sharp and brisk. My breakfast was a spartan glass of orange juice and two cups of coffee and then I took a long walk up and down the dunes. Afterwards I showered and came up to my study to work. I am, for the moment, vital, strong, resourceful, ascetic!

The secret, I think, is not to grow discouraged and resigned as one begins to slip from this level of excellence, but to fight every inch of the decline, like a frantic mountain climber struggling to hang on.

It is hard to know what this year will bring—what will be the triumphs or calamities and how the work on the novel will go. Above everything else work on the novel will be the substance of my life this year and next year and perhaps the year after that. That will be a different rhythm from the one involved in the writing of short stories, where one seeks to sustain the burst of lyrical energy only for several weeks until the story is finished

With the novel a certain pacing must be established, an approach that calculates the passage of many months and alternates moods of drudgery and excitement.

January 4
For several days the weather has turned warmer and the ice given a chance to thaw. Yesterday, for the first time since the New Year, the sun emerged from the thick clouds, reminding

me in a feeble replica of the sun of Greece I saw and felt last summer. Today the sky is gloomy and overcast again, the sun hidden once more, the wind blowing gusts across the ground, the air turning colder.

These last few days I have been slowly revising the first pages of the first section. As I redraft, new possibilities arise and I fill them in. I have added the burial of the church bell at the order of the Pasha of the province, "to ring for the souls of the Christian dead as a reminder of the benevolence of their masters." The stage is set more clearly in the description of the priest's house, the village square and some of the characters. In the early stages, the people and the land they occupy exist in a haze. Revision helps clear away that mist and I begin to see them more clearly.

Now the first section has also grown too long to stand by itself. I have decided to divide it into two sections, about twenty-five pages apiece. The first section as now planned will describe the village, introduce the priest, and end as he speaks with the youth, Manolis, before he departs to the mountains to join the guerilla band of Vorogrivas.

I have also been reading a good deal in the last few days. I know that many other writers refrain from reading any other writing while they are working, but I find other good work nourishing. My brain is so full of my own story and my own characters that ideas pop into my head as I read. I don't take characters or scenes from the other writers but find them stimulating my own thoughts. Those thoughts may have nothing to do with the book I am reading but I am sure a relationship exists.

Perhaps my urge to read as I write—everything from Rollo May to Kazantzakis' *Report to Greco* to Edmund Wilson's *To the Finland Station*—relates again to my willingness to speak of my work in progress. Many writers zealously guard what they are doing for fear of dissipating the drive and ideas in idle conversation. But as I describe scenes in my story to friends, I find myself ornamenting and adding as I speak, verbally revising before an audience. That may go back to the tradition of the storyteller, the spinner of tales, creating his stories before a living, responsive audience. Sometimes I even surprise myself, thinking I knew the tale and then discovering how it changes while I relate it.

Of course that same capacity for ornamentation makes me a prodigious liar. I understand that and over the years have tried to restrict my lies to stories, never using lies to enhance myself or to harm others. But when it comes to the stories, I am less concerned with the truth than with the tale.

January 5
The first finished copy of *In the Land of Morning* arrived in the mail yesterday. David McKay has done a lovely job of book-making; now we will see how well it sells.

As I hold the finished book in my hands, I see it as a culmination of all the long months of work, the scattered and discarded pages, the writing and rewriting, the moments of despair when the writer feels the book will never come to fruition. Then there are the months of waiting for the galleys to arrive and the months after that to see the completed book.

When my first novel, *Lion at my Heart*, was published in 1959, we lived in a suburb of Pittsburgh in a small house on Provost Road. Mark and John were small then, and our last son, Dean, had been born just a few months before. When the book arrived on a Saturday morning, we celebrated by marching in a triumphal procession around the house. I marched in the lead, holding the book aloft as a priest would hold aloft the chalice of communion, the two boys banging pots behind me, Diana bringing up the rear with the baby in her arms.

Since that festive day I have received that first book eight times, never with the same wild celebration but with undeniable pleasure. Somehow the finished book has survived the precarious process of creation. Afterwards there are other problems, sales and reviews, criticism and praise, but for one matchless moment the book has accomplished the immensity of the journey from dream to reality.

I think there is also a fragment of eternity attached to each book. That speculation may seem foolish because books can be burned, the plates destroyed, the text forgotten. But having been finished and published, the book makes a small, frail claim on the future, a tiny down-payment on immortality.

January 17
There has been no entry in this journal for almost twelve days now. They have been dreadful days when I have worked poorly,

doing little more than walking, reading, and pondering. Forcing myself to remain at my typewriter, I do a sentence and a paragraph over endlessly—fifteen times for the opening page of section two, sixteen times for the second page. The morning passes into afternoon. The mail arrives, my decision not to look at the letters aborted in my eagerness to distract myself... perhaps to unearth a particle of good news. When I return to my study and my desk, the remainder of the afternoon slips and fritters away. The day is done except for an hour or two I might salvage after dinner. The day is done and I am one day closer to the end of my life.

There are days I want nothing more than solitude, exile from my house, from Diana and my mother, from relatives and friends. I yearn for a series of uninterrupted days in which to work. But the prospect distresses me, as well, because I am bound to my family, love them, and, perhaps, need them close to me. The work on the book causes me tension as well. The project grows and I understand how much strength and vision I need. When I lose the excitement, I also lose the conviction that I can do this book. That is a terrifying and disabling prospect.

Today, for the first time in these last twelve days, I wrote well. There is nothing yet nearing a finished draft but some scenes are drawn with power. I wrote a scene between the priest and the monk based roughly on the character of Papaflessas, the demonic monk of the war of independence. In place of the commandment, "Thou shalt not kill," the monk affirms the new commandment: "Learn to love the fire." How many revolutions have been betrayed by leaders who mask their hunger for violence and murder in noble slogans and heroic symbols?

This has been a good day, for which I am grateful. I cannot spare the energy or the time for many bad days, nor can I afford the immobilizing hopelessness that comes with depression. Then the simple effort of raising my hand to strike the keys of the typewriter, becomes fraught with tension. Even my nerves resist, my heart and soul refusing to respond.

I will try to make tomorrow a good day as well. In that way, placing the bones of one day on the bones of the next day, I may someday make a book.

January 21

I have now worked through five or six complete drafts of the first two sections of the book. As I had originally planned, I opened the first section with the priest, Father Markos, at the end of a day of labor sitting outside his church watching the twilight. He meditates on the villagers and their way of life. The first omens of trouble are only hinted here. When he enters his house to cook his meager evening meal he is visited by two men who ask him to come at midnight to bless some of the villagers who are slipping away to join the mountain band of Vorogrivas.

The second section began with the priest in church early Sunday morning and the description of the service and parishioners. Afterwards Father Markos is visited by the monk Papalikos, who has abandoned the cloisters and is on some vaguely-described journey. He talks of the new commandment, ''Learn to love the fire.'' The scene ends and the priest goes to the cemetery, where he seeks guidance and reassurance from the bones of his ancestors.

In rewriting these sections I saw that an imbalance dissipated the growing tension. I had the feeling the monk's visit should be a climax, followed perhaps by the midnight blessing of the men going into the mountains. Perhaps the first section could remain fairly quiet and the second section begin with a storm, a driving rain, a strong wind assailing the village. The monk might appear out of the storm. While the wind howled and trembled the house, the monk and priest could sit before the fire and talk of the impending war. That scene might be the bridge to the scene in which the villagers take the oath of the Society of Friends before leaving for the mountains. That scene, in the shadows of the storehouse, could be followed by the priest visiting the cemetery, praying for some guidance from his dead, and, finally, seeing the signal fires on the towering mountain.

I work on these early sections slowly, with endless revisions. yet, every change may lead to other changes, so that beginnings and endings whirl around like a tiger chasing his tail.

It is too early yet for any soaring rhythm of work. This stage is plodding and relentlessly slow.

Painful and slow...slow and painful. There isn't any other way it can be done. That is the agony of a book.

January 28
After a lapse of two weeks of balmy and unseasonable weather, today winter returned. High winds and sleet have dredged up the lake so this morning I woke to the roaring of the water.

Friends were driving from Chicago to have dinner with us today but we postponed their visit because of the inclement weather. I have written instead and, perhaps for that reason, have put in a good day's work, the best in a week.

I worked on section one, reshaping the structure and movement of the scenes once again. I begin now with the priest in the village of Kravasaras. He rests outside the church in the twilight ruminating on the land, the people. Then he goes to visit his friend, the Turkish farmer Ahmed Bajaki. I am not sure at this point what will remain in the book or what will be rejected but the scene where the Turkish farmer talks of his love for the village and for his son is a gem. Certain scenes ring right from the beginning and that scene is one of them.

That section will end with the priest in church on Sunday morning, watching the pageant of parishioners, the old women like a cabal of witches, the patriarchal old men, the young men, the young women and the children. The section will end with the priest praying to God to make him strong so he might look after his flock.

The section following will be on the storm, the first meeting with the monk on his mysterious journey. Sitting by the fire, he will talk with fervor of the coming bloodshed. Then the final section will cover the midnight oath-swearing of the Society of Friends, ending with the priest blessing the men. The last pages will have the priest, unable to sleep, walking to the dark cemetery where the bell of the church has been buried. He will see the signal beacons on the mountain and those tiny flarings of light will form the transition for the following section, which begins in the mountains.

It has been, all in all, a good, productive day. The study is like a protected nest, the water roaring down below, the sleet striking the windows. How I yearn for a series of such days in this room.

February 1
It is another unusually temperate day for this time of year. After dinner this evening I walked along the dark beach, a flashlight throwing a beam before my feet. Now I am back in the study

and it has begun to rain in spite of the number of stars that were visible in the sky.

I finished a solid draft of section two this afternoon, climaxing the best week of work I have had since beginning the book. But even a good week of work is no more than a flashlight to guide my steps for a while in the darkness around my characters and my story.

Section two begins now with a fierce storm battering the village for several days, the priest huddling by the frail warmth of his fire. With a wild gusting of wind, the monk comes out of the storm to spend the night. This treatment is much more effective than the original scene that had the monk join the priest in church on Sunday morning, less static and more dramatic. After the monk's visit I show the villagers continuing in the pattern that prevailed before. In this way the priest can have his fears momentarily eased and can delude himself that perhaps the ominous winds of war will blow away.

Tomorrow morning I begin a totally new section, the one dealing with the bandit-guerilla captain, Vorogrivas, in his stronghold on Parnassus. It will be a difficult section requiring the recreating of the mountain fighters who never accepted the despotic rule of the Turks.

Afterwards there will be a section on the islander with his mystic feeling for the sea, who will become—like the legendary, Kanaris—master of the *brulot* or "fireship" the Greeks used to fight the heavier Turkish frigates.

Then there will be a section dealing with the wife of Prince Petrobey in the wild, male-oriented Mani, where the birth of a son was heralded as the arrival of another "gun."

All of these sections will be difficult, ambitious, challenging. Will I be able to pull them off?

February 12
There has been no entry in this journal for eleven days. Although there have been some working hours, there has been disruption and anxiety, even a few days of desperation again. In addition to the problem of the book's beginning, I have been waiting daily for the check from Doubleday that has not arrived. After a month of reassurance that it is coming, has been ordered, we received word that it required special approval. So I will sweat out that approval.

Meanwhile I have tried to keep working, making a tentative beginning on section three dealing with the guerilla captain, Vorogrivas. Although the thirty-odd pages of this section are still in a rudimentary stage, I have found a marvelous, leonine old character named Boukouvalas, an aging captain who had once led the band. I even know the heroic way he will die.

The main difficulty remains my inability to encompass the design of the book so that I know where the parts will fit properly. That is what makes writing so hard: to begin with a blank page and after struggling to fill it face another blank page and set down words and sentences on a series of pages. It is all fragile and uncertain markings made with a stick in the sand so that wind and water may erase them swiftly and leave one pathless. That marvelous rhythm I can recall with the earlier novels may be delayed or never arrive (God help me) with this book because of its complexity and length.

What I have accomplished so far is that at odd moments, at dinner or reading or visiting with friends, a line of dialogue pops into my head, a flash of a scene appears. That shows the book is at work inside of me. I must refine some of these rough nuggets while seeking the vein of pure gold.

These last few days the earth has been lovely under a clear, blue, and cold sky. Last night the moon, filling its earlier crescent, shone with a stark beauty across the lake.

Today the P.O.W.'s started home from Hanoi. The TV cameras invaded the houses of their families, showing the reaction of wives, parents, and children when the faces of their loved ones flashed across the screen. Every last quiver of longing and joy was communicated to millions of eager viewers. Even though I resent the intrusion—I feel like a voyeur—perhaps the years when we shared nothing but the grief and anguish make it mandatory now that we share the joy of those few who gain some happiness from that dreadful war.

February 13
Although the process of writing a book, drawing on the intuitive and the conscious, must remain fluid and not tightly structured, knowing where and how to end is a stunning advantage. In a book as panoramic as the one I am writing I had not dared to expect any light toward a conclusion for a long time.

Then, this morning, after working on section three about an

hour and a half, my eyelids grew heavy and my limbs weary. I left my typewriter and reclined on the couch, drawing the quilt across my legs. I don't recall sleeping. Perhaps I dozed a little, drifting on the waves of music playing softly from the record player.

I lay there thinking about the book and a scene unfolded for me—a scene perhaps taking place at the end of the revolution after ten bloody years of war. There is a schoolteacher in a village school trying to make his class of young children understand what has transpired. He talks of the great battles on land and sea, the struggle of devoted men, the tides of ambition, betrayal, heroism. He pours out his heart in an effort to make them understand the price that has been paid for their freedom. At the same time he feels a futility because they remain restless and inattentive.

In that moment I remembered an exquisite story from Nikos Kazantzakis. A village schoolteacher in Greece, haranguing his young pupils, is distracted by a bird that comes to perch on the ledge of the open window. The children and the teacher fall silent as the bird sings a melody of beauty that transcends words. The teacher understands that his rhetoric is like the flailing of wind and that the bird's song is Greece.

Suddenly, overwhelmed and excited, I knew that I had my ending. I wasn't sure where the scene would take place, who the schoolteacher would be, but I knew that was the way I would finish. The teacher would comprehend the futility of words to capture the vision, falling silent before the bird's lovely song.

In that awesome moment of revelation, I believed the story from Kazantzakis had been sent to help me, to provide me a beacon, a lighthouse eye, that might, in time, draw together the disparate strains of the book. Swept by gratefulness, I began to cry, feeling once again my links to some force of roots and faith that sustains me like comrades as I plod on my weary and often perplexed way.

February 16
A heavy snowfall fell during the night. When we woke this morning the shrubs along the drive were crested by a foot of snow. As I shoveled the short span from the house to my study I saw the frozen perimeter of the lake along the beach. In the still-

unfrozen water, chunks of ice were hurled about by the waves that surged and fought as if resisting the final effort to imprison them.

I had a good day of work today as I finished a full draft of section three on the mountains and the guerilla band. Once again the direction and emphasis I planned has been altered by the writing. Captain Vorogrivas is overshadowed by the character of the old guerilla captain, Boukouvalas. In the final scene of the section he sits before the fire and tells the men about Suli and the women of Zalongos. When he describes the women, trapped by the pursuing Turks, dancing with their children in their arms and then leaping to their death from the mountain peak, his power dominates the section.

Reading the scenes this afternoon to Diana, I was surprised how well they move. Yet I know this is still an early draft needing numerous revisions. The arrival of the young Manolis Kitsos from the village has not yet been included. Tomorrow I begin another draft that will have to include him. Perhaps in the scene when the old captain Boukouvalas tells his story, the young newcomer can listen to him with admiration and awe. Vorogrivas, watching from the shadows outside the circle of the fire, might feel the stirrings of jealousy. That must be handled deftly, revealing the perplexity of feelings Vorogrivas has toward the boy. I think Diana is right in suggesting that his first reaction should be one of a father for his son. The awareness of a physical attraction must come later.

I read somewhere that the way Dylan Thomas wrote his poems was to start each revision from the beginning of the poem, writing and rewriting from beginning to end. That is the way I rewrite my chapters, from the first page, repeating even those scenes that seem all right. How much shorter and easier it would be if I could go directly to the places where the revision was needed, since so much in the draft remains unchanged. But as if I were a runner who needs to return to the blocks each time he stumbles on a hurdle, I have to keep going back, building up a rhythm that propels me along.

A writer can spend years hoping to discover shortcuts to make the act of writing less arduous and slow. He will find that no such shortcuts exist. If we grow as human beings, looking upon the complex world with a maturing eye, the process of writing can only grow more difficult.

February 19

How tangled are the feelings we sustain about the aging of those who are close to us.

Tonight, as we were finishing dinner and watching the news on television, my mother came and sat in the rocking chair. Short, fat, all her energies required to push herself in and out of bed, or to move from room to room, she carries with her an aura of resignation and depression. One can wish her alive, enjoying even the meager satisfactions she has remaining at 86 and understand at the same time that she would be better off dead.

Looking at her now I remember her as she was once, full of vigor, strength, acerbity. I remember her standing like a sentinel beside my father's hospital bed during those last months of his life. I remember her in the kitchens of my childhood, assembling pots and kettles, a dozen brewings and bakings going on at once.

Now she has become a sour, unhappy old woman. She is slipping further and further into her haunches, walking in a curious curvature, almost like a hunchback. She whines about the house being too cold, complains about this, laments about that, terrified to face the few hours when we might leave her alone. She needs company, people to talk to her beyond the contact with us. Company and activity have always been the blood flow of her life. In the isolation of our house in the dunes she languishes, living hopeless as a prisoner. I understand her distress and try to be patient, but she weighs like a mountain upon Diana and only slightly less upon me because most of my day is spent up in my study. What can we do with her if she is not to live here with us? My nephews and nieces would be willing to take her for brief spells but she does not want to go. If there is any justice, she deserves some attention in her decline. She deserves consideration for the years she has worked and served so many people, for the unqualified love she has always given us. If it were not for the flowing of her passion and her blood, none of us, sons and daughters, grandsons and grand-daughters, great-grandsons and great-granddaughters, would be alive.

But all my worthy resolutions weaken in her disgruntled presence. She is just one more of the burdens and dilemmas that disrupt our lives.

February 26

It is Saturday afternoon and we are waiting for good friends to arrive from Chicago to sit, talk and eat with us. The day is a lovely one, the air as sweet-smelling as a day in early spring. Most of the heavy snow which fell last week has thawed and the ice floes float like miniature glaciers in the grey-blue water. I am sure there is much more winter before us, but a day like this one comes as a harbinger of spring.

There is a comfort in being washed and dressed in clean clothing awaiting the arrival of friends. The table is set, the kitchen is warm with the fragrant smells of Diana's cooking, the washbasins are scoured, clean towels hang on the racks, and there is a festive ambience over every room.

This morning I worked a few hours on section three. I have been struggling with this section of the guerilla camp all week and have managed to bring in the volunteers from the village. I wrote the first meeting between the handsome youth, Manolis, and Vorogrivas. In the ride down the mountain to raid the Turkish convoy, I try to show the effects of that meeting on Vorogrivas. For the first time in his long years of war he feels afraid without understanding why. But on the threshold of love, life becomes precious. Not understanding this change that has taken place in him so swiftly, he hurls himself into battle recklessly, scorning a wound or even death.

I have had second thoughts about the way to end the section. In earlier drafts I have old Captain Boukouvalas at the campfire relating the exploits of the women of Zalongos, but perhaps I need to dwell more on Vorogrivas and Manolis. I must write several versions of the ending and test them against each other.

Above all I must take care that I only lightly touch upon the captain's feeling for the youth. It must be an attraction that has not yet become desire—the first quiver of love only a crack in the spirit of that stern and disciplined man, but a crack that suggests the demolition of the world he has known.

I usually work with the blinds drawn because of the distracting panorama of pines, lake and sky. Today, anticipating the visitors, I have drawn up the blinds. Looking across the splendor of the landscape is soothing to my senses. I love this study, my typewriter, my books, and my music. If I leave it for travels elsewhere, the travel should be temporary, so that I can always hold before me the prospect of returning to this haven once more.

March 2
Today I completed the fourth full draft of section three, with many more drafts for individual scenes and pages. I have worked for two and a half weeks on the section and I still feel it is too loose. I will decide by Sunday whether to begin still another draft of the sections or go on to section four which tells of Leonidas Kontos on the island of Psara. Even if section three needs additional work before I move on, I have begun to feel more secure in the characters of Boukouvalas, Vorogrivas, and the youth Manolis. Even discarded pages and rejected drafts serve a purpose in the structuring of character.

The last few days have had temperatures in the forties and fifties, strange for this time of year. Tonight in a drizzling fog I walked for almost an hour, a flashlight sweeping a beam before my feet. Seeing the slopes of sand on either side of me, I imagined myself in the mountains with Vorogrivas, the two of us trudging back to camp. I spoke to him, and then felt a flutter of fear because I thought I heard him answer.

Tomorrow I drive into Chicago to speak to a luncheon gathering at the Art Institute. After all the lecturing I have done and will probably do in the future, I resent speaking now. These lectures interrupt my work and the value of my days now must be measured by how much time I spend at my typewriter. The social side of my nature must be made submissive to the private side that needs to write. Later on the social side may have its revenge!

March 6
Last night a morbid, shattering dream woke me. I recalled running through the darkness, a terrifying, directionless flight from something nameless that pursued me. For a long time I could not get back to sleep. Then this morning I woke with a pressing ache in my chest and feared I was having a heart attack. The other symptoms began to appear, chills and my palms sweating. I stayed in bed for a couple of hours and when I finally rose to phone the doctor I felt weak and ill. He told me he did not believe the symptoms were a heart attack but I made an appointment to go and see him tomorrow. Meanwhile the pain has remained with me all day, not becoming any more severe but simply a steady ache.

The same fertile imagination that functions to my advantage

in writing serves me badly here. I move as easily into the condition of illusory illness as I move into the make-believe of
characters and story. It is hard for me to separate the reality
from the fanciful.

Even as I grow calmer, accepting that I was not suffering a
heart attack, I could not work. The day passed for me in a
curious and resigned nostalgia. The temperature rose into the
sixties and the sun came out, the air smelling of ice and sand as
if warning them to prepare for the season of thawing.

Our eldest son Mark was here, preparing to begin rehearsals
tomorrow on the children's play he will be doing at the Ramada
Inn. We sat together on the terrace, reading and talking a little.
When Diana returned from shopping she observed that I
resembled some fabled invalid buttoned up on his porch,
catching the final rays of the expiring sun.

This evening I walked for a long time, breathing deeply as if
seeking to draw life-giving air into my body. I heard the sound
of a train in the distance and saw the stars glittering brightly in
the sky. I felt myself a boy again, in the country under the stars,
waiting for the train that would carry my father to me. I
remember him, dead now for so many years, and his memory
and memories having to do with my childhood swept me with a
wistful sadness. There were the scents of other springs, the fear
of the morning evoking earlier fears.

Is it a fear of dying? Perhaps. A fear of leaving before my work
is done. Maybe. Yet I have moments when the thought of death
is appealing, those days and nights when I feel a weariness that
sleep for a single night will not refresh.

I will remember and use this day—a lovely day shaded by the
resignation and nostalgia my fear and distress imposed on
me...almost as if I were at the end of my life and were being
given one final lustrous and fragrant forecast of spring to
console my end. Whether that is true or not, I will remember
and use this day.

March 17
Today the fury of winter returned. The water is heaving and
tumultuous, the waves battering against the retaining walls,
splashing over the rims. The black, menacing clouds gust sharply
across the sky. Far out in the lake the water is black and choppy.

I have been working on the sea and island section for a

number of days now but have not worked well. The mail is disruptive each day as I await the first reviews of *In the Land of Morning*. There were some fine reviews, one mildly unfavorable one, and then a venomous, malicious assault in the Sunday *New York Times* book section. I have never met the reviewer, know nothing about him, and find it hard to fathom his hysterical outpouring of poison and invective.

Perhaps it is the fury some of these death-directed pygmies feel when they are confronted with life in a novel, life that sustains some love and hope. They live in cages of their own disorders, embittered psychotics who cannot transmute their conflicts into art and envy those who can. Unleashing their venomous fury vents their frustration.

I remember Steinbeck's bitterness at the carping and malicious critics who decried his receiving the Nobel Prize. He called them "sucker-fish" and in the end ceased reading what they had to say about his work, whether they praised or condemned him. That might be the ultimate wisdom so one isn't unbalanced by either censure or praise. But the sensitive, perceptive review of *Morning* by Thomas Lask in the Saturday *New York Times* cries for a response. How can a writer resist someone understanding what he has written?

But today, the conflict of sky and water all around me, my perspective and equanimity returns. The water in upheaval sends currents out to seas and to other continents, north to where icebergs loom in cold depths, above the wrecks of ships littering the ocean floors. The earth seems in harmony and timeless as I return to my section on ships and the sea.

April 19
I haven't made an entry in this journal for almost a month now simply because I haven't worked at all. I have been traveling to promote *Morning*, to Cleveland, Detroit, Denver and Salt Lake City. Once more there is the cycle of flights and journeys, meeting people for the first time, speaking words that have been spoken before.

In Cleveland my fellow authors were Marilyn Sanders and Henry Cabot Lodge. Marilyn was a bright, gentle, chain-smoking and hoarse-voiced lady who had written a biography of Dorothy Thompson. She is a writer like myself, part of a struggle we both understand. Henry Cabot Lodge, on the other hand, moves in the ambience of Presidents. He was courtly, handsome, impeccably tailored, and scrupulously polite. He does not really have to huckster his book of memoirs, but I think he travels because he misses the limelight. He sits like a dignified, thoughtful statesman until it is time for him to greet someone or sign a book. Then he glows with a distinctive heat. Perhaps that is the colophon of the old statesman or politician when he gets close to people, like a firehorse whose nostrils flare with nostalgia as he hears the sound of the firehouse bell.

Marilyn spoke first. I followed her, leaving Lodge for last, a position befitting his eminence. I spoke of life and death and read the final pages of *Morning* where the old priest stands on his porch staring down at twilight beginning to obscure his neighborhood. He is pondering the passage of time and the stratas of sediment and bones and artifacts layered in the earth. After I finished and sat down, Lodge rose to follow me. He cast a puzzled, uncertain look at me, one swift, bewildered glance suggesting he wasn't sure what the hell I was talking about. No man could have followed me without making some gesture toward what I had said, some acknowledgement of those shades of darkness and light. But like an ambassador or politician, he thrust forward along his own track, relating a few charming anecdotes, smiling benignly, reassured by the admiring faces of the ladies in the audience who stared up at him.

When I walked to my table in the adjoining lounge where we sat to sign books for those ladies wishing to purchase them, the lines at Lodge's table were much longer than mine. That does not suggest that fiction is dead, simply that fiction readers can be deflected by celebrities!

May 20
Some weeks have passed without an entry in this journal. My working pattern has been disrupted by the publication of *Morning*, by the traveling, by the futile efforts to find the rhythm again. Then, too, there is worry about finances for the fall, bills to be paid. For a while it seemed I might take a year's residence at the University of Utah, but that didn't work out. Again we are talking of moving for six months to Greece. All these distractions do not encourage concentration on the book.

When I am immersed in the book, writing can be an exciting

and fulfilling experience. When I am distracted, everything seems distant and cold. It is like the difference between making love to a woman one loves and love with a woman one hardly knows. Perhaps that isn't a good analogy. But it is true that the personality of the typewriter changes when the rhythm of work is lost. The keys seem cold, the words strange, the emotions remote. I sense then that the characters and story have faded into some obscure and impersonal background. I must find the spark to make them burst into life again.

These last weeks have been wet and dreary, cold and damp, winter unwilling to give up. But this morning the day bloomed magnificently and as I walked with Diana along the lake and into the woods I saw how much the trees, shrubs and flowers have flourished in the weeks of rain. As the sun breaks free of the dense clouds the earth appears to burst into summer.

In the last few days I have begun working again on the island section, meeting the problem of the character of the sea captain Leonidas Kontos. I must show how the islanders are influenced by water, by the coming and going of of ships and by voyages and journeys, but it is slow, arduous going through unfamiliar territory. I read books on ships and the sea, make notes on the construction of sailing vessels and peer out across the lake for the sight of a sail. All of this is an effort to lighten fingers that strike the typewriter keys with a curious, leaden descent. Feeling better today, I am hopeful the writing will improve and there will be reason to record some small achievement in the journal.

Add to the other distresses that our son, John, has not been feeling well. A couple of weeks ago I picked him up at college in Kalamazoo so he could visit the doctor in Chicago. His illness was diagnosed as a virus. He returned to school in a few days but could not function. He has come back home to rest and rely on medication. I know that at twenty a youth takes good health so much for granted that illness is frightening and disabling. John complains of a feeling difficult to define—nausea, nervousness, headache, a general weakness, lassitude and depression. We worry about him and that becomes a distraction, too, but concern for someone loved is an essential part of life.

May 29
After about seven weeks fighting an assortment of pressures, I finished section four on the islander Leonidas Kontos. The pages are better now in portraying him as a strong, reliant man, dedicated in his purpose and committed to freedom for all of Greece. In this struggle for freedom, he feels that the island captains, the men who have learned to chart their course by the stars, will be the leaders of the revolt. As I finished the last eight pages of the section through a half-dozen drafts, some of the excitement of the book tingled in me again for the first time in almost two months.

Yesterday was lost once more when I drove mother to the cemetery for the Memorial Day observance of my father's death. The memorial *kolyva* I wrote of in *Stelmark* was once more in our car, although it was a smaller tray. Diana resented my being pulled from my work. I went reluctantly but as my mother sat beside me I was gripped by an inability to make her understand. Her life is drawn in clearly defined areas of "right" and "wrong," "good" and "bad."

In the more than twenty years my mother has lived with us, compounding our own personal difficulties, Diana has become obsessive in her resentment. I resent Mother myself, feeling an elemental pity for her. I haven't the courage or selfishness to put her out or to try and find another home for her away from us. That might unleash a whole band of furies of guilt and despair when I remember she has nothing and she has always felt her home to be with us. So we go on, our own problems complicated by her brooding presence, her endless plaintive plea to us to raise the thermostat because she is always cold.

I don't want her to suffer but I often make a silent plea that she die, since I don't know any other solution. Yet I admire her strength, the things she has done, her will of iron—all those things that keep her alive. And who has the right to deny any human being the freedom to hang on to life?

June 23
A series of strange days. Last Saturday the worst storm in my memory battered our house, bending the limbs of trees almost to the ground, driving leaves with such fury they remained stuck against the glass of the windows. The sky was full of turbulent black clouds that whirled low over the black water.

For several weeks now I have been writing and rewriting the section or chapter on the Mani, making an effort to capture some of that arid and male-dominated world. I have gone through a half-dozen rewritings and have the chapter at about 32 pages now, ending as I projected the ending in the synopsis.

One of the problems has been the character of the revolutionary leader Theodoros Kolokotrones, the heroic figure who dominates the history of the revolt. The position he holds in history gives him the status of a legendary chieftain like Achilles. How to make this real man come alive in the pages of a book poses a fierce dilemma. In an effort to know him better I have read and studied his memoirs. Other writers of that period described him as having eyes now wild, now soft and caressing, his nature as being tempestuous, generous, suspicious, erratic, proud, compassionate, stern, brutal, gentle, and on and on and on. . . .

Yesterday was the first day of summer. John is still at home, not yet well, and will not be able to return to school for the summer quarter as he had wished. He seems to be a little better, but his progress is slow and he looks peaked and frail. We all worry about him and yet there is nothing we can do.

June 26
This evening, after reworking the last five pages of the chapter for three days, I finished an acceptable draft. I have chosen to tell the story through the viewpoint of the wife of the prince of the Mani, Katerina Mavromichalis.

Through her eyes, that oppressive sense of a male-dominated society gains force, yet despite what is temporarily satisfactory, I see so much more that needs to be done. If the last few pages where Katerina feels she is being ravished by the God of War, Ares, are to be made believable, more of the haunted sense of the Mani must come through. The reader must understand these things that might happen among the ghosts, phantoms, and spectres, in the midst of a superstitious people who believe in dreams and their divinations. I considered and then discarded having an old woman divine such a dream earlier in the chapter.

I also wrote several drafts making the scene an actual nightmare, then discarded that treatment as well. In its present state the ending is ambiguous. The reader (as well as the writer!) is not certain if the woman is actually assaulted by the God of

War or if her fear and dread of bearing still another "gun" makes her imagine that her husband is the baleful god.

The chapter will have to be reworked. There isn't any assurance in thinking about how to do it best. The material simply has to be worked and reworked.

I am five chapters into the book now, a total of about 155 pages. The war has not yet broken out and I am not sure I have things under control. I am feeling and fumbling my way, hoping the material sustains drama and excitement.

Where do I go after chapter five? I am not certain, but I will have to formulate a beginning for what might become chapter six. Perhaps it will include the priest and primates on the road to Tripolitza, the machinations of the monk, Papalikos, and the accidental, contrived, irrevocable starting of the revolt.

Then I think chapter seven will need the terrible revelation of the massacre of the Turks in the village. The slaughter must spill blood on the pages and, in the end, sorrowfully and yet joyously and triumphantly, the bell of the church must be excavated from the cemetery and placed into the bell-tower where it rings for the first time in a hundred years....

August 4

I rose at dawn this morning, anxious to get to work on the final pages of chapter six. Yesterday I etched in a framework of the action from the time the priest departs the monastery of Aghia Lavra to his arrival in the village. What I hope to show is the storm of war rising all around him as he travels by cart, then by boat and finally by donkey. Near the end of his journey he grows more frantic to reach his village, as if it will be a kind of sanctuary from the madness and violence gathering around him. At the outskirts of the village he sees ominous plumes of black smoke in the sky above the houses, and he knows he has arrived too late.

It is a difficult chapter because he will discover the bodies of his Turkish friends piled in a burning heap in the village square. Among the dead are Ahmed Bajaki and his son Hassan. The priest's grief must be a wild and tangible thing, and in the depths of that grief he must hear the bell of the church tolling for the first time in a hundred years.

The great problem of this chapter ending is to fuse these contradictory elements, his dark despair with an uncontrollable joy when he listens to the bell that had been buried for so long, the bell his grandfather and his father never heard ring in their lifetimes.

The completion of this chapter might be the end of part one of the book. There might be alterations, characters added or deleted, but I feel a cycle completed in these two hundred pages.

For a while last evening I felt the excitement I remember after writing the church celebration in *Morning*. I felt something spark alive then that carried me along with the turbulence and power of a tidal wave. The book roared with a movement and purpose of its own. In such moments I have learned not to question but to accept. Another writer once called it ''like taking God's dictation.''

And so with mingled dread and anticipation, my soul both burdened and winged, I begin again with the beginning of this new day.

August 20

I cannot help wondering what this autumn and winter holds in store for us. John's illness, stretching interminably, affects us all. At times during the day when I am working I think of him and feel a quickening uneasiness in my pulse. The other night, whether from his frustration, despair, or terror, I thought he might not make it until dawn before we took him to the hospital. He seems frail to me, his wrists thin, his eyes blacker than usual. He is struggling himself to understand what has happened to him and we can do so little to aid that struggle. We are awaiting word from the doctor this morning about when to take him in again for new examinations.

It is consoling how a family draws more closely together when it is faced with adversity. Dean has been especially patient with all our concern for his brother. He comes from school into a house that cannot be cheerful or reassuring. Yet I know he has his problems, as well.

I am back again today to chapter six, after an erratic week. There were several good days of work but the rest was fragmented by taking John to the doctor and by my own depression. The chapter sits on my desk, forty pages that need additional reworking to be shaped and sharpened. The difficulties grow and the problems gain in magnitude with each day's delay.

Sometimes I think this book will take years and years to write or may never be finished. Then I remember what John Steinbeck wrote in his *East of Eden* journal: one day at a time, one step at a time, one page placed upon another, until the book is done. When I despair of finishing I am also consoled because I have two hundred more pages now than I had nine months ago.

September 3
This morning I finished another draft of chapter six that brings part one to an end. Obviously it is not a finished draft, I know, but it is an acceptable draft that will allow me to move on. Perhaps the material I may obtain on a trip to Greece this autumn will give the pages greater richness.

I am fairly well satisfied with the final pages where the priest finds the funeral pyre of slaughtered, burning bodies, and, even as he mourns, hears the triumphant pealing of the bell. Now I move on. So much remains to be done: the pile of discarded pages mounting on my desk growls for more food because only through endless drafts do the finished pages assume proper shape.

Later today we will go to my nephew Frank's house for barbecued chicken and ribs outdoors. The multitudinous segments of our family will gather in bedlam and confusion but, at the same time, exude a gratifying warmth.

I am uncertain at this point whether to move on or whether to return to page one and make one final redrafting of the two hundred pages to send to Doubleday. I'll make that decision tomorrow. This morning I will allow myself to feel that at least to this point I am finished.

For that much I am grateful.

September 10
After almost ten days of relentless humidity and heat, the last few days have cooled, the scents of autumn growing stronger. We are in that period St. Augustine called "the dead summer's soul." It is a good season for me—I feel a surge of some seasonal adrenalin in my blood. There should be a few weeks of slowly cooling weather, the altering colors of the foliage, the nights closing in earlier. Finally, we will enter the hibernation of winter.

I have begun another draft of the two hundred pages. When I

am finished with them I will send copies of the manuscript to Sandy at Doubleday and to other friends, Kimon Friar in Greece and perhaps Constantine Trypanis. They may help me with their reactions. Again, by returning to the beginning now, like a runner retracing the ground he has covered, I build up an impetus that should carry me into part two. Even as I retype and change pages in part one I find myself thinking ahead, my thought flying forward like seed for the chapters ahead.

This morning I woke early, around 6:00 a.m. I stood for a while on the terrace breathing in the cool scents of dawn, watching the slow, breathless emergence of the light. I thought of my niece, Barbara, who has been very ill but came to Chicago from Spokane yesterday to share the christening of my nephew Steve's and his wife Dena's baby girl. All of us, including our John, were touched by her coming, in spite of her illness, to, as she told us, "reassure everyone that I am not as ill as you imagine." Her brother, Mark, the young pediatrician, arrived during the evening, driving in his camper from Des Moines with his wife and five children to spend several hours at the baptism and then drive back home again.

The far-flung perimeters of our family were drawn together in the important and sustaining bonds of love.

September 13
The work has gone well these last days. I have been at my typewriter early and worked straight through the afternoon. The retyping of another draft of part one has had relatively minor changes. In a few places I temporarily bogged down, as in the first meeting between the guerilla captain Vorogrivas and the youth, Manolis. But by working hard I broke through the barriers. This morning I am finishing the guerilla chapter, reaching the point where the old, grizzled Suliot captain Boukouvalas tells of the women of Zalongos.

The oppressive part of the last few days is that our valiant Barbara is growing worse in the hospital in Chicago. She does not respond to treatment, her lungs collapsing, her body malfunctioning. The doctors are guarded in their prognosis and I am afraid they think she will die.

There is death all around us, each and every day, coming to the young and to the old, to those with families and to those alone. What consolation do we have, those of us who survive?

Nothing but the knowledge that time will efface the distinction between the living and the dead. In ten, twenty, thirty, forty years, we will all have joined that immense legion. Those of us who now bury our dead will in turn be buried because that is a destiny we accept as we first enter life.

September 22
Today I noticed the foliage changing on the trees, the first scarlets and russets appearing among the green leaves. Driving along the bog, I saw flocks of birds gathering for their winter migrations. The days are lovely, cool and clear. The water of the lake is a brilliant blue. The sunsets have a grandeur, as if seeking to leave a memory of majestic color before the paler constellations of winter.

Today I mailed part one to Sandy at Doubleday, the first six chapters, a total of about 45,000 words. Looking back over the ten months that have passed since I first began writing, perhaps I should have worked harder, been further along. But I am pleased with the quality.

With part two the war begins in earnest in the mountains, in the plains, at sea. Characters will die and new characters will be introduced. The old captain, Boukouvalas, will die in battle, Vorogrivas and the Turks fighting for his head. Kontos with the heroic admiral Kanaris will use the first fireships at sea. Psara will be devastated just as the old magistrate on the island prophesied. Kolokotrones will march north from the Mani, through the Morea towards Tripolitza, almost lose his life at Karitena and fight at Dervenakia, the first important battle of the war. There is stirring in me a vague conception of a family of volunteers coming from Crete to join the revolt. In Constantinople the enraged Sultan, furious at the revolt of his Greek subjects, will hang bishops and priests and crucify the Patriarch Gregorius, afterwards giving his body to the mob. Prince Ipsilantis and his army that invaded the provinces will be destroyed.

The most difficult problem will be to introduce the myriad voices of the characters. Each character must be independent of the others but must be linked within the framework of the story.

I have traveled a considerable distance since beginning and yet I have so much further to go. How many more months will pass before part two is finished?

October 3

A telegram came from Sandy at Doubleday this morning responding to the block of 200 pages of the manuscript I mailed him ten days ago. He used words like "ecstatic," "marvelous," "masterpiece." Of course that pleases me, and yet I have waited for word from him calmly. I have worked too long not to understand the quality of what I have written. But I had no way of knowing how others might react, whether the pages would produce lukewarm praise or even criticism. I am grateful that the response has been enthusiastic.

That telegram has helped me gird my spirit for the assault on book two.

October 7

Beginning part two is like starting the book again. I feel secure in the foundation, but I must continue a clean, dramatic movement. I will have to try several chapters and pick the one that seems the most natural development from chapter six, with which part one ends.

I lean now toward a chapter expanding the part Kolokotrones plays in the early months of fighting. After the victory at Kalamata, he moves north to lay seige to Tripolitza, is nearly killed and his peasant army is dispersed. There must be a scene in the church where he prays in remorse and gratitude for being spared and sees the tears on the face of the Madonna in the icon. He is inspired by the mystical revelation and drives his men to build breastworks and fortifications against the next onslaught of the fearsome Turkish cavalry. The men grumble at the burdensome task, but when the Turks attack again, the Greek strategy prevails...the withering fire from behind the fortifications scatters the cavalry. That is the first significant Greek victory of the revolt.

But this chapter requires a viewpoint character. Since Kolokotrones is a historical personage, I would prefer not using him. Perhaps I can have a lieutenant or an aide comment on Kolokotrones' strength and weakness, be privy to the moments of fear and the moments of resolution. After resolving this chapter I must return to the narrative of Vorogrivas and his band and then go to sea with Leonidas Kontos.

There are many difficult chapters ahead of me and at this stage

I have only the vaguest conception of their order and content. I know the book will build toward the fall of Tripolitza and the butchering of the Turks in the captured city. That was an orgy of bloodshed brought about by the wrangling and bickering of the Greek captains, like the wrangling and bickering that can take place in any assembly of Greeks today.

I have made no final decision yet on my trip to Greece. The question now is whether I can go alone since Diana will not be able to make the trip with me. Perhaps a delay until spring will prove just as fruitful, but I yearn to make the trip now to renourish some of the wellsprings I draw upon for the writing.

October 12

What has happened before has happened again. Once more the story alters direction, asserting a life of its own. I started the chapter on Kolokotrones moving north from Kalamata and somehow, I am not sure how, I have been launched into a chapter on Crete. The chapter begins as word arrives on the island of the outbreak of the revolution. I am excited as the scenes grow and flower.

There is a Cretan father, black-shirted, black-booted, a patriarch with seven or eight married sons and one unmarried son. They are fiercely independent highlanders. We open with the chapter, the start of part two, as a group of kinsmen from Sfakia urge the father to attack the Turks in Retimo. The father knows something of the reprisals that unplanned forays cause and he refuses. He sends his unmarried son to bring their other kinsmen together to move into one of the great Cretan caves, from which they will hide and fight.

In the mountains there will be a sculptor's studio, and there will be a lovely young apprentice that the son will meet and love, a love story that will become, hopefully, a vital dramatic segment of the book.

There is a chance to do so much here with the Cretans, drawing on the island's rich history and myths. Future scenes come flashing and leaping to mind. The son, romantic and impatient for the revolution to begin, matures through battle and suffering. Perhaps the father is captured and tortured, and the son rescues him in a great, warm scene of reconciliation.

I am aware that the tension built up through the end of part one with the priest returning from the village may be dissipated by another long chapter that does not actually begin the war. But I will start my drafts and see how they go. I have been hesitant about moving my story to Crete only because Kazantzakis uses Crete so brilliantly in *Freedom or Death*. I will move warily and gently in his massive footsteps, believing the spirit of that great and good man will guide and strengthen me.

Thinking of Kazantzakis I am reminded of his burial site on the fortinago bastion in Heraklion: the magnificent view of the town, mountains, and sea. The tall wooden cross that marks his grave bearing the inscription, "I do not hope for anything; I do not fear anything; I am free." With faith in Kazantzakis and with a longing in my blood, I move my story to Crete and will bring my Cretan family to life. I think they will play a rich, substantial role in my book.

October 27
I returned home last night after four wearying days in New York, days of rain, crowds, turmoil. There was a long, volatile meeting with a Greek director who might direct *Morning* should the film finally be made.

There isn't any patience in New York. Cab drivers snarl, people push, everyone rushing and frantic. Nelson Algren's comment about the citizens of Chicago might apply more aptly to the citizens of New York, that "they have the faces of occupying troops." To cross a street means running a blockade. I had some fever and nausea while I was there and spent part of a day in bed.

A highlight of the trip was a long lunch with Sandy Richardson in the cloistered elegance of the Century club, a serene oasis in the teeming disorder of New York. He spoke at length about the novel chapters he had seen so far. His enthusiasm seems total and unqualified and he spoke of the work as a kind of symphony. His opinion is only that of one man but he is a professional who would not be inclined to praise if he felt criticism would help the book. We spoke also of the help I would need from Doubleday if I wanted to keep writing and he pledged to try and get that help.

The journey back to Chicago seemed endless—the ride to LaGuardia by taxi, the boarding of the plane, the delay in taking off, the delay in landing at O'Hare, the wait for the Hammond-Gary bus, the stops along the way. Finally, I arrived in Gary where John and Dean picked me up.

Then I was back in the disorder of our house, Diana ironing, my mother shuffling through the kitchen, the boys watching a Steve McQueen film on television. Yet in all the chaos there is a warmth, a closeness that leaves me feeling empty when I am away from it. But, after a while, how restful it is to shower and wash away the soot, sweat and grime of cities and travel, climb between clean sheets, and sleep well for the first time in four nights.

This morning I rose, feeling rested, and after driving Diana to the train for a trip to the dentist in the city, settled at my table before my papers and my typewriter. The day is wet, gray, and clouded. But in my study the music of a Brahms quintet soothes me, the lamp glows across the desk, and typewriter, books, couch, pictures, manuscript all seem part of an orderly and significant world.

Preparing to return to the chapter on Crete which begins part two of the novel, I spend an hour reading brief sections from the manuscript experiencing the pages once more as Sandy may have read them. The characters came to life as I read, and I was filled with emotion. Holding the two-hundred pages that represents the work of a year, I began to cry. I think I cried for many reasons, for gratefulness because I felt the work strong and fulfilling. I cried, too, because I was fifty years old, most of my life behind me. I cried for Diana, as well, growing older with me, no longer the slim-legged, pretty girl she had been so long ago. I cried for the weakness and disorder of my years, for my absurd posturings and fantasies, for all the foolish and senseless things I had done, thought, experienced. Yet, in that moment, all the years and events seemed validated by the work.

And I marvel again, and cry for that, too, at how so weak, battered, and aging a fool could produce characters and scenes that are so moving, vital, and true!

November 2
These are long, lovely days in the full splendor of autumn. The trees have turned varying shades, the foliage gleaming golden, scarlet and purple. Once more the smell of the earth seems definably tinged with summer's passing, a brief vivid transition before the winter. Even to call this season autumn, to speak the word aloud, carries connotations of that sad, burnished passage.

Last night we went into the city and saw Mikis Theodorakis in concert. I found the evening an incredible experience. He is a tall, gaunt, monolithic-figured man, dressed in a black linen jacket and trousers that remind me of the garb of the Vietcong. Intense, passionate, vibrant, he conducted the singers and the group of about eight musicians on the bouzouki, guitar, piano, and drums. The songs he sang were mostly revolutionary ballads of resistance and protest, and, near the end of the program he grew more impassioned. One of his hands clutched the microphone while the other gestured like a sword at the band. In a strong, harsh voice he sang of prison, loneliness and terror, of the will and need to oppose tyranny. Members of the audience were caught up in his passion and responded with shouts, cries, a thunder of clapping which I joined heartily. I came to understand once again the enormous difficulty of my own task in the book. Kazantzakis, Theodorakis, Seferiades, Vassilikos, Yannis Ritsos, all the poets and novelists and composers who fought for freedom by opposing the tyrannies of dictators...any of them would probably have died for their faith, yet here I am born in a distant land, having visited Greece only a few times, seeking to untangle in dramatic terms the anguish of that hunger for freedom which burns in Greece like a flame. These men live defiantly while I seek to define and interpret defiance.

Perhaps my concern was also the concern of Kazantzakis who felt that Alexis Zorbas was a "true man" and that he, Kazantzakis, was simply a "pen pusher." I am a pen pusher, as well. Yet the image of that free and natural man, Zorba, lives today because of Kazantzakis. That might validate the pen pusher's role, as a mythmaker, as a recorder of the struggle.

So I return to the book this morning after the concert, renewed in my determination to accomplish the enormity of the task. I return to the demanding Cretan chapter, now and then glimpsing a vision of what it should be, then losing that vision in the slow, labored pounding out of the weak, ineffectual words. But somehow I must make language, scenes, and people encompass the intensity of those fleeting visions.

Nikos Kazantzakis, my Cretan father and my Cretan brother, grant me your blessing for I feel my frailty and weakness and have great need of your solace and your faith....

November 9
Suddenly winter has arrived with a vengeance. For several days now the wind has whipped up the waves on the lake, stirring them into a tempest. This morning some snow fell—strange after the months of summer and autumn. A hardy geranium, the last flower in the pots on the terrace, was still red yesterday. This morning the petals had withered in the frost that came during the night.

My sister-in-law, Marvel, has been visiting us for several days now and last night I spoke to my brother for a while on the phone. He is diabetic, suffering arteriosclerosis and edema, and has had both legs amputated. Having just been through a gall-bladder operation, he is to go through another operation for cataracts in both eyes, that veil everything in shadows. When we spoke I felt some of his despair. He has persevered through all his tribulations but now the wellsprings of his hope seem near an end.

Each time I see him in these last years, I am shocked at his decline. When my mother spoke to him on the phone—the two of them bound so strongly together—he cried. I think he yearned to see her once again but knew that his health and her age made that unlikely. She had been a whirlwind for him in the days of his troubles, all her strength and great spirit mustered in his defence. Now, white-haired, grown deaf and old, she exchanges a few feeble words with him. I can imagine him remembering how often she came to help him in the past. But she is helpless against the adversity he faces now.

Meanwhile, the snow sweeps a lacework across my windows. The sky is so dark it might almost be twilight. In the pages of my book I still struggle with Crete, advancing a paragraph at a time with agonizing slowness. When Andreas sees Voula for the first time, something of her grace and beauty must spring off the page—something, too, of that fierce world in which they live.

Later today, we are driving into the city to visit the doctor and, afterwards, go to the theatre. I would rather remain here and work...work...work...work....

November 15
The day is stormy, the sky almost black, the lake roaring, and, from time to time, a hard rain lashing at the windows. But it has been a good, exciting day of work for me.

I began redoing the earlier section of chapter seven. Instead of beginning with the Sfakian, Cosmatos, riding up with his band to bring Andreas and his father the news that the revolt has begun in Greece, I start now with the captains joined in two days of futile meetings. Knowing something of the volatile Cretan temperament, the warlike disposition of the Sfakians, they would not wait for the mainlanders to revolt but might chafe to take the lead themselves. By introducing several captains, two Sfakians and a cannoneer who had fought with Napoleon, arguing with Andreas' father, I show the dreadful rivalries and jealousies. I think the chapter is stronger now.

In the morning I will begin again, starting from the first part of the chapter and pushing forward, hoping the impetus will carry me still a little further. I am excited by this chapter, so excited it interferes with my ability to sleep. I read some of Douglas Dakin's fine book on the Greek revolution, and some of the Alvarez book on Samuel Beckett. Scenes, lines and characters kept springing into my mind, a process taking place independent of the books I am reading. I suppose this means my own work is now a force that draws fuel from everything I read or do.

I am still uncertain about postponing the outbreak of revolution. The scene of violence in the village of Kravasaras suggests the following chapter should continue that movement. Instead I have gone to Crete to develop more characters and another background. I hope the new section will be fertile and interesting enough to justify the delay. Then there is the love story between Andreas and Voula. Will they find happiness or even fulfillment?

How strange, in a way, to create characters and not be certain what will happen to them. Each draft sharpens their natures and helps me understand them. Their images grow clearer, their faces and voices drawing closer to me. They wait, suspended like statues into whom I am breathing the warmth of life. They wait for the destiny I am providing them, uncertain whether it will be joyous or tragic. At this point, neither I nor the characters know.

December 5
The first snow of the season fell this morning, large flakes glistening on the boughs of the great tree outside my window. For a while they dissolve and, as the flakes become thicker, they

whiten the trees and the ground.

I am working on chapter eight, returning the story to Vorogrivas and Boukouvalas in the mountains. It is an immensely difficult section that carries the guerilla band from their stronghold into the first battle of the war. Vorogrivas and his men will fight furiously to impede the advance of Turkish and Albanian troups from Lamia. In this battle the old, lion-maned Boukouvalas will die and Greeks and Turks will fight for possession of his great head.

Images of the old guerilla, festooned in his armor, kneeplates and breastplates, riding like an avenging demon into the battle, sweep over me. I can feel the terror his solitary charge wreaks among the Turks and the way they fall back momentarily at the sight of him. When he stumbles and falls from his horse, Vorogrivas, Manolis and the Greeks will surround his body to protect him from mutilation.

The Greeks must stem the advance but lose the battle. They will retreat to the mountains where, wounded himself, Vorogrivas will grieve for the death of Boukouvalas. The young guerilla, Manolis, might make an effort to console him. This relationship must be handled delicately. Perhaps the end of the scene might have Manolis sleeping near Vorogrivas.

The battle scenes need a quality of violence, frenzy and death. Ed Lueders wrote me after reading some of the early version of the book that when skilled writers describe war, some truly stunning scenes are achieved. I hope that proves true for me. I know the turmoil and thunder I feel as I contemplate the scenes and all I need to do is to render them onto the pages of the book. God, that's all!

December 9
The first anniversary of this journal. One year ago today I made the first entry and began the writing. I started this morning by reading some of the early entries which chronicle the struggles in the beginning chapters. In one way so little has been accomplished in a year and yet I am so much further along than I was when I started.

A long, good day of work today. I wrote and rewrote the chapter where the guerillas ride down to raid the Turkish column. Old Boukouvalas pleads to be taken along. When Vorogrivas refuses, the old captain demands he be thrown to the wolves since even that death would serve more purpose than his slow, useless decay. Then I plan a scene in the village with the mother of Manolis and another scene with the priest. In the morning I will begin drafting the journey into battle by Vorogrivas and his men.

Last night, with my nephew and niece, Steve and Dena, here to help us decorate the Christmas tree, I had sharp pains in my left arm. I thought at once of a heart attack and became apprehensive that something would prevent me from completing the book. But I lasted through the night and in the morning felt better and grateful.

The scene with Father Markos and Vorogrivas in the cemetery is causing me trouble. I envision the two of them in the shadows while revelry and music sound from the village. Around them crickets trill, an owl cries, a dog pursues and catches a hare, barking in jubilation.

I can see the scene but I cannot define what the men should say to one another. I write pages of senseless dialogue seeking an entry into a meaningful exchange. The priest might speak of war and ask about the way it brutalizes men. Vorogrivas might answer impatiently.

Adding to my problem is the uncertainty I feel about the chapter to follow. Perhaps when I write the battle scene at the end of this chapter, I will open a path for the one to follow.

Tonight I reached page 266. Am I moving too slowly? I am still in the first month following the outbreak of war. If I am still in 1821, how long will it take me to reach 1824 and 1825? I must find a place to stop long before those years or the book will take as long as the war.

But I have had a good day of work on the first anniversary of the beginning. I am grateful.

December 13
All day it has been storming, the lake hurling waves in across the beach. The wind shakes the windows and my study seems to roll like a ship at sea.

For two days I have been struggling with the final pages of chapter eight, the battle between the Greeks and Turks at the bridge. As the discarded pages pile up I understand this scene is one of the most difficult I have ever attempted. If I have written emotional, dramatic scenes in earlier novels, the scene where

Alex kills his brother Manuel in *The Odyssey of Kostas Volakis*, the scene in *A Dream of Kings* when Matsoukas battles the dead husband's spirit for possession of Anthoula, the bathtub murder scene in *In the Land of Morning*, all these scenes have only had two or three characters.

But to render the chaos and frenzy of a thousand men at war, to describe that carnage, is to attempt a mural where the other scenes have been cameos. I see fragments that I link together to fashion the whole. The scream of a wounded horse, the cries and pleas of injured men, wolves slipping down in the darkness to forage among the bodies. In the lull between attacks, the birds shriek overhead and the sky reflects the crimson of blood.

There isn't any other way to do these scenes, I suppose, than to write them over and over again. From a page I may salvage a single decent image and use that in the following draft. That has worked in the past but for the last two days I could not reclaim even those few good images, unable to transfer them from my head onto the paper. This morning, with the storm outside aiding me, I begin again. Tonight after dinner while I walked around the yard for almost an hour, lines and words kept whirling in my head.

Although I have never seen war except in films or in scenes I have read in books, I have the task of depicting war—distorted merciless, chaotic. In battle there are no heroes or villains, simply men fighting and dying, frightened, stunned, resigned.

Tonight I feel exhausted. If I do not claim I have been in a battle today, I have been witness to war, reaching deep into myself, drawing upon those primitive sources of hate and murder that exist in us all.

Aman is the Turkish word for mercy. If I thought it would help I would cry Aman...Aman....But even if someone heard, how could they help me? A writer must write alone.

December 15
I did not feel well today. Once again I had cramping pains in my chest that made me think my heart was faltering, foreshadowing an attack.

The cramps began last night before I went to bed. I tried to reassure myself that my senses were heightened and everything about me distorted while I worked so closely on the book. I rose at 5:00 a.m. to drive Dean to school, where a bus would take him to a debate meet. After driving back home and returning to bed, I had a fearful dream. In the dream I was having lunch with a writer friend in a Walgreen drug store. My friend ordered wine in spite of my telling him Walgreens did not serve wine. As he left, a group of men called to me to join them at another table. I did not recognize them but found their faces menacing.

Then I was somehow back in my house, finding every room littered with refuse. The kitchen sink was filled with dirty water and a hand severed at the wrist floated in the scraps. In my dream I knew the hand belonged to my son, Mark, and in a moment he entered the kitchen to show me the bloody stump of his wrist.

I cried out then and the dream tangled. A veiled woman stood in a corner. With the same prescience I had about the severed hand belonging to my son, I knew the woman was the long-dead Naka, my childhood guardian. When she raised the veil I saw her decomposed face, bone visible beneath shreds of rotted flesh.

I seemed then to become aware that I was dreaming and hurried to find Diana. I screamed at her that I was locked in a terrible dream and if I were not awakened, the dream would hold me forever. Diana tried to reassure me I wasn't dreaming. I kept trying to convince her, pleading with her to wake me. As proof of the dream I pointed to our dog Perky resting in a corner although she, too, had been dead for a number of years. I do not recall if I convinced Diana, but my own screams finally woke me.

What a strange, horrifying dream! In thinking about it afterwards I understand that for days I had been writing of the carnage of war, slashed heads and severed limbs. Between the cramps and my fear of the night before, the two worlds had fused into a nightmare. That is the price to be paid when the life of the book grows real.

Some of the horror I felt must be the way men feel in war.

December 16
Today I felt better, the cramps gone except for an occasional twinge. When I first rose this morning I rode my bike, straining and pushing, seeking to reassure myself that, if my heart was faltering, strenuous activity would swiftly kill me.

Now, in my study at the end of the day, I have written for

hours on the complex pages that conclude chapter eight—the battle to hold the bridge when the last Greeks are saved by the wild charge of Boukouvalas. In the crimson light of the setting sun the armored old man, strapped to his saddle, comes riding like the wind. At the sight of him, kindled scarlet by the sun, the Turkish troops panic and flee.

I can envision that inhuman, thundering ride but the problem of describing it on paper is shattering. Several days ago, working on this chapter, I did 19 drafts of page 272. I have rewritten it again seven or eight times. I will never again write a page 272 without remembering this obstruction.

Now with a 46-page draft of the chapter completed, I will try in the morning to redo the last ten pages a few more times. Then I will begin the chapter over again because there is too much material now. Having suffered to put it in, I must now trim it down. Even if I manage to finish it in a satisfactory way, the next chapter will encompass the first of the battles at sea between the Greek brigs and the Turkish frigates. That chapter should be a peach, as well!

I am old enough and have written enough books to know that there isn't any easy way to write.

December 21
The last entry in this journal implied I was about finished with chapter eight. As has been the case many times before, the work turned out more extensive. I have been working a week until this evening, when I finally finished a good draft of 54 pages, the longest chapter of any written so far.

There are some fine scenes—the cupping of old Boukouvalas, the scene between Vorogrivas and the mother of Manolis, the scene with Vorogrivas and the priest in the cemetery...finally, the death of Lascarina and the great last charge of Boukouvalas to his death. There is too much material in the chapter now, but it also has the richness and depth and will be easier to prune.

We had the first massive snowfall of the season yesterday. Yet the earth layered with snow is lovely. Today, more snow fell to add a half-dozen more inches to that already on the ground. The lake is turbulent, the water shaded the hue of dark olives, the sky full of dark, seething clouds. These are good days to work and I have worked well.

After about a year of work I have about 70,000 words. I must begin to move more rapidly. I think now that chapter nine will be the sea chapter, the small island of Psara joining the revolt. Leonidas Kontos will go to sea with the naval hero Kanaris and they will use the first fireships against the Turkish frigates. Chapter ten remains uncertain. Chapter eleven may be a return to Crete to continue the love story of Voula and Andreas. Then, in chapter twelve, which should conclude part two of the book, there will be the fall of Tripolitza and then the Congress of Greeks at Epidaurus in January of 1822. That is where I may finish. I may have to juggle and alter the sequence of these chapters later on, but the short story discipline I practiced for years helps me here. I can conceive of each chapter as a self-contained section.

If I had chosen a smaller canvas, perhaps telling the story of a single family or concentrating on one phase of the revolution, I might be finished by now. But I am sure I would not feel nearly as elated as I am with the canvas I have assembled.

December 23
I am still not finished with chapter eight!

Once again the writing changes the conception. As I worked the pages where old Boukouvalas makes his charge and is shot off his horse, I planned to have the Greeks and Turks fight for possession of his head. But as I wrote those pages I felt the magic that surrounds the charge, Boukouvalas almost an extension of the sun that reflects his silver breastplate and jeweled sword raised above his head. How would the Turks, as superstitious as the Greeks, react to that demented assault upon their army by a single man? Would they not panic and flee, seeing before them the vengeful ghost of a warrior they thought dead? They flee and the old man stumbles from his horse and is killed in the fall. In this way the scene will also reveal the way in which a myth is created. In the years that followed, that legendary charge would be embroidered to suggest he not only dispersed the Turks but also that he killed a score of them, as well. It is fitting, somehow, that the man who relates the myth of the dance of the women of Zalongou in chapter three should himself end as a myth!

December 30
I continue to work on chapter eight, feeling like Sisyphus chained to his rock. Everytime I feel I am about finished, something

needs to be changed once more.

After the frenzy of the charge by the old captain, there has been the problem of capturing the turmoil, disorder and madness of the battle. Perhaps it cannot really be done in words. Films of battles can use the camera to create multiple images and distortions. But the writer is required to write one coherent sentence and then follow that with another. Words have to be used with some regard for their meanings and the sense they make when they are put together. So the struggle to find the right words go on. Wasn't it Mark Twain who said that the difference between the right word and the almost right word was the difference between lightning and the lightning bug? All I want my work to be is lightning!

We are coming to the end of the year. There has been more snow and the weather has been colder the last few days, the sky overcast and bleak. Tomorrow is New Year's Eve. Diana has taken a pair of ducks from the freezer and with Dean, John, and mother, possibly Mark, we will eat a quiet dinner, say a quiet prayer, give thanks for all the things we are grateful for and hope we hold our own for another year.

Meanwhile the tangle of ways to get money goes on. I have an offer for a non-fiction book on Greece that I may be able to do in a few months. There is also real interest in producing my novel *In the Land of Morning* with provision for me to do the screenplay. We may have to go to Rome to see the director who is interested. I don't want to interrupt the novel with any of these distractions, but I may not have a choice.

I'll make a small entry in this journal tomorrow evening as the old year flickers out.

1974

Harry Mark Petrakis

January 1, 1974—Midnight
Another year is beginning. We saw the old one out quietly, Diana, John, Dean, mother, and myself eating the roasted, delicious ducks, toasting one another with cold duck. Shortly before midnight we watched the celebrations from State Street and Times Square on television.

Revelry and celebration at the beginning of another year seems superfluous to me now. I can remember so many year-end festivities where I drank too much, laughed, and danced. Perhaps fifty is a milestone on the journey from high-spirits to somberness. Perhaps I understand now that another year does not require bacchanalian carousing, simply some resolve and determination to do one's work.

I am well into the novel and that is an advantage. There will be distractions this year, I know, things I must do for income that will deflect me from the book. I must try to balance those things I am forced to do against the emphasis on the major work.

I pray for health, spirit, hope...now, in the silence of my study, listening to the sound of rough water in the lake, I pray for the courage and the joy to do my work. I must make 1974 a good year! I am fifty now and a wasted or unfulfilled year means one lost year out of the limited supply of time that remains to me. The irony is that when we reach a point in our lives and become mature enough to understand that time is precious, the amount of it we have left is diminished.

One more year: I meet it now with my buoyancy somewhat curbed and, yet, determined. I must assemble the force and spirit to do my work!

January 1
The day began with snow flurries that added another inch to the snow that had fallen during the night. When I rose to make coffee, the overcast day suggested still more snow. But the sky cleared, blue and fiercely cold.

I made an effort to work, anxious that this first day of the new year be a good and productive one, but I found it hard to concentrate. I worked several hours and with each page I moved forward I became aware of something wrong with two I had left behind. The day started with my typing revisions on page 265 and ended with several hours of work this evening on page 261.

At this rate I shall be back to the beginning of the book by the end of the year!

But I can accept the cogent reasons for going back. The chapter on Vorogrivas and the death of Boukouvalas has many good scenes but I think I have made the characters too introspective, too gentle, too concerned with the feelings of others. In the scene where Vorogrivas visits the mother of Manolis, I have them reticent and considerate with each other. That is wrong! They are enemies and rivals for Manolis. She must be contemptuous as he talks about Manolis becoming a warrior. He must grow impatient and angry. When he relents slightly and offers to send her word about the welfare of Manolis, she must reject his pledge as unnecessary. She will tell him then of the carnation and rose that bloom in her garden, flowers the old women of the village whisper are the eyes of God's son, portals to keep death from entering the house. As long as the flowers bloom, she will know her son is well.

So, tonight, and I am not sure what brought the awareness to me—perhaps reading Tolstoy or watching one of the episodes of *War and Peace* on television—I realize I am not finished with that endless chapter yet. I must rework the character of Vorogrivas. He is a fighter, a man bred to war, ill at ease in the confines of village and house, suspicious in the presence of women. His character and that of the mother of Manolis must steam and sizzle, not whisper like teapots.

Another danger is that of making characters too similar—Vorogrivas and Kolokotronis, for example; Manolis and the young Cretan, Andreas. I must give them distinguishing characteristics to overcome the problem of drawing on a broad canvas with a multitude of characters.

Sometimes in anxious moments I see the sections of the book like an immensely complicated puzzle where the parts can be fitted in different ways to create deceivingly beneficent designs. How does one know where they really fit best?

A few months ago my editor, Sandy Richardson, said my chapter endings did not derive from conscious effort but from some indefinable sanctuary of creativity which writers may draw on intuitively. Perhaps he is right. So along with the work there must be a prayer....

January 6

I have finished still another draft of chapter eight and yet am still not satisfied with the battle that ends the section. I am also apprehensive that the love of the captain for Manolis skims the surface instead of gripping the implications of the attraction. The feeling of love that Vorogrivas feels is new and startling to him since he has suppressed all feelings of tenderness and affection. Suddenly the young man focuses those emotions he had thought dead. But regardless of my concern I will now leave the draft as it stands, since most of the 50 pages are good.

Today, Sunday, I have begun reading materials on the sea to provide the background of chapter nine. This will carry the story to the island of Psara, to the sea captain Leonidas Kontos who will join the struggle at sea. All day I make endless notes. In the morning I will draft a rough synopsis of the chapter. Some scenes I see vaguely now—the captain's farewell from his wife, Aspasia, and his daughters; Hadji Yannaros, the old magistrate, saluting their departure. The chapter must end with the Greeks using the first *brulot*, or fireship, against the Turkish fleet.

From the mountains to the sea. From guerrillas to seamen. That is a leap I will have to make.

January 13

After almost a week of snow the weather turned freezing. Snow is frozen on the roof and on the railings of the terrace, forming glaciers of ice along the beach. After months when we could hear the water, the freezing of the lake's surface brings a curious, unreal silence. Last night when John and I walked along the beach road, we could hear the water cracking up against some patches of loose ice, as if it were trying to break free.

I have been working along slowly, very slowly, on the island chapter. As difficult as the earlier chapters have been, this one is even harder. I haven't any knowledge of the sea, or ships at war. I have been reading sailor's diaries and sea journals, studying manuals on ships, foremast, mainmast, outer jib, flying jib...all the parts of the vessel, and the ways in which cannon are loaded and fired. After all the Errol Flynn sea movies I have seen I have never noticed the way a cannon must be withdrawn from the gunslot to be loaded!

During the night I had a dream that I was somewhere in

Greece in a small village house, feeling melancholy and depressed. A woman entered and asked me in Greek what was wrong. I could not answer but she read my despair in my silence. She left and returned bringing a lovely little girl, no more than ten or eleven. The mother told me I could caress the child but made me promise I would not have intercourse with her since her virginity had to be saved for her marriage.

With an innocent and indescribable sweetness, the child caressed me and allowed me to caress her. We were shamelessly intimate with each other and all the time I was conscious of a strange, nostalgic delight, as if I were being returned in some magical way to my own childhood.

When I woke, remembering the dream, I thought of the final scene in Bergman's great film, *Wild Strawberries*, when the old man looks across the river at the idyllic vision of his childhood. And I thought, too, still caught in the warm pliancy of the dream, of the ways I could utilize that emotion in the book.

For some reason I seem to be starting later and later in the morning, as if delaying the agony of the work. I shave and shower, take a bracing walk in the cold, clear air, breathing the crisp temperature into my lungs. I return to the house, drink a fourth cup of coffee and ascend the stairs to my study with feelings of both anticipation and dread. By the end of the day I seem to have accomplished so little, a few pages I know will have to be rewritten.

Tomorrow, John and I go to the doctor again. We will try to resolve some further course of action for him. We will also have the doctor examine me to see if I am well—I mean well in spite of my dry, burning eyes, aching back, and assorted debilities.

January 15
A magnificent day! After a week of sub-zero temperatures and hills of frozen snow, today a thaw began. Late in the afternoon the sky was streaked with pink and scarlet streamers—a sky reminiscent of the January sky two years ago that I described while writing the last pages of *In the Land of Morning*. The cycle comes around once more.

Yesterday the doctor found John had recovered physically and told him he thought his condition was now emotional, a residue from the long months of the viral disorder. John and I reacted with disbelief, almost despair. Then we decided the diagnosis might perhaps rid us of the uncertainty about how much might still be physical and how much emotional, and might allow us to concentrate our energies on the area needing improvement. Afterwards we both felt better and went to a Chinese restaurant for sweet and sour duck.

The doctor found me fairly well except for a slight rise once again in my blood pressure—not serious, but higher than it should be, tied undeniably to my weight. I must try to lose some more, but it is difficult. The compulsion to eat a good dinner satisfies the tension built up during the day.

Meanwhile, today I worked on chapter nine, moving forward a miserly two pages. I feel I am trying to budge massive stones.

The entire background is so unfamiliar that every sentence requires me to pause. I return to the beginning of the chapter and rewrite, a new line here, another line there, building additional impetus, hoping I can go further than the draft before.

Tonight Mark came from Chicago and we ate and watched "War and Peace" on television, the final episode in the 15-hour BBC production. So very lovely! One finishes viewing the episodes with a conviction that so much of life is determined by chance. There are interruptions, as well, as we are caught in the great events, upheavals, and wars. Afterwards the stream of life resumes for us, shattered love is mended, children are born, dreams are reawakened. The young feel the way is the future and the old look back with nostalgia. As I watched the lives of those Russian families I identified them with the life of my own family, with Diana and our sons.

Afterwards, before going to bed, I walked around the yard in boots and coat, exercising, thinking, breathing the sharp night air into my lungs. I saw Diana baking in the kitchen, her dark pretty face visible in the window. Mark wrote or read up in my study, the light from there shining down across the snow. I thought of life and death and being fifty years old. And I murmured a prayer that I work well tomorrow.

January 24
After working well through the weekend, pushing forward on chapter nine to page 301, Monday became a disaster! Sitting on the edge of my bed to put on my socks, I pulled up rapidly and felt something tearing in my back. So it was back into bed for the damn recurrent back trouble, the muscle spasm that develops

from the weakened lower back and twists my body out of shape. Examining myself naked, I am stricken to see my hip tilting to the right, my frame resembling a lopsided pear.

Although the pain hasn't been as severe as in earlier bouts I have remained in bed with heat and some pills prescribed by the doctor. Although I spend the hours reading, I am anxious to get to the typewriter. Yesterday I crept up to the study and managed to write a half-dozen letters. When I finished I could not straighten up and limped down the stairs. In bed I feel fairly comfortable, although I am frustrated and impatient. Today I am trying to write for a few hours again but by the painful ripples that sweep my back, I know it is too early to start work.

Discipline, energy, will, all these are blunted when disorders and illness take over. To creep slowly through the house in the middle of the day, wearing bathrobe and pajamas like an invalid, is maddening.

Even now as I write these paragraphs my back begins to hurt again and I am apprehensive that by not remaining quiet, ministering it with heat and rest, I do myself further damage and impede my recovery. So to hell with it! I will carry my failing, wretched and complaining carcass back to bed!

February 2
The whole wretched business of my back might have been worse. About ten days have passed and I have been mending slowly. For about a week I have been getting to my typewriter, working for a few hours until the ache banishes my ability to concentrate. I lie down for a few moments, but the only comfortable position seems to be in bed with a heating pad applied to my decrepit frame.

The last few days have been better and I have managed to write for six and seven hours at a time. For a few days the weather turned springlike, the temperature setting a record in the fifties. Almost all the snow has thawed and, sometimes, at twilight, as I walk from the study to the house a faint scent of spring touches my nostrils. Or is it simply a longing and memory of spring that erupts in the deep womb of winter?

The book goes very slowly. After the lost days of writing, even though I read for hours, the chapter section with Kontos at sea drags on. I struggle and suffer over each page.

In addition to my own disorders, we have been besieged these last two weeks with deaths. The first was a ninety-one-year old man whose wake lacked only cocktails to make it a total celebration. That is the way death should be greeted, a courtly traveler carrying away the shells of men and women who have lived long, full lives.

A few days after the old man's passing, a family friend who was just fifty-eight died ignominiously while sitting on the stool in a hospital toilet.

Then my nephew Leo's father-in-law died and his death touched us closer than the others. He was a good, proud man with frailties but also a generous man who lived with raw courage through his own illnesses. I remember him with affection.

These days I am conscious of death, illness, disorders. My dreams are a tangled crossroads, a spider-web of paths at the end of which I see fragments of faces and hear snatches of voices from the living and the dead.

In reading through some of the books on Greece in these last few days I ran across a verse of Hesiod that I may use in the foreword to the novel. He writes of the Greeks:

This is the race of iron. Dark is their plight.
Toil and sorrow by day are theirs, and by night
the anguish of death; and the gods afflict them and kill,
though there's yet a trifle of good amid manifold ill.

February 11

This morning the clouds of yesterday were gone, the snow moving eastward, leaving us a bright day of sun and blue water visible beyond the rim of the frozen lake. As the day progressed, the water drove the boundaries of ice closer to the shore.

Despite the magnificence of the day I feel leaden, without any spark, and am not sure why. The worst of the back problem seems behind me and I have managed to work each day. I write several pages and am barely finished with them when I see ways to improve them. I rewrite endlessly and one draft seems no better than an earlier one once it is on paper.

For the moment I seem to have lost any guiding vision, that quick, volatile leaping that leads from one small awareness to another revelation. I think that vision has to do with the feeling that the characters are under control rather than floundering. It is like watching or directing a play enacted on a brightly-lit stage where the characters respond at once to my instructions. Now I feel the stage darkened, the characters shrouded and motionless. Sitting in the audience, from time to time I cry out a command. On the stage a figure moves stiffly and awkwardly and then freezes once again. I try another command, still another. The characters ignore me, the stage remains dark. I sit slumped and depressed, continuing to mumble ineffectual directions that are ignored.

It has taken me three hours to write a single page and I know that will not be the final draft. At this rate how long will a book of six hundred pages take to write? Feeling melancholy and resigned, I resist sadness. The sun beams in across my desk, across the stack of discarded pages that has grown to be a foot high in the fifteen months since I began the book. On the top of the stack the bronze priest glistens, the light reflecting from his surface.

Tomorrow may be better. I hope so. Meanwhile, I will sit and stare out across the ice floes, at the blue water, at the green pines, and take what pleasure can be taken in simply being alive.

February 17
This morning I took a walk, still favoring my back, but breathing in the magnificent days with its portents of spring. Yet my dark mood continues. I wake early in the morning, while it is still dark, and once awake find it impossible to sleep again. All the problems, tensions and dilemmas whirl in my thoughts. My son, mother, money, contracts, the book...finally, I rise and go to the kitchen for orange juice and coffee to start my day.

Afterwards I work for a few hours at a time on the book. The sea chapter moves slowly. There are some good scenes but they are still written too much with my head buried in books on ships and the sea. These details stick out in the manscuript like foreign substances put in for "color": "The masthead lookout's cry was muffled by the wind and the lively crack of sails."

Do sails really crack? I read somewhere that they do and I have inserted the reference. Maybe that makes me more conscious of it than a reader might be. I know I have never before written in such detail of ships. Perhaps a series of drafts will blend the facts more naturally with the story.

My dear niece, Barbara, is back in the hospital in intensive care. The little gnarled old guard at the gatehouse here in our community, who could barely see as he waved us by, has died from a bleeding ulcer. My mother grows more obstreperous every day, shuffling miserably from room to room, radiating her wretchedness across everyone. Yet it is not her fault; it is simply that she has lived too long. At least that's the way it seems to me now.

I am rereading the *Letters of Kazantzakis*, the biography compiled by his wife, Eleni. Those few hours I spend with that great man's spirit and vision lighten my own soul. In the beginning of his years of writing he would ask Eleni to read something he had just written and let him know if she thought it worthwhile. At the end of his life, after so many books, writing his spiritual autobiography, *Report to Greco*, the same uncertainty about what he had done prevailed.

That follows a pattern: the burden of creation for the creator, feeling simultaneously the fever of joy and the fever of doubt. After one finishes a section of writing, the spirit cries, "It is good!" and then, falteringly, the cry becomes, "It is good, isn't it?"

All his life Kazantzakis dreamed of being an ascetic who could master the hungers of his body. But in early pictures of him, he had the advantage of an ascetic's frame. My stocky carcass seems built for gluttony and excess.

The sun has changed stations in the sky once more. I can see that by the way the light reflects different portions of my desk at the same time each afternoon. The strip of sunlight moves daily, across the bow of the model brig, across the mound of discarded pages held down by the bronze priest, across the bottle of green Airwick.

Nearing the end of February, feeling the cold of winter deep in my bones, I read Kazantzakis and dream of the sun of Greece.

February 25
These are strange and lovely winter days that I enjoy, despite the persistent ache in my back. A few days ago a storm struck the lake, twenty-foot waves breaking across the beach. When the storm diminished I saw the water hurled up by the waves had frozen into white, sculptured forms. As the water froze, the silence returned.

I have been working better for several days now, still on the sea chapter that threatens to capsize me. Building to the end of a 50-page chapter, I have Kontos and Kanaris launch the first fireship. In the two or three pages I rewrote a dozen times today I had the ship used as a fire carrier belonging to Papanikolas since he is the personage history has recorded using the ship for the first time. But in describing his feelings I thought about how much more poignant it would be if the ship to be sacrificed belonged to Leonidas Kontos, the principal character of the chapter. So I rewrote the pages to make that change.

It is strange how writing fashions the changes, changes that cannot be structured by thinking or planning. The process is so difficult to explain to young or tyro writers who want to be assured of everything before they begin writing. Most of what we discover comes by writing and not by planning. It isn't until we put words down on paper that we understand what is taking place. From the pages of writing, another direction is suggested, and the possibility of new scenes is born. That is elementary but it is also a truth that must be rediscovered by everyone who writes.

After seven or eight hours at the typewriter today, my back aches and my eyes burn. But I wrote a lovely page, about the coming of sunset on the night Leonidas Kontos will sacrifice his ship to the flames, clouds and stars and moon rising like mourners. One page to make the day worthwhile.

March 19
I have been uncertain how to proceed after finishing the sea chapter. I tried sketches on events and characters. One character kept intruding, throwing a web of fascination across my plans: Papalikos, the wolf-monk, modeled broadly on the historical figure of the monk Papaflessas. To enter his viewpoint for a section seemed to provide challenges and opportunities. So much of the war was shameful, false leaders sacrificing morality and decency for their own aims. Intrigues and machinations were rampant. In using Papalikos, I would have a participant in the intrigue and deception.

Three days ago I began the chapter, slowly working forward a half-dozen pages. The following day I began the chapter again, firming and expanding the foundation. Papalikos, scourging the other Greek leaders, flees because he fears they will assassinate him and takes refuge with a handful of his followers in an

Arcadian mountain village. He sees a woman there he is drawn to, but he is more deeply attracted to her daughter, a golden-haired little beauty of about ten. There is a chance for contrasts here, to reveal the innate brutality of the man and yet also show some vestige of tenderness about him as well.

This chapter might begin as he takes lodging in the woman's house. He abuses the mother but treats the child with care because he is awed by her innocence and beauty. To curry his favor, the woman tells him of a farmer who has hidden gold. Papalikos plots to steal the gold cache because the money will provide him an army of men to do God's will and free Greece. The scene where he threatens to kill the farmer, his wife and their two daughters could be strong and graphic.

Afterwards, the gold in his possession, Papalikos prepares to leave. Filled with a sense of power and a movement to violence, he yearns to ravish the child. But her sweetness and innocence deter him and he leaves her untouched and unharmed. The chapter will show him as brutal and immoral, willing to use any means to achieve his end. But he must also make a small claim upon our sympathies because he could have harmed the child and leaves her alone.

That is the plan of the chapter as I see it now. But tomorrow may change it, and the writing may alter it. The book has its own life and sometimes that life asserts its own direction, and purpose.

I have had a cold the last two days, but have managed to work on the chapter, feeling the excitement driving me. My back still aches, and John is still not well. So once more Greece, Easter in Greece, seems to be fading.

March 27
It has been unseasonably cold the last few days, but each day is still a harbinger of spring, the calendar ignoring the weather. Today I walked for an hour, along the lake, up the hill and down to the tennis courts. The green surface is deserted now, but I have vivid memories of the courts crammed with players, the whack of balls, the leaping and running. I hope I can play this year.

Yesterday the muscle spasm in my back returned and when I undressed I saw the weird twisting of my body. What brings on the cursed crookedness? I have been exercising diligently to strengthen myself. But the spasm and pains continue, if not severe at least persistent. Today after I had worked for some hours the pain grew stronger and I had to lie down. Enough! I refuse to allow this journal to become a medical record of my misery.

There is enough illness and misery around. My brother-in-law, George, suffered a heart attack and will be in the hospital for perhaps six weeks.

Today I worked on the Papalikos chapter. The pages move slowly, his character and the story developing as I write. I envision a final scene where Papalikos kills the farmer. The scene remains vague and I move toward it through the shadow.

Yesterday, to rest my back, I sat in my rocker and read the Pandelis Prevelakis book on Kazantzakis, *The Poet and His Odyssey*. How beautifully he renders the visage and soul of that dedicated and incredibly disciplined man! How Kazantzakis worked from dawn until dark, possessed by the fury of creating! I feel pale and trivial beside him, mourning my disruptions, my starts and stops, my petty disorders. They keep multiplying. Looking at my right hand this evening I noticed that several of my fingers were knobbed and swollen. Arthritis? Perhaps an occupational hazard of writing that produces crooked fingers as well as a crooked back.

In the Prevelakis book I found a reference to the Cretans having an inherent love of freedom. They were, in Prevelakis' words, shepherds of shadows. And I thought of that as a possible title for the book, a title suggesting the gathering of those elusive shadows. *The Shepherds of Shadows*...the best projected title so far.

April 1

For the past four days the writing on chapter ten has gone splendidly. This evening, after about a dozen revisions of the final three pages of the section, I finished a sturdy draft. I am as excited by the section as I have been with any other portion of the book.

Yet, in spite of the excitement, these last few mornings have been agony in getting started. I have had excuses, some real and some contrived, but all calculated to prevent me coming upstairs to begin. Once started, however, the joy of writing takes over, with all the surprises and revelations good writing provides the writer. When everything comes together, the book glows with life.

At the end of this chapter, after killing the miser, the monk gathers his men to depart from the village. In a final scene the little girl, barefooted and barelegged, runs alongside his horse and tosses him a single yellow rose. He scents her fragrance in it, feels the smoothness he imagines her body to have as he puts the petal to his lips. Then he crushes the flower, hurls it away, and rides on to war. Those are the bones of the end of the chapter but I feel it has power.

There is a scent of stronger spring in the air today, after a thunderstorm swept away some of the debris of winter. And after an endless winter, how eagerly we wait for spring!

My damn back may be decrepit, I may have frailties and my spirit may have lapses, but, by God, sometimes I put words and sentences together as if I were the healthiest devil on earth!

April 7—Palm Sunday

Today the full force of winter returned. There has been a frigid wind, a bleak drizzle, and tonight the surf pounds the beach. It is as if the winter, angry at being forced to relinquish its grip on the land, is mustering its forces for a few final assaults.

For the past few days I have been reading and sketching the sequel to the Cretan chapter seven. I will have Andreas and Voula and the clan move to the cave. As I read or walk along the beach I see the scenes and hear dialogue from the chapter; Voula might be betrothed to another warrior, a man that arouses jealousy and hate in Andreas. They will have a confrontation over her. The fragments of the chapter float unmoored in my head, waiting to be caught in a net and drawn together.

Mark left today for Albuquerque and then will move on to settle in San Francisco. He gave up his studio apartment in Chicago, found an actor to play his role at the Children's Theatre, and brought a carload of his books, clothing, and papers to us. In just the few years he has been in that tiny apartment he, too, has begun to accumulate the assorted flotsam and jetsam we all acquire in our lives.

Tonight Diana and I miss him. We might not have seen him that often while he lived in Chicago, but we knew he was only an hour away, could always come home for a meal or to walk the beach and woods. But he began to feel it was time for him to leave and perhaps he was right. There isn't any reason to remain rooted at twenty-five. So he packed up the old suitcase once owned by Nick the Greek and I drove him downtown to the Palmer House to catch the airport bus after first dropping mother and Diana at church. I hugged Mark goodby and watched him walking away, another young man on his way west, into adventures and experiences unknown to any of us now.

After mother, Diana and I returned home, as I lay on the couch in my study I read of Crete. While dark clouds swirled across the sky, my thoughts wandered to Mark in his plane, and I thought how much more poignant their departures are for us than departing is for them. And I remember a line I put in *The Odyssey of Kostas Volakis*, where Kostas observes that a father lives in his sons in a way the sons can never live in the father.

May the good spirits look after the young man. We don't love him any more, I am sure, than other fathers and mothers love their sons, nor is he more deserving of a fortuitous destiny than other boys...but simply because he is a good and gentle young man whose poems and heart speak the quality of his soul. And I am sure some of my pensiveness and nostalgia will find its way tomorrow into the chapter on Crete.

April 27
It is a hot and balmy day. Last night I spoke before a library association in Oakbrook and Diana and I remained at the hotel overnight. This morning we drove back home and I have spent a listless afternoon.

I am tired, with that curious weariness that settles over me after I have spoken to an audience. They gave me a standing ovation at the end of my talk and about a hundred people passed to shake hands and have me sign my name on small cards they could place in my books at the libraries. I had that sense of communion with people, a kind of spiritual link that came through the talk and their response. Their faces and the words they spoke to me revealed how much they had been touched. I am not sure just why I reach the spirit of an audience as I do. Perhaps it is because I talk candidly of my own life, foolishness, aging and the shadow of death, threading these things together in a way they can identify with their own lives and longings. At times like that I feel a kinship with my father, the priest.

Working on the screenplay of *In the Land of Morning* since I returned from the meetings in New York, I have had to put the novel aside. That disheartens and saddens me, but I am far enough along to pick up the story once again when the time comes. After another lecture before a temple sisterhood tomorrow I will have the rest of the week to work on the script. Friday I leave for Louisville, Kentucky, to to a special story on the 100th Kentucky Derby for the *Chicago Tribune Magazine*. John will come with me as my official photographer, and we are both looking forward to the experience despite the pandemonium we will find there.

Meanwhile, Andreas, Voula, Kyriakos and the other Cretans in the chapter I am working on will wait silent and motionless in the shadows, waiting for me to breath life into them again.

It is strange that this turning of the season, this premature hurling into the heat of summer, fills me with melancholy. Perhaps it isn't the weather but the residue of the lecture, so many people whose faces pass in an instant, who speak a few words to me, clasp my fingers and then disappear. So many good people that I will probably never see again.

May 8
Winter has returned! I find it hard to believe that just last week we had hot, sunny days. The last few days have been rainy and cold, temperatures plummeting into the 30s, the sky seething with stormy clouds.

John and I drove to Louisville last week. There was a crowd of almost 175,000 there to watch the running of the Kentucky Derby. Visitors and citizens were all caught up in that madness. From the motels that triple their rates to the taxicabs that triple their fares, the city was one massive, inexorable claw of greed. I saw the Derby as a shabby relic of some past glory. By the frenzied labor of public relations people, aided by hundreds of newspapermen and newspaperwomen who swarm over the track, the mediocrity of the event is obscured. Somehow in all the trivial sound and fury I must find a story.

Back in Indiana I did the Ridge Book Club lecture yesterday and will speak at Chicago State College on Friday. That will finish my lecture obligations for this spring. Then as soon as I can finish the screenplay I can return to the novel. I am consoled by knowing I have driven deeply enough into the soul of the book that I will be able, God willing, to regain the challenge and excitement.

Tonight we carried a small white cake with three candles on it into the dining room for my mother's eighty-sixth birthday, or perhaps it is her eighty-seventh birthday. Diana, the boys and I sang happy birthday to her and kissed her. How strange it is when one considers how long she has dwelt on this earth—so many years longer than I have lived.

While in the earth my father waits for her to join him.

May 12—Mother's Day
When I rose this morning about seven the sky was a stunning blue, the air cool and clear. Taking a series of deep breaths seemed to fill my body with some vital, life-nourishing vapor. Now, two hours later, the sky has filled with black and purple clouds, the lake altered to a stormy, tumultuous gray. So swiftly does the earth change its face!

On Friday I finished my last lecture. Afterwards we stopped to eat and drink a little wine at my mother-in-law's house. Yesterday dragged listlessly while I made a few half-hearted efforts at the screenplay. Although I know a good screenplay might enhance our chances to make a film of *Morning*, the novel haunts me like a love I have been separated from for a while. The truth is that I don't want to work on anything else but the book now. But reason advises me to hit the screenplay hard and afterwards muster my forces to return to the novel.

We had a letter from Mark yesterday in San Francisco, a seven-page letter full of lovely thoughts and phrases about love, faith and life. He sounds even more involved in the religion of the Guru Mahara Ji than he was in Chicago. Diana was depressed by the letter and I had mixed feelings. He may be filled with this life-force and it may help him, but I don't like to envision him existing in some spiritual cocoon, a young fakir able to sleep on a bed of nails and yet unable to live.

I fill these pages with musings about life and my days, feeling a void, a lamentable emptiness in place of the fountain of the novel. I must try to return to it soon.

May 23
Just as one begins to despair of summer ever arriving, a magnificent day dawns, a sharp, bracing coolness in the air, ripples of

warmth riding from the sun.

I finished the Kentucky Derby story yesterday and mailed it to the *Tribune*. Today I tried to start back on the script. I worked a few hours while the sun taunted me through the drawn blinds. Finally, I gave up, stripped down to trunks for the beach. I took John Beecher's book of poetry that I will review for *Book World* but I could not concentrate on reading. I came back to the house for the mail and there was a sad, moving letter from a good writer friend who feels his personal life is coming apart. He writes that of his numerous friends I am the only one who seems able to write and keep his personal life intact.

I wonder sometimes if I am really keeping it intact or whether I am padlocked by the years. I know what a sensitive, special woman Diana is and I love her very much, feel linked to her in so many ways. Yet I am sometimes lonely, need different kinds of love. Yet I have no great temptation to change the structure of my life. There isn't much I want out there that I do not keep hoping I can find here.

Tonight I drove mother to the store in town. She seems to be sinking daily into a disoriented daze. I feel sorry for her as she sits trying to read, hour after hour, rising with a groan, shuffling stiffly from her room to the bathroom and back to her chair again. She is always cold, and keeps pleading with us to turn up the thermostat. To hear her laugh is a rarity, and yet why should she laugh?

And John is not well. He suffered his illness for all those months, fighting his own fears, while the roles of those around him became confused and overlapped: internist, psychiatrist, father, mother. I know he is suffering, and yet I don't know what we can do to help him. Perhaps there is nothing to be done except try not to panic...only watch and wait.

Meanwhile, the book sits in the shadows, no pages added to the manuscript for weeks now. And with the script to be finished, I am not sure how soon I will be able to return to it. God help me make it soon.

June 5

Today is my 51st birthday and it has been a good day. I started working early in the morning on the film script and worked through most of the afternoon. In the late afternoon Diana came up to the study and we made love. Afterwards, feeling buoyant,

I played two sets of tennis for the first time since my back injury in January. I returned to shower, to a good dinner with a few glasses of wine. . .and so to the end of a day.

Hopefully by the end of this week I will have about half the script to send to New York. Then I will try to finish the remaining half as quickly as I can and return to the novel. I feel like a lover absent from his beloved. But there is also a relief in not having to struggle to create. Yet, without work on the novel, there seems little material of consequence to add to this journal.

Tonight some good friends came to eat a birthday dinner with us. After the meal, as we sat around the table, my mother, sensing compassion from our visitors, trudged to her bedroom and returned with her scrapbooks. She seems to have a compulsion to prove her life worthwhile, pointing to this photograph of her with a congressman, this letter of commendation from a mayor, this award from the Red Cross. When our friends warmed her with their praise and admiration, she returned to her room and brought out several plaques from organizations for her meritorious service.

There was a sadness about the event and as I passed her room late tonight the room was dark except for the small night-light she has always needed, like the light in the room of a child. Perhaps she slept dreaming of her small past glories.

Will I someday pull out reviews and awards and the letters from eminent friends when friends come to visit the house of my children? No man can know his destiny.

July 29

This marks the longest gap in this journal since I began writing it in December of 1972. It has been a frustrating, unproductive period. Perhaps the absence from work on the novel explains the difficulties and problems. So many dilemmas are unresolved, relationships smothering, my life in a kind of shambles.

I am working on the articles for the *Chicago Tribune* as well as the story for *Today's Health* that I have delayed for weeks now. In addition I am doing a review for the *Tribune's Book World*. Even the amount of work I have to do would be tolerable if at least I could work well. But a strange apathy hangs over me and the days slip by. I am getting plenty of sun, play tennis every day or every other day, have gotten brown and healthy-looking. But the work drags on without spark, every line a struggle.

Even this entry in the journal seems dislocated and rambling. Have I had a stroke? Rage and frustration feed at me and I feel an impatience and fury against everyone around me.

John was away at Kalamazoo, and the one morning in two weeks he returned home Diana and I argued. How stupid that was, because he heard us. He must feel his presence adds to our tensions. He must also feel that it would better for him to move away from the house. I think both Diana and I understand that may be best for him although we would prefer to keep him here so we can try to respond with what help he needs.

If I can stay calm, avoid making any hasty or desperate decisions, then perhaps we can survive this tense period as we have survived others before. But I have the maddening feeling that I must break free!

August 4
I woke this morning near 5:00 a.m. and noticed the darkness is lasting longer, the cycle of summer passing into autumn. In the early spring one yearns for sun and warmth, to peel away clothing, feel the soothing water. Then, as the summer moves on, a cold, bleak day arrives and one feels attuned to another season.

Meanwhile, while I have still not returned to the novel, that time is growing closer. The *Tribune* articles are finished and also the cover review for *Book World* that should be done today. I will return to the screenplay and if I can finish it early in September I might still make the trip to Greece this year.

This has not been a good summer for me. In some ways it has been physically beneficial. But emotionally I have felt depleted, dissatisfied with my life, angry with my frailties, and with those around me. I have taken my anger out on my mother and Diana, blaming them for things that are not their fault.

I must try to be grateful for the things I have. In the book by Archie Lieberman I have just reviewed, an Illinois farm mother quotes a poem by Walt Whitman that ends:

Whoever is not in his coffin, and the dark grave
let him know he has enough.

In my saner moments I realize I have enough. Perhaps the longing to work on the novel, to pour out the emotion that whirls within me, produces this malaise, this aggravation.

August 19
Today I began working on the novel again after an absence of
several months. Starting was painful and all morning and into
afternoon I whirled with excuses for delaying a beginning still
one more day. Then when I picked up the last few chapters I
had completed, I was caught by the tragic coincidence that I
should be writing of Greek-Turkish battles in a time when
Greek and Turkish blood is being spilled again on Cyprus. The
newsreels the last few weeks showing frightened, desperate
refugees are the faces of Greeks as they might have been at the
time of the revolution. The terrain is changed, jet planes swoop
overhead, but the shadow of old hatreds remains unchanged.

The Greek Junta led by the colonels machinated an attempted
takeover of the Makarios government on Cyprus and the Turks
invaded the island. Under the threat of war between Greece and
Turkey, the Junta fell and the democratic Constantine
Karamanlis returned from exile to Athens to form a new government. For a few days jubilant crowds filled Constitution Square.
Theodorakis, Mercouri, all the political exiles were welcomed
back. But as the agony on Cyprus continued, the Turkish army
invading and occupying more and more of the island, jubilation
has turned to frustration and anger by the Greeks against
Turkey, America and Kissinger. Thousands of Greek-Americans
gathered in Chicago today in protest and the Greek restaurants
throughout the city closed their doors in a one-day strike.

Now, under these shadows, I return to the novel.

I have started with the Cretan chapter revolving around
Andreas and Voula. Working through an early draft of that
section, I will move on to Vorogrivas, the guerilla captain, and
the death of the old Suliot, Boukouvalas.

My plans to travel to Greece, possibly even to Turkey in
September, remain in limbo. The threat of war between the two
countries makes a postponement likely. I can probably finish the
novel without making a trip, but I know that a journey there
would strengthen and authenticate the book.

We will see what happens. Having started once again I will
keep going, making only brief detours for other work I have to
do. There is so far to go, it is true, and yet I am 90,000 words further along than I was two years ago when I first began putting
tentative words on paper. Characters have been born during
this time, fleshed out, becoming as real as human beings for me.

August 27
For the last eight days I have been working well. I finished a good draft of chapter seven, Andreas in Crete, and mailed it to Walter Hamady for the small gift edition he wishes to publish. Then, through the next five days I finished the death of Boukouvalas scene, which ends chapter eight. I think it is much better now, particularly the final pages where Boukouvalas comes charging the Turks at the bridge, his appearance striking terror into them because they believe he has returned from the dead.

In these last days of work I see the possibility of a tighter book, eliminating Kolokotronis at the battle of Valtetzi and going directly to the Kontos chapter with the fireship and then proceeding to the Papalikos chapter where the monk murders the miser for his gold. If I went from there to chapter eleven, following Andreas in Crete, his battle to the death with Kasandonis over Voula and his banishment from the cave, then I might finish the book with a single long chapter on the seige and fall of the fortress of Tripolitza.

A problem I must resolve for that last chapter will be whether it is written from the viewpoint of a Greek attacker or a Turkish defender. What must come across is the tragedy of war, the failure of principles when men are possessed by greed and lust.

As now planned, the book might finish with about 120,000 words. That would not be a long book when compared with *War and Peace* or *August 1914*, but would be twice the length of most of my novels. And it would contain in the twelve-odd chapters a microcosm of the larger canvas, love, hate, vengeance, the myriad forces arrayed against one another in war. The important thing is that the finished book must hold together, the parts fitting smoothly, so that in reading it one senses the fusing of passion, patriotism, hate and terror.

Will I make it to Greece this fall? A decision will have to be made soon.

September 5
Today is the anniversary of the fall of Candia, Crete, to the Turks in 1669, an item gleaned from Llewellyn Smith's fine book on Crete, *The Great Island*, which I have been reading.

On Sunday my back began to hurt again, whether from the

hard sets of tennis I played on Saturday or from the long hours at the typewriter, I don't know. I made the Pan-Icarian lecture and the following day, rainy and cold as a day in late autumn, several of my nephews, nieces and their children drove out to visit us. We had a pleasant afternoon while we talked, laughed and drank. The following day I rested in bed, a heating pad on my back. Last night John rubbed my back with ointment, as he used to do in the spring.

Resting a good deal of the time these last few days, I have been reading, almost three books in three days: *The Great Island*, that I mentioned, and *The Killer-Angels*, a really splendid novel on the Civil War that encompasses the viewpoints of Lee, Buford, Longstreet and other generals during the three days of the battle of Gettysburg. I was excited by the book and depressed, as well, because it opened new dissatisfaction for me about my own work.

The achievement of the Civil War novel is the ways in which it weaves men and war into a moving tapestry, a sense of how battles are somehow decided by human frailties. Across the book broods the majestic and mythic vision of General Robert E. Lee who was so convinced that an army survives on faith and spirit that to order a retreat would forever destroy their will and capacity to fight. Believing that with his heart and his head, he ordered the senseless, brutal assault on Cemetery Ridge that Longstreet knows will be a disaster.

Dealing with the Civil War in America provides a writer a mass of material, diaries, and memoirs. There is so much less available material on the Greek War for Independence. Still, that was the war I chose and I must fill that canvas with the drama of the events and the heroism of individuals.

I tried to work today and spent several hours struggling at the typewriter but a melancholy made the day unproductive. When I went downstairs in the afternoon, mother complained to me about Diana having gone out and left her alone in the house. I tried to explain to her that I was just across the terrace and up the stairs in my study but that didn't seem to appease her. John is also tense tonight and came up to my study after dinner to sprawl across the couch. While he rested I sat in the rocker under the small beam of the lamp and read a lovely essay by Loren Eiseley on enduring the night. He quotes the words of St.

Paul: "Beareth all things, believeth all things, hopeth all things, endureth all things."

I hope to God I can bear, believe, hope and endure. . . .

September 17
These are lovely autumn days, the final golden period of the summer, with the children back in school. The beach is as solitary as it is in winter. The beauty of these days is marred only by my wretchedness. I went to the doctor on Friday with pain in my abdomen and back. He found my blood pressure higher than it should be and my prostrate (that ripe fruit of middle-age males) swollen and tender. Two doctors prodding and pushing fingers and instruments up my anus crowned several days of misery.

It is hard to work under these conditions and meanwhile I haven't made any decision about going to Greece in October. But I have decided to write letters to all the members of our family living in Chicago, suggesting that I fabricate a lie for my mother, telling her that I will be leaving our house for the winter to teach, Diana coming with me. That will mean my mother must begin a series of visits to my nephews' and nieces' houses.

On Sunday, to break the news to her, I drove her to church in Chicago and afterwards to the cemetery to my father's grave. When I told her about my plans and that she would have to stay in other houses for a while, I was surprised at the quietness of her reaction: "Do what you have to do for your family," she said. "I won't be lost." Her response was calm and lucid, as if the confusion and senility she manifests some of the time were suddenly cleared away.

She has lived with Diana and me for more than twenty of the twenty-three years since my father's death. I know it bothers and will bother me that I should be driving her from the house she feels is her home, where she feels she belongs. Standing beside my father's grave, over the earth where she will be buried someday, I ask him to understand, that I do it for Diana and John as well as myself. But I know the responsibility is mine.

September 19
It is still another lovely day, soft and scented with the coming of autumn. But my work has been frustrating because I am revising

the screenplay according to changes they sent me from New York that seem to make little sense. My mother remains unaware, I think, of the maneuverings we are undertaking to get her away from here for the winter. Somehow she seems calmer, strangely bearable. Perhaps that comes from our knowing that in a few weeks she will be gone.

This evening some neighbors joined us for dinner. I felt curiously detached, hearing their voices as if from a great distance. The long, interminable evening dragged on and on. After they left I walked in my circular pattern of exercise in the yard, wary of aches, abdominal pain, throbbings from the baleful prostrate.

I am up in my study now, a little before midnight, swept with a depression and loneliness... a sense that the path ahead is fraught with endless dangers. I feel I lack vigor and discipline, letting the precious days and hours escape. I must finish these screenplay revisions and return to the novel. I have moments when I believe I may not be far from the end and other moments when I think I have months and months, perhaps even years, still ahead.

And I am beset by this dreadful feeling of isolation, no one really understanding my problems or able to help me. Buddha was right, "Follow thine own path alone, O my heart, O old rhinoceros." Perhaps tomorrow will be a better day.

September 28
Yesterday I mailed off the final pages of the revised screenplay. Hopefully I am finished now.

Today I began work again on the novel, struggling to get started. That is the paradox. All these months I have yearned to be working on the book, counted the days and nights, and now with the prospect of starting, I squirm to find excuses not to begin. Perhaps my spirit resists returning to the labor.

Chapter eleven picks up the story of Andreas on Crete, the clan assembling in the cave. I started page 371 a dozen times today, one clumsy sentence leading painstakingly to another awkward one. I wrote one paragraph twelve times. Slowly, laboriously, a word is improved, a sentence is amended so that at the end of about five hours I have finished a page and a half. Yet I can't even be sure that will be the final page.

In the house my mother is packing for her departure to the

first of my nephews' houses. She believes we will be leaving this house soon ourselves. I see her shuffling about and have pangs of guilt and remorse. But I believe it must be done. Too much depends on this coming winter.

Next Friday I begin teaching a writing class at Columbia College one day a week. By the 11th of October I must make the decision about Greece. The advantages are that I will be able to verify locales I am using, absorb atmosphere and a sense of place. The disadvantages are that a trip may break the rhythm I pick up now as I return to the book.

There are days, walking or resting, when I think I might finish the book by next spring. At other times I feel there is more than a year's work ahead of me. I know it is the best writing I have done, but there are flaws. I know that as well. Having aimed high, I must not settle for less.

So, at this end of September, two days from our 29th wedding anniversary, melancholy and aching with assorted disorders, I gird my fiftyish loins for another assault on the mountain.

October 7
This has been a series of stunning days, the leaves beginning to turn to burnished gold, pale crimsons, faded browns. Once again my ailments shadow the season. The prostate flared again and when I used the prescribed medication, I broke out with a rash all across my body. Then four days ago I developed a neck spasm that hurt constantly. I missed my first writing class at Columbia but made the lecture at the Third Unitarian Church. While I have not written these past few days, with a heating pad applied to my neck, I have been reading and finished the trilogy of Bruce Catton's history of the Civil War. The tragic dimensions of that conflict have made me think through my own novel again.

What is the central theme of my novel: The futility of war? The tragedy of men pitted against one another for their beliefs? The striving for freedom? God, there is so much to be decided, planned and written. After finishing the last moving pages of Catton's final book I came upstairs to look at the pages of chapter eleven, wondering if I can work a few hours.

Joseph Heller spent thirteen years doing his first novel since *Catch 22*. Having been on my book only two years, I have eleven to go. Even in jest the thought hurts me.

Meanwhile this evening we plan to drive my mother to my nephew's house, the culmination of the huge lie that we are leaving so she must go.

October 10

My neck still feels as if a strong hand has gripped me by the throat, threatening to throttle me. But in spite of it I have worked well these last days on the novel, writing and rewriting for hours at a time.

When Andreas joins his family in the cave where the clan has taken refuge, he must dread going underground. When he first sees Voula, he must be furious at her for rejecting him. As the men move out to attack the Turkish garrisons, Andreas must fight recklessly, almost as if he is courting death, to prove he is braver than Kasandonis, the captain who is betrothed to Voula. Both men must be established as stout warriors in preparation for their battle together, a contest to match the one where Digenis wrestles Charon on the marble threshing floor of Death.

My pattern of work continues as it has gone in the past. I push forward a few disjointed pages, simply putting words down on paper to match the flashings of thought. Then, using these scenes as a rough track, I begin them over and try to pull more coherent paragraphs and scenes together. In this way scenes are born.

I project this chapter will be between forty and forty-five pages with certain key scenes. In one the old bard sings to the clan around the fire in the cave of the great history of Crete, the epics and poems of their heroes. Then there will be the scene where Andreas and Kasandonis battle for Voula, leading to the older man's death.

In the end, and this may not even be included in the present chapter, Andreas will leave Crete, forsaking Voula as his punishment for killing Kasandonis. What happens to his father, brothers and the clan? I don't know yet, but I hope to unravel that tale.

I say a small prayer that my aches, prostate and back, and undetermined other disorders don't disable me so I can keep writing. Amen!

October 14

The gray, overcast days are beginning, a somber foreshadowing of winter. I continue the slow, labored movement back into the rhythm of the book. Pages done over and over, sentences revised a dozen times, while I grope for the spark.

On the Cretan chapter I have carried the story through the first months spent by the clan in the cave. When word is brought to them of the massacre of a Cretan village by Turkish troops, the men choose lots to determine which ones will go for vengeance. Andreas cheats to be sure he is among the men who go. Following the story line I work along for pages of what seems, even after rewriting, mundane material and then, suddenly, an image is captured—the first stunning view of the stars for the men who have spent months buried in the cave. And, riding through the burned and pillaged village, as they pass a shallow grave where the Turks have thrown the bodies of the dead Cretans, a hand rises from the ground, the pale lifeless fingers seeming to point them on their path toward vengeance.

Stumbling through my days, working for a couple of hours, I lie down to rest my back, go downstairs to take aspirin or robaxin, return to the typewriter again, start the paragraph at the beginning of a page...write...rewrite...rewrite, so that there are eleven page 380s and ten page 381s and so on. An ant moves at a faster pace!

October 19

There have been several days of magnificent autumn colors, a fleeting, final burst of fall. Tonight it turned sharply cold and the wind rose. Suddenly, the roads are covered with leaves swept mercilessly from the branches of trees.

Yesterday I went into Chicago to teach my class, spending the time telling stories and letting my students talk. This morning I started on the Cretan chapter again. The battle scene where the Cretans attack the Turkish garrison has been done eight or nine times now. Although I have never experienced war, one does not need to murder to know the feelings of a murderer. One does not need to go wild with jealousy to understand what jealousy is like. However, transposing those feelings into pages of good writing is something else.

The scenes written and rewritten give birth to other scenes.

Like the first stroke of a brush across a canvas, arm and spirit moving toward one vision, suddenly, intuitively, hand and brush alter direction. By a flash of insight they find their way to another movement and vision born out of what has come before, but impossible to reach without that intermediate step.

The creative process is a mystery, even to the creator. The secret, I think, is to know how firmly to guide and yet remain sensitive to the intuitive aspects of the work which seek their own expression.

Something I said to my students in the writing class yesterday comes back to me now. There are times when the writing is like the violence of a blow and times when it is like the caress of love. Was that profound or simply obvious?

Tonight we played ping pong with neighbors. The physical activity helps release tension. Back home now, I make this entry in my journal, hearing the wind gathering strength for winter.

I pray it is a good, productive winter and a healthy one physically and emotionally. Is that asking too much?

October 23
How strangely life aids the rhythm and development of the book. On Saturday we had invited friends to dinner. Several of them had to return to Chicago early for a concert by the composer Yannis Markopoulos and the Cretan ballad singer Xelouris. Although we had not planned to go they urged us to join them. We attended the concert that I found an incredibly moving experience.

For the first time I heard the santouri played, an instrument full of mystery and resonance that created a sound unlike any other I had ever heard. There was a Cretan lyra player, several young women singers and Xelouris whose harsh, throaty voice evoked the passion, the heroic stance, and the agony of Greece. He sang songs of love and life, songs of journeys and of home, songs of the roots and songs of loneliness and exile.

In the darkened theatre box, Diana beside me, our friends around us, I was moved to tears several times. I think I was touched by the beauty of the songs and for other things: for the singers so far from their land, for the suffering of Greece, for Diana and myself growing older, for one of our good friends and his wife about to bear her first child, for the book that must be finished, for my sons, for my mother, for my home, for my dead father, for his island, blessed Crete....

On the following morning I found the songs and the music sifting their way into the book, into the pages of the Cretan chapter I am struggling with now. I can see the watchful, haunted faces of the men, women, and children of the clan as the old minstrel singer brings out his santouri and plays for them by firelight.

In such eerie ways do the book and life join hands again, giving me that sense that I am being provided some guidance and help, perhaps even from the spirits of Crete.

This afternoon I phoned and made reservations for a flight to Greece on November 6. I hope I can go. I have never seen Greece and Crete in winter and the prospect of the trip excites me. Tonight I walked briskly around the yard for an hour, warily awaiting pains and aches. I have two weeks yet to strengthen the back, heal the prostate, mend my wounds and prepare my spirit for flight!

November 2
Having postponed the departure for Greece until November 11, I am trying to put the Cretan chapter into publishable condition. Should anything happen to me on the journey, I think enough has been written to make a book.

But then, at my niece's house, my mother fell for the second time in several days. Perhaps it was simply an accident, miscounting her pills and taking one extra that might have made her sluggish or dizzy. It is bad luck for that to happen to her, adding to the grief that we are not there to look after her. I know I must bear the responsibility for sending her away. The reasons I have done it, for Diana, for John, for myself, are sufficient, but that doesn't mitigate the remorse. Once again, one can only feel the poor woman has lived too long.

Sometimes, in moments of despair, I too have a feeling I might have lived too long.

November 5
Winter has arrived like a fury. All day yesterday a hard, cold rain battered the house. Last night I walked around the yard for exercise, bundled to my throat and carrying an umbrella. Today, election day in the country, I worked almost all day trying to complete a good draft of the Cretan chapter.

Whether the proximity of the trip to Greece unsettles me or that I simply have not yet recovered the spark and rhythm of the book, I plod and struggle. From ten this morning until almost four this afternoon I retyped page 402—not revising sentences and words, but simply desperately probing to find a direction. I have scenes, but they don't lead anywhere.

After attacking and destroying the Turkish garrison, the men make camp. I need to send Kyriakos, Andreas' father, away from the tension developing between Andreas and Kasandonis. The father would act as a moderating influence on his son. Then I conceived of having the father wounded in the battle and that meant going back some pages to rewrite that scene. So in a draft completed this evening near seven o'clock, the wounded Kyriakos leads a group of wounded men back to the cave. Andreas is left behind and I must now build to the great fight he has with Kasandonis over Voula.

I hope to finish before leaving for Greece, but physically I feel so wretched today, so full of aches and pains, that I think I must be mad to travel. Somehow I drive through my days and accomplish some work. Perhaps Greece will provide the spark I need.

Now I will cover my typewriter and go downstairs for the rest of the night to listen to the election returns, to hear if the bitter fruit of Watergate has reaped a harvest of demolished Republicans.

November 13
The first snow of the season, several inches of heavy, wet flakes adhere to the bare branches of trees and mantle the earth. Driving in from Chicago tonight I passed under a canopy of lovely, snow-laden trees.

But the unhappy news is that my mother is in the hospital. She has been diagnosed as having heart acceleration, edema, and related ailments. The day before she entered the hospital Diana and I went to see her where she was staying with my sister in Chicago. I sat beside her while she lay in the big bed, slipping from rational moments into moments of confusion. She told me how she could not bear to move from place to place. I felt pity for her and for all of us.

When I spoke to the doctor about her he told me it would be prudent for me to delay the trip to Greece. I have postponed it for another week or perhaps for good. Everything seems to grow harder. Driving home from work in Chicago the other night, John triggered some eruption of despair. He couldn't sleep and rose and dressed and walked along the beach at dawn. When I got up at seven we talked for several hours. I came up to my study feeling drained and depressed, wondering how long he must suffer and what we can do to help him. I wondered whether the Doctor he is going to is the right one, and so on and so on....

He has so many questions about illness and life that no one seems able to answer...not the doctor, not Diana, not me. So we struggle along from day to day and from night to night.

I am tired and feel old and helpless. The Cretan chapter remained inactive today. I could not seem to work. Tonight at dinner John seemed better after having slept most of the day. Sleep is the easiest thing in the world to do as long as you're not afraid you won't sleep. Then it becomes a monster. I hope to God John doesn't have to experience that agony.

November 15
A long hard day of work, and a good draft of the Cretan chapter has been finished. Rereading it this evening I see flaws. Too many "souls," too many "Cretes," too many "stranges." But there are fine scenes, too, in the pages where the clan descends into the cave, the old psalmist singing, the *rhymadore* playing his santouri, the fight scene where Andreas kills Kasandonis.

The total of 55 pages comprising this section doesn't yet hold together as tightly as I would wish. In the morning I will begin again, working for a tighter draft.

My original conception was to carry the story with Andreas banished from the cave to the mountains where he would live on the run, harrying the Turks, finally rescuing the clan when the Turkish Bey sets fires in the cave entrances to suffocate the Greeks. But as the section expanded I realized it would need at least twenty more pages. That means I will need a third Cretan chapter, whether for this book or a later one remains to be seen.

What is missing in the book so far? The sequence of chapters bothers me and sometimes the Cretan sequences seem an intrusion, not really part of the original structure of the novel. Perhaps that, too, is a warning from blessed Kazantzakis. He is helping me with the Greek revolution, but Crete must be left to him.

Now, before going to bed, I will make some notes on ways to tighten and control the chapter better as I begin to rewrite tomorrow. Even as the trip to Greece remains uncertain, at least I can work.

November 22
I have had a week of good, substantial work, and another full draft of the Cretan chapter is completed. I think I can move on now. Having worked through the scenes with care, making some radical alterations, I managed to cut ten pages from last week's draft. The biggest change comes in the battle between Andreas and Kasandonis. In the earlier versions I had Andreas angry and bitter, full of hate and determined to kill the chieftain. But in rewriting I understood that his reckless challenge to the chieftain would be reevaluated during the hours he waited for the battle at dawn. As he sobered he would be ashamed of himself and remorseful. That would provide him a greater sympathy and he would begin the fight believing he deserves to be beaten. But he defends himself, unable to extinguish his will to live. Then, by a fluke of the struggle, Kasandonis is impaled on Andrea's knife and dies. Afterwards when he is bound and returned a prisoner to his father and the clan in the cave, Andreas silently accepts his banishment from the cave. He finds reason for survival because of Voula. Knowing her fierce grief for Kasandonis, he vows to redeem her with his own love.

There are things in the chapter that still bother me. I am uncertain whether Kasandonis overshadows Andreas, making him more sympathetic. I am also apprehensive that these two Cretan chapters somehow intrude upon the structure and flow of the novel, suggesting they belong in another book. Perhaps when a number of additional chapters have been written, these Cretan sections can be excerpted. I will wait and see.

Finishing the chapter last night, today I drifted, uncertain where to go. I need to cover the early march north of Kolokotronis after the surrender of Kalamata. That may be the next sequence. Meanwhile I have the articles to do for the *Tribune* and for *Today's Health*, and that is always a disruption because I have to leave the book.

Greece is out, at least until next year. I will have to continue writing the book without the spark Greece could have provided.

Today the nineteen-year-old son of a doctor in Porter died,

after struggling for a year and a half against leukemia. In his final year of life he spent his time tutoring deprived children. Despite his weakness and pain, he worked with dedication for the election to Congress of a fine history teacher named Floyd Fithian, who is running from our district. The newspapers reported that Fithian was at his bedside a few hours before the young man died.

I wrote his father a note of sympathy, but what can one really say? I think of my own sons and the sons of other parents and feel the dimension of the loss. This last year and a half we have struggled and suffered as John has suffered with his illness, emotional as well as physical, and although we have often been frightened we keep hoping he will be all right. Watching a dying son has to be worse than anything we have endured so far.

I still pray at night before going to sleep, a solitary prayer of despair or gratefulness to some Kazantzakian God because things could be worse. Yet, each day offers some new proof that life is blind chance. God comes to exist as a personification of our longings and our faith. Why then, against all reason, do we continue to pray and to believe in what is unbelievable?

November 30
A week of travail and distress. On Thanksgiving Day we went to my nephew's house where my sister and my mother, released a short time ago from the hospital, joined us. My mother sat at the foot of the table where I have seen her so many times over the years but she was changed, drained somehow, her spirit gone. She seemed confused, weary, almost anguished. She was exhausted and wanted to go to bed. We got her up to one of the children's beds and covered her when she complained of being cold. We brought her a heating pad that she placed on her stomach. I sat beside her, trying to think of words and phrases to console her, but she kept asking over and over, ''What will become of me?''

Finally, she got up, wanting to undress to go to bed and had to be told that she wasn't in her home. She would return with my sister to her apartment. She came back to sit at the table, evidencing some slight interest in photographs of the grand-children.

I could not help remembering her spirit in past years, that same indomitable spirit we resented because it made her irritable and demanding. But there comes to me a vision of her sitting helpless in her room in my house, reading her papers for hours at a time. We did not appreciate how blessed we were simply to have her feeling well. While we resented her abrasiveness, that same vigor drove her to dress each day and force herself to go on. Now, from what my sister tells us, mother remains in bed most of the day. When she gets up she is confused whether it is night or day, where she has been, or what is happening to her.

Something will have to be done. She cannot remain with my sister in that small apartment. Another sister is ready and willing to have her come to her home in Independence, Missouri. I am afraid it is like sending her away to die.

The family look to me for decisions and anwers I don't have. I think of returning her to our house, but then if she becomes an invalid, what will we do? What will poor Diana do? She would bear the brunt of that illness as she has borne the brunt of mother for more than twenty years.

How responsible am I for what has happened to her? I know that her age and generally deteriorating condition has been taking place for years. But how much of her disruption, the falls at my niece's and nephew's house, the heart acceleration...how much of this has been produced by the move? Guilt weighs on me, I am sure, but there is also remorse. We had held on with her for so long, perhaps we could have held on a while longer.

And still I am working along on the book, reading more again this past week in Gordon, Finlay, Howe, trying to pick up threads to link the sections.

Walking around the yard tonight, in the circular pattern of my exercise, I had a vague vision of the ending of the book, utilizing in some way the parable of the thrush from Kazantzakis. I am far from certain yet, but in the way I have felt during the writing of previous books I am probing toward an ending, I envision a man matured in ways by suffering, granted near the end of his life a glimpse of the eternal, inextinguishable flame that is Greece.

I see this so tenuously, feel it really more than see it. And my mother's agony adds somehow to it, her own suffering and impending death interwoven with the suffering and death of which I write. Those glimmerings of my own betrayal, well-intentioned and logical as my motives might have been, somehow again link into those complexities that make up the lives of human beings.

Life and death...the passing of time...the passing away of a little mountain of a woman. God grant her a quick, tranquil passing into death and yet, the other evening, walking along the beach road and praying, I could not really pray for her. There is so much suffering around, so much agony, so much pain greater than hers or mine. I could only pray for some enlightened awareness to allow us to make decisions that will minimize her distress and decline.

A quiet death is a luxury today. Maybe each age rediscovers that inexorable truth. A tranquil death has always been a luxury.

December 2
Once again the book changes. Now the vision I felt so vaguely the last few days has altered. Using as a narrator and lighthouse eye the character of the young warrior Elias Mavromichalis, son of Petrobey, seems much too limited now, his outlook on the conflict too martial. In his place I now have the conception of another character, a teacher-scribe-historian brought by Kolokotronis from Zante to record the history of the struggle for freedom. He remains shrouded in mist for me now and yet I think he may well become the most important character in the novel, drawing all the strings together, seeing the action of the battles, and yet understanding the conflict in terms of history.

I conceive him to be a mild-mannered, scholarly man, versed in Herodotus, Thucydides, Xenophon, and Plutarch, a theorist in terms of revolution and a veteran only of textbook battles. He would be an Ionian Greek who feels the cause of Greek freedom but without the passion that Kolokotronis and Petrobey bring to the conflict. From the victory at Kalamata, the teacher (I may call him Xanthos) follows Kolokotronis north to Karitena. He is witness to the rout of the Greek army, almost loses his life with Kolokotronis, shares with him the vision of the Virgin Mary in the church where they have fled for sanctuary.

Finally, the teacher-scribe would be my recorder at the siege of Tripolitza, describing the agony of starving Turkish men, women, and children. Tempered by the bloody reality of suffering and war, the teacher changes, his humanity overcoming the more limited scriptures of patriotism and country. By the end, preparing for the song of the thrush, I see him in a monastery where children are gathered. He makes an effort to speak to them of freedom, war, and suffering, and rambles on and on. A child asks him to hush and he sees the attention of the children drawn to the open window where a winter thrush is perched, singing a lilting song. He falls silent, suddenly and profoundly aware that something deeper exists beyond words and explanations. The ancient, enduring qualities of the Greek soul are contained in the song of the thrush.

Ahead of me are months and months of work, endless pages to be written and rewritten, massive problems with the final work still in doubt. But at the same time I have a vision of the last mountain I must ascend to complete the book, the most forbidding mountain, but the one also where from the highest peak all the mountains and plains, valleys and rivers of the book will become visible.

That is the vision and all I have to do now is find the means to make it bear fruit. Spirit of my revered dead, help me.

December 16
These are dreary, overcast December days, one falling fretfully into another. It is an unhappy December in so many ways. Mother has grown frailer, longing to stay in bed, unwilling to dress. Yet we have made the decision to move her from my sister in Chicago to the home of my sister in Missouri. Diana is flying her there on Wednesday.

It is hard to explain or make those around me understand my feelings. I know she has never really understood me, never comprehended who I was. But she has lived with us for so many years since my father's death and I somehow feel she is my responsibility. Seeing her at my sister's for the last time last night, her hair long and almost snow-white now, her face grown frailer, her small hands with the veins and bones clearly visible, I felt a great surge of pity for her. I understand her worth as a person because she has done so much in her life for so many.

I have the feeling that sending her away to my sisters is sending her into a kind of exile to die—not that my sister and brother-in-law won't look after her, because I know they will do that as well as they can. But she will be removed from the majority of the family, removed from all the associations she has back here. Maybe she will grow more alienated and confused.

Even now she forgets she has seen me or spoken to me on the telephone the day before.

I continue not feeling well. The prostate doesn't hurt as much but still aches sometimes, as if to remind me it is still there. Last Thursday to make sure there wasn't any malfunction of other organs I took X-rays, sitting in a wraparound smock in the hospital X-ray department. A score of men sat on either side of me, a morose assemblage with shoes and stockings sticking out beneath their gowns. I had the X-rays and then had to void for the final picture. Whether through tension or fear, I wasn't able to void. I tried unsuccessfully for almost half an hour, holding up the line of men waiting to use the X-ray machine. Where is dignity for a man who cannot even piss?

Soon it will be Christmas. The *Tribune* article is done. Time seems chewed away, and after the beginning of the New Year I will have to work out still some additional revisions on the screenplay of *Morning*.

Meanwhile work on the book proceeds slowly. I am reading, making lengthy notes, walking the circle of my yard, breathing in the cold night air, willing myself into the heart and spirit of my teacher-scribe. I finished a careful reading of Xenophon a few days ago, and the *Persian Adventure* will be immensely useful to me, I know, with its descriptions of men at war in the mountains.

Perhaps even the sadness of this period because of my mother can be used and find its way into the book. Perhaps the passing of one old woman can in some way reflect the emotion of my scribe, Xanthos, as he looks out over suffering Greece.

December 24

Tonight is Christmas Eve, the sky is overcast, the clouds are heavy with snow. The winter is upon us in earnest. A few days ago a half-dozen inches of snow covered the earth, and the pines, with trappings of white make a stunning sight.

Most of my days now are spent reading and making notes, writing trial pages in an effort to develop Xanthos, assimilating the writings of Xenophon, Plutarch, and Thucydides.

I have not yet unraveled the scribe's character or his relationship to the other characters. What are his feelings upon arriving in the Mani? What does he think of Kolokotronis, of Petrobey, of the other chieftains? As soon as I think I have one question answered, three more appear. There must be in the hundred-odd pages of the two chapters dealing with Xanthos a development of his vision. Pedantic in the beginning, made complacent by his readings of history, the actual experience of war changes him. Through witnessing and sharing suffering and death, he develops a greater humanity. At the same time he comes to understand the capricious, unpredictable elements and cross-purposes of the revolution, reflected in the captains and chieftains.

The song of the thrush remains a beacon for the end of the book. Even that may change as I approach the final pages. These coming chapters frighten me. They will be the most difficult of the novel to pull off because for the first time my narrator is someone who sees beyond a single action to the totality of the struggle. His tragic vision will lead him to understand that in any war there is cruelty and inhumanity on both sides.

The book's ending must have the impact of that final moment in Xenophon when, after two thousand miles and four months of marching, fighting, struggling to escape from the wild tribesmen of Persia, the Greek soldiers reach the water that will carry them home. They mass on the hilltops and raise their voices in a great roar, crying out, "Thalassa! Thalassa!"—"The sea! The sea!"

Meanwhile, tomorrow all the good relatives will gather here, their numbers grown by a dozen from last year. The day will be full of noise, shrieks and laughter, affection and warmth. We will eat and drink too much. Then, performing the conclusion of our time-hallowed ritual, they will depart. In the shambles we will have renewed the bonds of love that embrace us all.

Mother enjoyed these celebrations, usually sitting close by the fire to keep warm, not saying a great deal, but content to watch and absorb the tumult of the gathering, seeing the fruit of her generations around her. She will miss it this year for the first time.

Tonight Diana, John, Dean, and I will exchange a few presents around the tree, eat a little, sip some champagne. With our toasts and prayers, we will send love to our Mark, who is in California, and to Mother in Missouri.

December 31
A cold and somber end to the year with illness all around. Diana is down with flu and fever while Mother has become ill in Missouri. My sister sounds more concerned each time I speak to her on the phone. We decided earlier today that if my mother did not improve, they would put her in the hospital.

I try to appease my remorse by remember her recurring complaints and grievances, the house was cold, her room too drafty, why did we have to go out...one lament following another. Yet she was the woman who gave birth to me, helped mold the clay that makes me who I am. She was also the most compassionate human being I have ever known, always concerned with the poor and the dispossessed. As a child I remember riding a trolley with her as she carried a basket of food to some lonely old woman.

Now this woman who helped so many others needs help. She is ill and across the country in California, my eldest brother and her first born child, the one who in his youth needed her protection and support, has entered the hospital for cataract operations. His condition is complicated by his weakened heart and by the diabetes that has cost him the amputation of both his legs. When he lost his second leg, we kept the news from my mother. Now I have the feeling that their destinies are linked together once again.

I am an observer and yet also a participant in this drama, seeing the ironies, the complexity of relationships, love and sorrow and remorse. God, how it hurts sometimes to live....

Tonight, at midnight, I will come up to the study and make a short entry in my journal. Tomorrow is the beginning of another year—perhaps the year in which I finish this work or the year when it finishes me.

1975

January 12, 1975
I have been in Missouri a week now, spending most of my days and nights with Mother, who is in the hospital. My sister Tasula had her admitted a few days after New Year's and I flew to Missouri a few days later. From the airport in Kansas City, my sister and brother-in-law drove me to the hospital where they had been giving Mother a series of tests. She had one bowel X-ray taken and they had given her castor oil afterwards to flush the barium from her system. So, for several days and nights, her pattern of activity was to struggle from her bed to the portable commode, shitting, then going back to bed, a nurse and I heaving to help her. Unable to control herself she would shit again in bed, the nurses having to change her and her sheets, the routine repeated, bedpan, commode, shit.

Through those dreadful days misery made her incoherent. At times she did not know me, thought she was back in Chicago, in my home, in one of my nephew's houses. She would call out in Greek to Diana or to one of my nieces.

The tests proved her clear of any disorder, no trace of malignancy or stones. But the tests also exhausted and tore her up. Yesterday her bronchial tubes congested and they put her on oxygen. The medication they administered to her started the relentless diarrhea again. They have also inserted a catheter that causes her pain. Meanwhile she grows weaker and the doctors don't know if she will make it through or not.

The night her congestion began it grew rapidly worse and my sister and I stayed with her most of the night. The gurgling sound of her labored breathing under the mask is chilling, like life bubbling away. I had written of that sound in *A Dream of Kings*, when Matsoukas visits Cicero in the hospital, and I have a recollection of hearing it when Naka lay dying in Woodlawn Hospital.

For the first few days while I sat with Mother, I found myself unable to control my tears. She is an old woman with little to look forward to but a few moments when she might hug one of her grandchildren, and one must believe she will die. At the same time she has always seemed so indestructible. To see her battling for life now is to be forced to join the struggle because if her life is long, eternity is longer. Her struggle isn't graceful because there isn't any grace or dignity in illness or age, but it is a struggle. The doctors are fighting, the nurses are fighting, my sister and I are fighting, and the old embattled wreck, Red Cross veteran, and campaigner of a thousand raffle ticket drives is battling because she doesn't know how to give up. Now and then when a nurse's hand touches the raw flesh of her buttocks, she snarls, proving the eagle has not yet become a dove.

How painful it is to see her trying to stand, a nurse holding her on either side, white socks crumpled about her ankles, clumps of fat sagging at her thighs, trying to fit the commode to her behind. She is breathing harshly, her hair is disheveled, her chin is trembling. The thought strikes me that from this battered woman I came to life. I want her dead and at peace, but then she coughs and I move quickly to see if she can spit up some of the phlegm. Why? To ease her suffering? To help her live? Perhaps to relinquish the neutrality of the bystander? All around us in the rooms of this hospital, illnesses and dyings are taking place. But one still fights for each life. Everything is complex, mysterious, soiled, somehow pure.

If my mother dies now her problems will be over. She need make no more journeys except for the final one that will bring her home to her parish and her church, and then the brief passage from there to the cemetery where she will take her place beside my father.

If she lives and comes out of the hospital, we will have to do something about her. We might try to bring her home and find a woman to help us with her. I don't know what else we can do. She loved the lost ones, the weak and infirm inhabitants of the world. Now that she has joined them, how can we forsake her?

February 7
My brother Dan died today. He came through the cataract operation several weeks ago but afterwards grew weaker with complications developing. I spoke to his wife Marvel several times by phone and she told me he was failing. Early this morning she phoned to tell us he had died. Tomorrow I will leave for Los Angeles to attend his funeral, and then Marvel and I will return with his body to Chicago so he might be buried in my father's plot.

Meanwhile my mother had been discharged from the hospital in Missouri about ten days ago, returning to my sister Tasula's house. She seemed physically better but was confused and incoherent, uncertain where she was. She kept crying out for one of us during the night so that no one in the house could sleep. I had to go to New York for a few days then, and Diana came to Missouri in my place. Mother didn't improve and, finally, returning from New York to Chicago, I located a bed for her in what seemed a good nursing home, my nephews and sisters and other brother, Mike, agreeing to share the considerable expense. Heavily sedated by the doctor, my mother flew with Diana from Missouri to Chicago. I met them at the airport and we drove directly to the nursing home, where my younger sister Irene, met us. As the nurses undressed my mother and put her to bed, Diana, Irene, and I standing close by, I had the feeling she thought she had come home.

Yet that veil of confusion might protect her now as well. There isn't any reason to tell her of my brother's death. I remember the fierce and enigmatic bond that always existed between them, a bond so strong that when we were young I felt she would have sacrificed all of us for him. Over the years that have passed since then, I have come to understand that if she loved him a little more, he was, after all, her first-born child. Perhaps, too, her mighty heart had enough love for all.

Will she go on living for a long time, or, now that Dan is gone, will she try to join him soon? Perhaps that is why she has been crying and moaning these last weeks, a distress that does not seem to stem from any discernible pain. There is so much about love and death that we can never understand.

When I return from Dan's funeral in California, God willing, I will try to return to the book.

February 14
I flew to California on a 747, a monstrous plane that seemed reluctant to rise from the earth into the air. The day was overcast and after takeoff we climbed above the clouds into a blue and sunny firmament. In Los Angeles we landed in a dark, dismal rain. Marvel and Dan's daughter, Barbara, and her family were waiting for me. My son Mark was there, as well, having come down from San Francisco, the first time I had seen him since the Easter Sunday he had left Chicago. He was bearded, shaggy-haired, obviously poor, but serene. I embraced him, feeling it good to see and hold him, whatever the reason that brought me to California.

We took Dan's clothing to the mortuary. Marvel selected a coffin and we waited in one of the parlors while the undertaker dressed Dan. His wishes were that his casket be closed but we saw him for a final moment that night before they sealed the coffin. He looked at rest, that cold, liberated peacefulness of death. He wore his artificial legs on his stumps and the sport shirt buttoned at the collar I had seen him wear so many times.

Tears did not come to my eyes then or during the funeral in the church, nor back in Chicago at the graveside, with all our relatives and some friends standing around the casket suspended over the open grave. There were tears in many of their eyes but I could not cry. I cared for Dan, too, particularly in these later years when we had become closer, but I could not mourn for his death. He had suffered so much, through one amputation and then another. He had little to look forward to but more suffering. Death is often maligned as an enemy. But I think that Life, relentlessly refusing to give up the tiny, final spark even after living has become hopeless, Life then may be the foe.

I thought of my mother in the nursing home while we buried Dan. After the funeral luncheon, after eating fish and drinking wine, several of my nephews and nieces with their children went to visit her in the home. She was pleased to see them, unaware that they had come from the graveside of her first son. "I am so happy...." Diana told me she spoke those words. "I am so happy to see you all."

And there was one, final gesture, one strange, sensitive touch from the grave. Dying with only meager possessions, Dan left his clothes to a mission, his physical therapy equipment to a therapist who had helped him, and his four pieces of fine luggage to my son, John. That was the only bequest he made to anyone in our large family, as if choosing the one most in need. His gift was an optimistic omen, a sign of encouragement and hope, as if he were saying to John, "You will become well and you will travel."

Now as I write these words and think of that kindness from the grave, I feel tears in my eyes. In the end he fooled us. Nothing he could have done would have so balanced the scales as that simple inheritance.

Another part of the mystery, the dying of that solitary, enigmatic brother and his final bequest to my son.

February 15
An ice storm this morning covered the earth with a frozen, glistening crust. I walked down carefully for the paper, avoiding the driveway that was slick as an ice rink, treading through the grassy dune instead. Back in my study I see the lake white and still, in the distance a span of blue water.

Marvel returns to California tomorrow. My brother is buried and my mother is in the nursing home. That is the beginning of this new year.

I am working on still more revisions of the screenplay but am anxious to return to the novel. Walking around the yard tonight, my booted feet crunching the ice into slush, I thought of my characters. They reside in shadows for me, pushed away by all the things that have transpired. I am sure a trip to Greece, so long postponed, would spark them and the book again.

The major part of the winter seems to have passed in this time of troubles. In another month to six weeks, spring will be here. How lovely and renourishing it would be to welcome spring in Crete and Greece, then return to plunge vigorously into the last sections of the book. Is that a fanciful dream? The next few weeks will tell the tale.

March 23
This has been one of the longest stretches without an entry in this journal since I began in December of 1972. So much has happened, yet nothing has happened. Work on the novel has come almost to a standstill while I struggle to finish the screenplay, redoing the endless changes they suggest from New York, while I hope but doubt they know what they are doing. In addition I have been teaching a writing class once a week and am working on several articles. Then I have been saddened and worried about mother.

Each time I visit her in the nursing home I am swept with a pervasive agony. I see her there among the poor, aged wrecks, the broken bodies, the senile minds, and have the feeling she does not belong among them. A few members of the family visit her in addition to myself and Diana, but when she sees me she pleads to come home. There are moments I am tempted to bring her home, but there is Diana to consider and there is John.

I understand the dilemma is not merely my concern about the reaction on Diana and John if I were to bring her home, but my own uncertainty about whether it would be dangerous to change her environment again. If the change doesn't work out it might even be more painful to return her to the nursing home. If we brought her home, what would we do with her here? She might sit in the sun as summer comes, seeing about her the movement of healthy people, hearing the voices of her family instead of the voices of strangers.

Perhaps it is too late. The family, loving her, are still willing to accept the necessity of her confinement. Yet she looks to me for possible salvation. She pleads with me to take her home. She tells the nurses that her son has purchased the nursing home. She asks them to look after her and her son will take care of them. They grin and giggle, think her funny and cute, take her to the bathroom, pull down the diapers they have pinned on her, pull them up and pin them again. The Welsh nurse on the first floor told me of old women who carried on about going home for months and finally grew resigned, quiet and hopeless. There is a horror in that kind of defeat.

Meanwhile, tomorrow, I will make the long delayed flight to Greece. I will go for three weeks to assemble atmosphere, trying to reignite the spark of the novel. When I return, we may come to some decision about mother unless a decision has already been made for me as she slips deeper into futility and hopelessness. Am I expecting more from Greece than it can possibly fulfill? Will I be able to return and finish the book or will I come back smothered by more grief and frustration?

Follow thine own path alone, O my heart, O old rhinoceros. . . .

March 28 (Nauplion)
Greece!

I am finally here, achieving the journey so long delayed—a good, but long flight and then the taxi from the airport to the Amalia Hotel in Constitution Square where I found all the staff I had seen on previous visits. I had forgotten the tumult of Athens and after the stillness of home it was like having rivets pounded into my head. I couldn't sleep the first day or night and by the morning of the second day was heaving with weariness and futility. I lay sprawled across my bed thinking I had been mad to come, that I should be home writing, that I had no reason to cross half the world with so many unsettled elements in my life.

Some of my depression passed as I walked about the city. On earlier trips I had enjoyed breakfast at Zonars, the sidewalk cafe on Acadimias Street. The mornings are still too chilly to sit outside but I had orange juice, feta cheese, croissants and coffee inside the dining room. The place was crowded and full of strident voices arguing politics. With the fall of the Junta, the Greeks have again found their voices, bristling with adjectives, saturated with scorn, anger, indignation. A stocky man at the next table rattled on in such swift Greek I couldn't quite make out what he was saying except that every third word was "psofios," which translates to "rotten" or "putrid." I had never heard the word expressed with so many nuances fusing to an unmatched, irrevocable contempt!

Then, walking down the wide Panepistimion avenue, I saw my first rally in Greece, hundreds of young Communists preparing to march to Constitution Square. Formed in a line from one side of the street to the other, their arms linked, great red banners unfurled before them, they swept on like a tidal wave, immersing taxis, buses, pedestrians that came to a jumbled stop. Here and there a few clusters of police stood on the sidewalks, almost indifferent, as if understanding that after the years of the Dictatorship this release was healthy.

That night I slept better, and the next day spent several hours at the Press Ministry, establishing my credentials and receiving a letter asking all authorities to cooperate with writer Pe-tra-keez as he wends his way through the Pel-op-pon-neez. In the evening I went to dinner with my dear friends Deno and Maureen to one of those places not yet discovered by tourists that Deno knows so well. It was called "Balcony of Hymettus," a huge room with a roaring fireplace at either end and marvelous food. We ate, drank, laughed and talked and I felt better than I had felt in months.

On the third morning I took the Key Tour bus from Athens to Nauplion, to the lovely Xenia Hotel that overlooks the sea and the great fortress of Palimidi where Kolokotronis was imprisoned during the revolution. With my bag packed, waiting for the bus in the hotel lobby in Athens, I visited the Historical Museum, going into the same gallery full of the pictures and paintings of the heroes I had seen on my earlier visit. Their demeanors were not as approving this time. They seemed impatient, irritated, anxious for me to eliminate delays and distractions and get on with it. Only old Boukouvalas, the real hero I modeled the Suliot captain on, seemed to smile down at me. After all, I had resurrected him for a noble death in his wild charge at the bridge before the forces of Pehlevan Pasha.

I had phoned Mihali, the young taxi driver in Nauplion who had driven me around Greece on earlier trips, and he met the bus when I descended at the Xenia. We embraced like brothers and then sat down at once to map our plans. In the morning we would begin the journey to Tripoli, then go to Sparta and Githion for the caves, to Monemvasia, and then into the deep Mani. From there we would drive north to Pylos, then up to Kalavryta for the monastery of Aghia Lavra, where the outbreak of the revolution is reputed to have taken place. We would stay in Patras for a night and then cross the Gulf of Corinth by car ferry to Missolonghi, where Lord Byron died. The trip would take between eight and ten days and then I will return here to Nauplion to record and expand my notes and impressions.

The spell of Greece is working on me again. Now, typing this entry in the Xenia, the strange, wild wind I remember has risen off the sea. I have heard it on earlier trips but now it wails with added fervor, as if I hear resonances I have never been able to understand before.

I am suddenly homesick. I think of Diana and my sons, my mother in the nursing home. Before I go to bed I will say a small prayer for all of them and I will sleep with the doors open so I can hear the rolling of the surf that reminds me of home.

March 29 (Githion)
We have finished the long, first day of our journey. I am staying for the night here in the Laconis at Githion, one of a series of bungalows overlooking an expanse of sea that batters in against the rocks with a thunderous roar. This time of year only three or four of the hundred bungalows are occupied. Once again I enjoy the sound of the water, even more turbulent than the sea at Nauplion.

Our day began when Mihali picked me up at seven at the Xenia, rushing around to open the door for me, smiling, bouncing, warm. His Opel is much older than it was on my last visit (nearly 200,000 kilometers) but I told him that I am older (300,000 kilometers). The little car still sparkles and he carried the bucket and rag and washes it whenever we stop. When we left Nauplion, driving through the cool, sparkling morning, we drove to the town of Tripolis. Since it was Saturday, market day, the square was packed with people milling about the stands and carts. The women wore the ubiquitous black frocks, mourning some relative who might have been dead for years. A few of the young girls wore print dresses. Mihali and I had a cup of Greek coffee to plan our route and then drove from the city into the mountains toward the village of Valtetzi. That site was the first victory for Kolokotronis and the Greeks, who took advantage of the mountainous terrain. We drove beneath the rocky, barren peaks where Kolokotronis and Elias Mavromichalis had placed their men. I had read of the battle but how much more revealing it is to actually see those ominous peaks under grey, heavy clouds and to understand how the Turkish cavalry would be helpless in the impassable mountains.

When we finally drove into the village of Valtetzi, it was deserted. Houses were boarded up or in disrepair, ivy climbing over eroded walls, winding across the broken shutters of windows. Wash hung in one of the yards but there wasn't a trace of a human being anywhere. On the stone steps of the lovely old village church there was an almost indecipherable inscription, commemorating the victory of Kolokotronis, a memorial read now only by roosters and vagrant ghosts. We spent about an hour in that eerie deserted place, never seeing anyone. As we left the village, driving past some ruined towers that were relics of the battle, bright little flowers sprouted up between the tumbled mortar and broken rocks at the base.

We stopped at the small museum in Tegea, a shabby building containing the relics of ancient Tegea. The guide and ticket seller, resembling hundreds of men one sees, were dressed in suits, shirts, and ties, impeccably buttoned, scrupulously polite, pleased when I spoke to them in Greek. The guide showed me a treasure, a recently-discovered head of an ancient statue concealed under newspapers because the government had not yet sent the official photographer and, as the guide explained to me gravely, "It would be a shame if strangers photographed it before us." At the end of our tour of the museum I gave him ten drachmas. He accepted the coins with a poised nod that told me not to be fooled by his worn coat and tattered collar or by his accepting a few drachmas that in more affluent circumstances he might have politely refused. When Mihali and I left the building to return to our car, both men came to the door. As we drove off they offered a gracious, seemly wave of their hands in a friendly farewell.

We drove south for Sparta, the town so renowned in Greek history. Little evidence of any grandeur remained in the shabby houses and the men crowded around the tables of the sidewalk coffeehouses. We came out of Sparta, driving east for a while, and then I saw a range of fierce, snow-capped mountains that formed an almost impregnable barrier for the Mani. I was awed by their majesty, kept looking at them until they receded in our approach to Monemvasia.

Kazantzakis calls Monemvasia the "Gibraltar of Greece," a huge mountain of rock that thrusts its head into the sky. Once again the impression I had from photographs was inadequate since no picture could convey the gargantuan form of the fortress. We lunched at a seaside restaurant and then, fortified by grilled fish and ample wine, Mihali and I climbed the great rock. The steep, rugged path up the side ascends through tangles of brush and masses of boulders, ending finally at the church of St. Sophia on the peak. The wind whistled eerily around our heads and I remembered how the Turks had occupied these heights at the outbreak of the revolution while the Greeks laid siege to them. For weeks the Turks were reduced to eating cats, rats and mice until, starved into submission, they finally surrendered.

From the steps of the church one looks down on the almost limitless panorama of southern Greece, an expanse of water and clusters of miniscule houses grouped in villages. The guerilla fighter in my book, Captain Vorogrivas, stood on such a peak and pitied the poor pygmies who were forced to live on the plains below. In that moment I understood the meaning of what I had written.

We resumed our trip again, weary now, but trying to get to Githion which is the gateway to the Mani. From there, early in the morning, we would start south for Areopolis and the deep Mani.

There is, I feel strongly once again, a regenerative quality for me in Greece. Each time I return I think this will prove a romantic illusion, but the land slowly mesmerizes me, absorbs my blood and spirit, refreshes and stimulates me. Now with my thoughts linked to my book, each day is replete with stunning sights and sounds I know I will use. I saw goats crossing the road today and then climbing an impossibly sheer wall of rock like comics walking on walls and ceilings. I saw a child chasing a chicken, running in circles, shrieking with a delirious joy. I saw and heard a shepherd play a reed flute to his flock, a plaintive wail that banished centuries. I smelled the fragrance of lemon trees, saw the twisted forms of olive trees resembling stooped, gnarled old crones. I admired a white-haired old farmer with a body as straight and strong as a young tree, moving with the graceful, unhurried rhythm of a man in tune with the earth. And, full of impressions, sights, sounds, the landscape absorbed through blood and spirit, the strange, and enduring sadness of these sturdy people and this eternal land seeps into my soul.

Now, honeycombed with weariness and once more consoled by the sibilance of the water, I will go to sleep.

March 31 (Pylos)
Before leaving Githion this morning, I ate breakfast in a huge, domed dining room that a young waiter unlocked just for me. I had my choice of a hundred empty tables and he took my order and went to the kitchen to prepare it himself. As I ate I remained the only occupant of the dining room, every bite of toast crunching loudly in the cavernous silence. Mihali joined me for a cup of coffee and even our cups and saucers clattered with the crack of breaking glass.

We drove from Githion to the caves of Dirou, descending on foot into the dark bowels of the underground. With about a half-dozen others we climbed into a long boat tied to a pier and with oarsmen at the bow and at the prow we navigated through a series of eerie, subterranean chambers. Thousands of stalactites hung from rocky ledges and crevices, dripping into the water. They formed strange, distorted shapes and visages pointed out by one of the oarsmen in a sonorous voice as the dangling carcass of a fox, the prow of a ship, the head of Charles DeGaulle. After a while, the dampness seeping into my bones, I thought of the underworld of Hades with Charos, the ferryman of Death, rowing us across the river Styx. Leaving that gloomy labyrinth, I was grateful to emerge into daylight.

From the caves we drove toward Areopolis, once the city of Tzimova that Petrobey Mavromichalis made his capital. From time to time we glimpsed the great ranges of Taygetus, other lesser mountains closer to us temporarily shielding that snow-crowned monarch until, crossing some hill, the awesome peaks loomed above us.

Rocks are a major part of the Greek landscape but nowhere else in Greece are they as abundant as they are in the Mani. The earth seems to have heaved up layer upon layer of rocks. They are piled into heaps, built into houses, bordered into fences, crumbled into the ruins of the great Nyklian towers of the nineteenth century from which the Maniots fought their wars against external enemies and against each other. What little land has been cleared produces only poor scrubs of vegetation, the olive groves full of dwarfed and stunted miniatures of olive trees. The only vegetation that seems to thrive is a plant that resembles a cactus, ugly-looking and vicious with prickly leaves, called an "ilex."

We were driving at the end of March and in this southern area it was already hot, Mihali and I sweating. I could imagine what the land must be like in the heat of midsummer, the sun blazing down on the rocks. Even the ridges that ran down from the mountains were as barren as the humps of massive whales, their surface creased and scarred by sun and wind.

Driving still deeper into the Mani, even the men and women walking along the road seemed different from the inhabitants of the rest of Greece. Their faces were sun-bronzed, almost black, their eyes staring at us with an ancient and inbred suspicion of strangers. One understands why the Turks did not ever totally conquer the Mani. Left to themselves the Maniots fought one another with the same relentless ferocity they turned against invaders.

I remember reading in Patrick Fermor's book on the Mani that vendettas and wars flourished because the poverty of the land could not provide sufficient nourishment for all and some had to be killed. Wars accomplished this attrition and feuds did the rest. If a Maniot was murdered, none of the murdered man's family was granted rest until he was avenged. From generation to generation the angry, vengeful vendettas continued until families were thinned out and the reason for the original outrage was all but forgotten.

Yet probably no other section of Greece made a greater contribution to the War of Independence. The martial, heroic clan of Mavromichalis alone lost more than forty men, fathers, sons, brothers, giving their lives for Greece and freedom.

Later in the day we drove north through Areopolis once more, following the lovely coast from Kalamata to Pylos. We arrived in Pylos at twilight, the evening mist shrouding the island of Sfakteria where Spartans and Athenians fought more than two thousand years ago. I registered for the night at a hotel called "The Castle." The place was a gross misnomer because the rooms were shabby, the linen was stained and tattered, bulbs were missing from the lamps. In the bathroom a toilet tank with the brand name "Niagara" released only a trickle of water.

Mihali and I ate dinner with Dr. Antonopoulos, a dentist in America who had retired to this city of his birth and become one of its patrons. Afterwards I walked along the harbor, peering out into the darkness where the lights of a few ships could be seen at anchor in the Bay of Navarino. This was the site of the great sea battle in October of 1827, when a combined fleet of English, French, and Russian warships sank a Turkish-Egyptian armada of more than eighty frigates and brigs. Although the revolution dragged on for another three years, that sea battle crushed the Turkish ability to achieve victory. During my last visit to Pylos I had been taken in a small boat onto the bay at dawn. When the early light is right, looking over the side of the boat, I could see the masts of the sunken Turkish frigates like shimmering ghosts on the bottom of the bay.

The night was fragrant and serene and I resisted returning to the dismal hotel. I walked from the harbor to the town square and sat under a pair of ship's cannon that commemorate the battle of Navarino. A pair of motorbikes came roaring up ridden by two men and a pretty girl, young French tourists. They cavorted and romped over the cannon, laughing and singing in the flowing tongue of their country, unconcerned with my presence. I felt like part of the cannon, hoary with rust and age, as they frolicked around me. Then they mounted their bikes once more, the girl hanging on behind one of the young men, and thundered off into the night. The cannons and I slipped again into shadows and silence.

April 1 (Patras)

When Mihali and I left Pylos early in the morning, it was raining and we drove several hours through the drizzle. The road from Pylos to Pyrgos passed the ruins of Nestor's palace. We stopped to walk around the grounds, looking out across the panorama of mountains and valleys that had been the view of the wise old king who counseled the Greeks at Troy.

We stopped for lunch in Pyrgos, at a cafe called "Achilleion" in a room where the tables had linen cloths and the patrons appeared decorous and affluent. Below us was another level of the restaurant, a bare-tabled emporium full of laborers and peddlers, waiters rushing around and patrons shouting for service. Mihali told me that if he were alone he would have eaten downstairs because the food there was served by the same kitchen that served us and was considerably cheaper.

Starting again, we drove along a road that I haven't traveled before, passing fertile farmland. We arrived in Patras, a city of about 120,000 people with hotels and houses along the harbor. Mihali went off on his own after seeing me settled in the "Astir," in a large, clean and comfortable room. Having slept little the night before in "The Castle," I showered, climbed wearily into bed, and slept as though dead.

At dawn we were on the road again, driving through the mountains from Patras to Kalavryta with our destination the monastery of Aghia Lavra. The day was overcast, with dark, swirling clouds that from time to time released a spatter of rain. The scenery of mountains was immense and majestic, reminding me of Taygetus and of the splendid mountains of Crete. We passed groups of men and women sitting beside a cluster of large milk cans. Having milked the goats, they were waiting for the trucks that would carry the milk to the plants where feta cheese was made. At another intersection men and women picked out, held, and slaughtered sheep for the morning markets. Beside a grove of trees we watched crows and ravens take off in a flurry of black wings.

The terrain we traveled had gotten a good deal of rain and in places rock had tumbled to the road, leaving barely enough room for our small car to pass. Mihali looked up at the slopes and crossed himself a number of times, while I felt a flutter of fear. To be crushed by falling rocks on one of those mountain roads would be a disheartening end!

From the town of Kalavryta, resembling many other towns we had passed, we drove up the road to the site of Aghia Lavra. I was shocked by the small, inauspicious chapel where history said the War of Independence began when Archbishop Germanos braced a flag out one of the windows. Hardly more than a handful of men could have crowded into that chapel and any flag stuck out the window would have dangled on the ground. The chapter in my novel I had written on the great meeting of archons and prelates could not have taken place inside that chapel. But a solution to my problem was at hand. There was a large church adjoining the monastery that had been built in 1830, the year the revolution ended. I decided to use that church as the site for my meeting and hoped only scholars and perceptive tourists would catch the discrepancy in dates.

Visiting the monastery, we were guided through the cloisters by an old white-haired and white-bearded monk with gleaming and perfectly proportioned false teeth. As he took us around he urged Mihali to have a second son so one could be given to the monastery as a young novitiate because only a few aging monks remained in the cloisters. When they died off, the old monk said somberly, "only the wind will be left to say Mass."

Another monk unlocked a room that contained the treasures and mementos of 1821 stored in glass cases. There were the faded banner of Archbishop Germanos, crosses and guns used by the insurgents, their documents and maps and proclamations. Each item in the cases was numbered and the monk put a record on an old phonograph and cranked the arm vigorously. As the record spun around a sonorous voice listed the number of the artifact and described it. After a moment or two the voice was garbled by the scratches and squeaks in the record. The monk lifted the needle and blew on it and put it down again. The scratching and squeaking continued and Mihali and I listened politely and gravely to the voice we could not understand.

Before we left the monastery we visited the small graveyard where, every few years, the bones of the dead were dug up and then stored in a shed. Peering in through the windows of the shed, we saw an array of skulls on a series of shelves, perhaps a score of them, surrounding the huge skull of what must have been an abbot or bishop. His skull was the only one that was joined to the crossbones. They rested against his robust jaw so that he seemed to be gnawing on his ribs.

The monks bade us a friendly farewell, asking us to return soon, advising us to visit a monument a few miles away on another peak erected to the "Heroes." We drove to that site, a stark, massive memorial built to commemorate the murder of

1300 Kalavrytan men and boys in a massacre during December of 1943 when the Nazis occupied Greece.

Mihali and I stood there silently for a long time. I thought again of how much Greece has suffered through invasions, famines and wars. The wind wailed about our heads and fluttered the hundreds of withered stems and dried flowers from once-fresh garlands and wreaths that littered the base of the memorial.

Back in my hotel in Patras, I typed for several hours to capture the countless sights of the day. I wrote about the monastery and the memorial and myriad other impressions. There were the lovely cypresses of Kypparisia; the wildflowers blooming in the crevices of boulders; the dark tents of gypsies dotting the mountain slopes; the heads of cattle tied to stakes in the ground so they could not eat the olives; the disfigured face of a woman in the doorway of a village house. As our car passed, I caught one fleeting glimpse of her, long enough to see her bitterness and hate of everything that lived.

All the events and scenes of the days drift together suddenly with thoughts of Diana, Mark, John, Dean, my mother. Earlier in the evening, from my balcony, I looked down on the ships in the harbor, the ferry that sailed from Patras to Brindisi, Italy. I watched the passengers board the gangplank of the ferry and with a flare of homesickness wondered how many of them were going home.

I think, as Kazantzakis wrote, that it is good to travel. But even as one travels one needs a place to remember, a hearth that one loves and calls home.

April 2 (Ioannina)
We left Patras early this morning, driving to Rion for the car ferry that would carry us across the Gulf of Corinth to Antirion. The crossing takes only fifteen minutes but the sea was rough, swells of water splashing over the railings and decks. Mihali rushed down several times to wipe the spray off his Opel.

When we docked we waited in the car for our turn to disembark and then drove north to Missolonghi, the city where Lord Byron died in 1825 and the site of the great siege that stirred the world to the plight of Greece. The city, set in the midst of swampy riverbeds that contributed to Byron's final illness and death, is shabby and unattractive. They have built a memorial park for the graves of the heroes of the War of Independence, reminiscent of the unkempt, neglected Tokhapi museum in Istanbul. Paint is peeling from the monuments, graves are weed-tangled, some markers obscured under brush, and mold has formed on the stones. The tomb of Markos Bozzaris has a small naked stone child pointing to the hero's name. The tallest monument in the park is Byron's grave, a life-sized statue of the cloaked "Pilgrim of Eternity" staring out across the shoddy gardens. Around Byron's grave are the graves of the volunteers from Sweden, Russia, and England. As we walked from the depressing park, we passed several unemptied cans of garbage that overflowed litter on the graves of Demetrios Sideris and Spiros Kontogiannes.

The historical museum was located in the town hall, where a little gravel-visaged man acted as guide for Mihalis and me. His voice trembling with emotion, he described the stories behind the paintings that hung in poorly-lighted alcoves up and down the stairs. Pointing to a painting of a grieving mother and child, the guide gestured to a pair of feet visible at one edge of the painting. He told us the feet belonged to the woman's husband, who had been killed. The woman had killed her child and afterwards would kill herself rather than fall into the hands of the Turks.

Mihali made the error of suggesting there weren't women like that in Greece anymore. The guide fixed him with a scathing stare and told him that in Albania in 1941 the Greek women fought beside their men against the Italians and one had died of multiple wounds in the guide's arms. Mihali beat an apologetic retreat into the shadows of an adjoining alcove.

On our way back to the car we passed a schoolyard full of young shrieking children. One golden-haired little girl reminded me so much of my niece, Chrissy Papangelis, that I leaned against the fence and stared at her in disbelief.

From Missolonghi we drove north to the old city of Ioannina, the beauty of its skyline with the minarets of mosques and the castellated fortresses in sharp contrast to the flat drabness of Missolonghi. The domed palace of the notorious Ali Pasha, who had ruled Ioannina in the early nineteenth century, had been converted into a gloomy museum with displays of scimitars, pistols and long-barreled rifles. But the grounds around the museum provided a stunning view of the Bay of Ioannina, and on the hillside, in a plot enclosed by a low iron fence was the grave of Ali Pasha. Sharing the same weed-cluttered condition as the graves of the dead Greeks in the Garden of the Heroes, Ali Pasha's plot had been neglected on purpose, unidentified by tablet or name. The guard in the museum directed us to it and while Mihali and I inspected the site, two young Greeks scaled the iron fence to stamp on the earth over the tyrant's head. The passage of more than 150 years since the death of the "Lion of Ioannina" apparently had not appeased Greek hate.

That night a severe storm struck the city with peals of thunder accompanying a heavy, driving rain. I lay awake in my hotel bed wondering if we would be able to travel in the morning. When I rose at dawn and peered out my window toward the mountains we planned to cross on our journey to Meteora, they were obscured in a dense fog. When Mihali came to pick me up, he assured me the fog would lift in a few hours and that it would be safe to travel.

We started out from Ioannina about eight, beginning our ascent into the foothills of the mountains. As the car cut into the misted, seemingly impenetrable barrier, the fog broke into ghostly patches that slipped like giant paws across the car's windows. For a moment we'd see the road and then the fog would swoop in again, fashioning a haze so viscous the hood of the car was obscured. I was tense and scared as Mihali drove the invisible road of the mountain with some canny, intuitive sense of direction. Even he grew nervous a few times, slowing to a crawl and making a hasty and furtive cross. I berated myself then for having ventured to Greece, fearful that the book and I would expire together in the mountains of Epirus.

Higher and higher we drove, the fog lifting enough in places so we caught glimpses of the sheer precipice beside the road and the cliffs and crags above us. Suddenly we broke through the crust and saw the sun, a core of glowing fire that blazed across a stunning vista of snow-mantled mountain peaks. The sight was so awesome and majestic Mihali and I cried out in unison. Then we drove peering out the windows, chortling and gleeful as children. We were in the resplendent Pindus mountain range of Epirus, the magnificent natural fortress inhabited by guerilla bands throughout centuries who had resisted Persians and Nazis. Once again I thought of my own Captain Vorogrivas, in my light-headedness almost expecting to see his stalwart figure poised on a crag above us. Swept by jubilation, I began to sing a Greek mountain song I had learned as a child. Mihali joined me, our voices rising buoyantly, while the Opel bounced and rolled over the several inches of freshly-fallen snow that covered the road.

We stopped for coffee and a glass of ouzo in the mountain village of Metzovos, whose houses were suspended in terraces below the steep crags. The air was incredibly clear and cold, a delight to breathe. We resumed our journey, ascending still higher toward the peaks. We picked up a hitchhiker, a grizzled old laborer who worked on the roads bundled up in a woolen cap and a thick fleece jacket. When he climbed into the car smelling as if he had not bathed in years, Mihali looked pained and quickly opened his window. But the old man was good-natured and garrulous, telling us in a dramatic monologue how impassable the roads became in winter, villages sometimes snowed in for weeks. One doesn't associate such cold and snow with Greece, but we were at the northernmost point of the country, just a few miles from the border of Albania.

When we began our descent toward Kalabaka, the snow disappeared quickly, the sun blooming over green, fertile valleys on the plain of Thessaly below us. We dropped off our passenger who expressed his gratitude by shaking our hands vigorously and wishing us a safe journey. Less than a mile further along the road we picked up another traveler, a lean, stern-visaged farmer who was on his way to visit his married daughter in Larissa. He spoke grimly of the plight of farmers who barely avoided hunger by scraping along with a few goats and a small patch of olive trees. In the areas where tourists cluster one sometimes forgets how poor much of Greece is and how the people struggle simply to survive.

We stayed that night in Volos, a seaport city of about 50,000 people. Mihali and I had dinner and then walked along the harbor, mingling with the crowds making their evening promenade. Back in my hotel room I typed the day's entries and wrote a letter home. The following evening we would be back in Nauplion. I will remain there for a week, assembling my thoughts and composing my notes. Afterwards I would return to Athens and prepare for my flight home. It is strange how little I have thought of home in these past few days. That is the magic spell that Greece weaves.

April 8 (Nauplion)
I have been in Nauplion for six days now. This Sunday morning, the final day of my stay, I dressed early and walked down the hill from the hotel to one of the old churches in the square. I entered the *pangari* shortly after the service had begun, caught at once by the chanting of the priest and the smells of candles and incense. I bought six small candles, one for each of the boys, and for Diana, my mother, and myself, lit them, and bent to kiss the icon of Jesus.

When I walked into the nave, I might have been entering a small Greek church somewhere in America. The men and women were neatly dressed, the faces of the children scrubbed clean. A baby wailed from a corner. The trustees had the austere demeanor of church trustees all over the world. Before the altar an old woman in black knelt and then leaned forward to touch the floor with her forehead. To one side a quartet of small girls stared intently and gravely at the priest. They were exquisite children wearing short bright dresses, their hair tied by bright strips of ribbon.

I suppose the ghosts returned for me when a small boy dressed in the gown of an acolyte emerged from the door at the side of the altar, carrying a candle. He resembled someone I had known and as I continued to stare at him, God help him, I understood why. He had a pair of ears that stuck out from his head like my own absurd appendages when I was about his age. And with that boy's ears as a lodestone to track the past, I could not help the tears which came to my eyes.

Were the tears a release of compassion for the boy because I understood from my own crucible as a child the jeers and taunts he had to endure? Were they for all the years that have passed since those Sundays so long ago when I was an acolyte and held a candle that reflected flame from the gilded vestments of my father? Were they for the years Diana and I had lived together, struggling from our youthful innocence to middle age, to where we stand now? Were they for our Mark and the pain of his passage from adolescence? Were they for our valiant John, who was caught in a whirlwind of illness? Were they for our strong-legged and clear-eyed Dean, awkward and earnest in pursuit of a dream? Were they for my mother, old acerbic hawk become a pigeon now, in diapers again as if she were a baby once more? Were the tears I cried for all these things and more?

For I stood in that church in Nauplion as if I were an apparition, a nameless stranger no one knew, knowing no one myself, yet recognizing the faces of men and women around me, images of those long dead or far away. In the mournful old women, dressed in black, I saw the lamenting old women of my youth. I saw a young man resembling my friend Zorbanos, a jowled man who might have been Mamalakis. A woman like Mrs. Petros and another one beside her like the white-haired woman in Chicago who lost a daughter, and Kopan, and Bessie's husband, and Mitchell, and a girl resembling the dark-haired, dark-eyed beauty in Koraes school I once longed for.

I thought of my father, his many years as a priest, the lifetime that has passed since he died. In the years that followed, my mother always sat on the aisle in the last row, people pausing to greet her on their way out of church. And then my thoughts flew from the church and I remembered climbing the rocks of the promontory with Diana when we were both so young, stealing peeks at her legs as we clambered up. I remembered our house in Pittsburgh and sliding down the snow-packed hill with Mark and John, and one wild ride on the back of an empty refrigerator carton that sent me crashing into a telephone pole and convulsed them both in laughter while I felt for broken bones. I remember the old house by the lake in Chicago, the beach deserted in winter, when Dean and I kicked a ball beside the water. I remembered the Sunday dinners with Diana's parents, my father-in-law shouting and urging us all to eat and drink, that good old man making us feel like kings. I remember Fox Lake and the cottage in the early morning, when dew glistened like webs of silver on the shrubs and I had no worry but the endless fields and pastures in which to play.

And I wonder what meaning the memories have, what pattern or sense in the jumbled recollections, lessons learned and forgotten, warnings and premonitions, remorses and regrets. The anvil strikes more quickly now, all of us moving more swiftly to the end. Naka was the first to die so she might set my father's table when he came, as she had set his table in our house for twenty-five years. Then my brother Dan joined them and one grave is left for my mother, and then two more plots for whichever of us comes next.

Now the sun shines brightly on the beach below my room, and the great mountain of Palimidi looms above my head, and my unfinished book lies beside me on the bed, and will I finish, and will it be as good as I want it to be and will...and will... and will....

I must stop writing now because I can no longer distinguish between what I remembered in the church and what I am recalling now. Yet that, too, may have its meaning, the way a thread spins out of ourselves, winding and unwinding, linking to the threads of others.

And when words cease to be written or spoken, perhaps then another kind of understanding begins, a silence that has to be mournful in a way because it encompasses what we struggle not to remember...the ways we have failed others, the ways we have hurt others, our inability to help others, our inability to help ourselves.

So from all those things, church, candles, incense, faces, family, wife, sons, mother, the living and the dead, what-has-been and what-will-be, sun, Greece, mountains, castles, work...from all those things one comes, in the end, to silence.

April 22

I returned from Greece a few days ago, making a fretful transition from spring and warm, balmy air to the cold and rain back here.

How to sum up those three weeks in Greece? First there were the few days in Athens, with depression mantling me like a shroud, the feeling of reluctance to leave my hotel room. As I began my journeys around the country, that therapeutic effect Greece has for me, and countless other travelers, began to spark my spirit. The days traveling with Mihali were marvelous— Monemvasia, Githion for the caves, into the deep Mani, Missolonghi, Ioannina, the snow-swept mountains of Epirus and, finally, Nauplion. In the final week of my stay in that lovely, tranquil town, each morning after breakfast I wrote on the chapter involving Xanthos, the historian. In eight days I produced a rough draft of almost forty pages! In the chapter Xanthos relates the background of the events in Mani in early March. When Kolokotronis starts his march north to lay siege to Tripolitza, Xanthos goes as his scribe and the march is described by references to Xenophon, Thucydides, and Herodotus.

The character of Xanthos is not yet clear. He is still too much a mirror for the character of Kolokotronis. I have not fashioned him individually enough yet. Only when he is moved, frightened, nostalgic, does a flash of the man he might be come alive. Yet, in fiction, this is the way a character is developed.

Now, back in my study, thousands of miles away from Greece, driving hard to finish, I look back over the road I have traveled to understand something of the journey still ahead. Illness, emotional disorders, depression, death has beset the writing yet the book has grown. I might have written this much in a shorter time but perhaps there is a rhythm a book acquires from a writer's life that takes into account the disruptions and lost time.

In these final months of work I will draw on the memories of Greece, those myriad impressions I have carried back here with me. I know I will conclude with the lovely story of Kazantzakis, the children and the song of the thrush. Toward that end I plod my way like an ant.

Meanwhile, in my first visit to the nursing home since my return, I found Mother drifting in and out of reality, pleading constantly to be taken to the bathroom. Sitting with her, I notice how frail she looks as she goes through the strange, distressing ritual of tearing and folding paper napkins.

I put her into the home. Whether that decision was right or wrong slips back and forth into my thoughts. I must try not to brood on that now since there is so much work to be done. Diana will help me by going into the city to visit her a few times a week.

Today has not been a good writing day. I am still looking for that rhythm of work. Perhaps tomorrow will be better. Kazantzakis, help me.

April 30

I have had good writing days and then a series of bad days. I am not sure just why. Last Friday, after teaching my class, Diana and I spent a couple of hours with Mother. She rambled thorough imaginary conversations with people who are dead. I found the experience agonizing, remembering how sharp and quick she had been. Perhaps the day will come when she won't even know us when we visit her.

On Saturday Diana and I drove to Ft. Wayne, where I spoke to a writers' conference. Having dinner with some of the conference directors, I drank too much, just about passed out when we returned to the hotel, Diana keeping a worried vigil. The following morning I spoke again and then we drove home through a heavy rain. They were three days lost, when every day is important if I am to finish by July.

Monday I worked on the Xanthos chapter. There are some good scenes but some weak ones, too. Part of the problem is the character of Kolokotronis, a giant of the War of Independence. Every word of dialogue I put into his mouth must be examined and reexamined to determine whether he would have spoken that way.

Yesterday and today have been plodding, arduous hours without a spark. Lacking that spark, the writing process is full of pain. I sounded so hopeful and optimistic a few days ago at the writers' conference before the participants. I wish I could muster more of that hope and optimism for myself now.

Tomorrow I will drive into the city and see Mother again for a little while. I don't look forward to these visits, but she must not feel forsaken. Friday I have to teach my writing class with half a dozen private conferences with students on their manuscripts. Some of the manuscripts are dreadful but even the worst writers have a great need to write.

Saigon surrendered today. The war in Vietnam is over after almost thirty-five years, a senseless calamity that our own ignorance and arrogance prolonged. Now, on the eve of the 200th anniversary of our own revolution, we must accept responsibility for having tried to thwart the aspirations of another people. After 150 billion dollars expended and after millions of dead Vietnamese and 55,000 American lives lost, their revolution has triumphed.

And tomorrow I return to my own bloody revolution.

May 3
It is the Night of the Ascension. Tonight in Eastern Orthodox churches across the world the lights are turned off at midnight and after a few moments hundreds of candles are lit to flicker in the darkness. I can remember what those Easter midnights meant to me as a boy, when I watched my father emerge from the darkness of the Sanctuary, candlelight glowing on his vestments. In the middle of the night we would return home from church to a bountiful table and delicious food. We would end our feast at dawn with the cracking of the blood-red eggs and then climb wearily into bed as the first light traced the rim

around our shades.

This week of Easter I did not go to church a single time. I think also it will probably be the first time in my mother's 88 years of life when she did not attend church at least once as well. I saw her yesterday. Each visit is a wrenching experience—her astonishment when she sees me, as if I have just discovered where she was and had come to rescue her. As she fumbles constantly with the paper napkins, folding and unfolding them, I try to calm and reassure her. I wheel her downstairs for a plate of ice cream and then take her back upstairs into the room of poor old women, to be tied once more in her wheelchair. Before I leave she asks me to take her to the bathroom. I wheel her to her room and get her out of the chair. Struggling to seat her onto the toilet, pulling down the heavy towel diapers she wears around her thighs is unreal and yet terribly real.

This morning, Saturday, after losing yesterday because of the writing class, I started again on the book. I struggle and twist and am still unable to ignite the spark. In spite of that impediment, I push on with the Xanthos-Kolokotronis chapter, carrying them from the victory at Kalamata to the defeat at Karitena. I am faced with the massive problem of moving an army.

The excitement I carried back from Greece has faded in these last days. Is it being back in the house with all the problems? Yet there isn't any use blaming others because the responsibility is mine.

It is near midnight now and in the churches they are preparing for the Ascension. I will go to bed soon, saying a prayer, even though I will not be lighting a candle.

May 12
Some good days of work on the Xanthos chapter, and the day before yesterday I finally completed a fair draft nearly forty pages long. There are some effective battle scenes in the chapter and some moving scenes of Xanthos in flight from the carnage of Karitena, following Kolokotronis who takes refuge in the small church in the village of Chrysovitzion. That is the scene where Kolokotronis prays before the icon of the Virgin Mary that weeps for him. In Greece I saw that icon with the worn track the tears had made. In the writing I must try to capture the emotion and supernatural quality of the events. I wrote that scene nineteen times yesterday, unsatisfied each time with the

result. Yet the preceding scenes are just as difficult. When Xanthos looks upon the battlefield littered with the dead and dying bodies, he hears the Turks slaughtering the wounded. I imagined the blood producing a scarlet mist floating over the bodies, a crimson haze to shroud the scenes of horror. My problem is simply to describe those scenes and convey that horror.

Some of the spark is returning, slowly, allowing me to work with a sharper, finer rhythm, pushing toward the end because I can see the end now. After nearly three years of research and writing, I can see the end. Sandy has written from Doubleday that if I can complete the manuscript by July 15, they will publish in March of 1976. Otherwise, unwilling to conflict with the turmoil of an election year, they will probably delay publication until 1977. A grim prospect. Perhaps the challenge of the goal will help me finish.

I have begun a final typing of chapter nine, the altered chapter that carries Xanthos on the march to Karitena. Then ten would become the sea chapter, the fireships, with most of those scenes already written. Eleven would be the chapter with Andreas in Crete and twelve the Papalikos chapter, where he hides in the village and murders the miser. I will need one final chapter, drawing all the threads together in the assault on the fortress of Tripolitza.

Afterwards I would like to go back through the manuscript one more time, trimming and tightening, putting in those thoughts that have developed in the writing of the later chapters.

To complicate matters, the last couple of days a dreadful cold has struck me, producing aches, pains, sneezes, and a stuffed nose. I take medication and today, in spite of feeling wretched, I managed to write for almost six hours. I hope to make tomorrow another good day. Wednesday I have a lecture in South Bend, Friday my writing class, and Sunday a lecture in Kankakee. These are interruptions that I resent now, but the fees help pay our bills.

I will bid Xanthos, my companion and friend, goodnight now. Let us both rest well.

June 21

I have had splendid weeks of work! Moving from chapter ten, rewritten several times, and then on through chapters eleven and twelve. Those three chapters encompass the first use of fireships in the sea chapter, the duel between Andreas and Kasandonis in Crete and, finally, the monk murdering the miser in the village.

Now chapter thirteen looms before me, in the viewpoint of the historian-scribe Xanthos, present at the siege and fall of Tripolitza, witness to the Greek massacre of Turks in that city.

The work has progressed well despite the misery all around me. I have been enduring pain running from my side up my back, diagnosed by the doctor as shingles. John is going through another tense period, beset by the feeling that he will never get well. My mother, in the nursing home, grows more terrified, confusing, despairing. Earlier today when Diana and I visited her, she raised her fists and cried out at us angrily because we left her alone with strangers. A nurse told us that even when she is strapped to her wheelchair, she will push and tug her way out into the hall, dragging the chair with her. We stayed several hours and managed to calm her down. When I kissed her goodbye she stared up at me with a stark and lucid despair.

Tomorrow morning I leave for a week to teach the novel at the Indiana University Writers' Conference. I have been worried that my own health would prevent my attending and that I would have to cancel at the last minute. I have taught the Conference several times before, and it is a hard week but an invigorating experience as well. Diana will join me for the final three days and we will return home together. Then I will have three weeks to finish the book by the deadline. Three short weeks to do so much.

But I know I can finish now, driving and pressing and writing and rewriting toward the end, like the men of the army of Xenophon after their perilous march across thousands of miles toward the freedom of the sea that would carry them back home. The first soldiers to reach the ridges and cliffs overlooking the water cried out, "The sea! The sea!" Men behind them heard and took up the cry in waves so an army shouted the enchanted word. So now, nearing my own sea, I raise my cry, "The book! The book!"

June 28

I returned home last night from the conference at Bloomington, Indiana. I found the week taxing but I also felt that I had dispensed a few small, supportive truths to the writers assembled there. They provided me a measure of their gratefulness and excitement which I brought to my own work.

In the morning I will begin the final chapter of the book. I am expectant, hopeful, eager, frightened. The end is near and yet I cannot be certain of the end. The chapters are powerful, and yet what will the whole of the book be like for those who read it?

I sent an additional 30,000 words to Sandy and he remains as enthusiastic about these sections as he was about the earlier ones. I pressed him for any doubts he might have, for any fragments he felt should be strengthened, but he remained firm in his admiration and support for what I have done. I feel that, too. Could we both be wrong?

Meanwhile, tonight in my study, I gird my spirit. Sorting papers, I look up at the picture of Nikos Kazantzakis on my bulletin board. Tears come to my eyes because I need just a measure of his discipline and his faith. I am going to finish this book now, I know that, barring some unforeseen calamity. But this final chapter may still be fraught with hazards. Feeling like the fetus that kicks and struggles to breath, from the moment the book is born, a new life has been created, a new form conceived.

In the morning I will begin with the armies before Tripolitza. I am sleeping in the study now, and in the darkness my characters wait for the ascent of tomorrow's sun. Help me, my Nikos.

July 3

I have had a series of fine working days. On Tuesday I completed a synopsis of about fourteen pages on chapter thirteen and then wrote the first five pages of the chapter. Working until late afternoon, I stopped to walk the beach in the sun, seeking to retain my excitement, to nourish my fervor.

Today, rising early, I rewrote those first five pages several more times, improving them although I am not certain that is the way I will begin the chapter. I have started with a description of the beleaguered fortress, Tripolitza, and the inhabitants under siege. Then I describe the captains and their armies that ring the city, like Homer describing and listing the captains and ships about to embark for Troy. I think that makes for a ponderous opening. I need a more dramatic vision. Realizing that Xanthos is my key, I will try to exhume his mind and spirit. This evening, after the day of writing, I read Stringfellow Barr's *The Will of Zeus* again, the scenes describing the Greeks battling against the Persians at Marathon and Thermopylae, seeking parallels, but, equally as important, seeking those resonances of the past that might echo in my own characters. Time and again there are passages from the poets or the historians that ring with validity for Tripolitza. When Odysseus says, "For a shame is this even for men that are not yet born to hear of, if we shall not take vengeance on the slayers of our sons and brothers," the rationale for the slaughter of the Turks rings clear. That slaughter is not humane, but it is in the cycle of history. For like the Greeks that assaulted Troy so many centuries before, once again at Tripolitza Greek armies laid siege to a great city, to snatch wealth and win glory. They are no longer the Achaean warrior-kings but men with names like Ipsilantis, Kolokotronis, Petrobey, descendants and inheritors of the world that emerged from that violent age.

There is so much I wish this chapter to include, so much that needs to be said. I am feeling the pressure of time, wanting to get the chapter roughed in so that I can begin revising and refining. The ending will be immensely difficult, but I feel it in my spirit as I felt the endings of my earlier novels. All I have to do, God help me, is write it true!

July 8
I have had energetic, productive days of work! They have not moved me forward very much but there have been good revisions through the opening pages of the chapter, a nuance here and a shading there. While the beginning works better, the chapter still bogs down after about eight pages with the historical material on the politics within the assaulting armies. I need to compress this material and concentrate on the drama.

Reading the previous Xanthos chapter tonight, I found it holding together well, the character of Kolokotronis consistent, the battle scenes ringing true. That chapter took two months to write and for ten days now I am on this new chapter...a more difficult one, I know.

Saturday I became uneasy about Mother and drove into Chicago to visit her. She was strangely detached, calm, untroubled. When I asked her a question, her answer was quiet and coherent. I took her to the roof of the home, the sun shining down on a few patients and aides sitting at several tables, Joe was out there with his patient and the talkative little woman in the wheelchair, and an older man being visited by his daughter and grandchildren. As I wheeled Mother past them, one of the little girls ran by, and Mother stretched out her hand as she might have reached out for one of her great-grandchildren.

We sat in the sun, and after about a half hour the roof was cleared except for the two of us. I walked her around slowly, looking up at the skyscrapers that loomed around us. I imagined residents of those apartments looking out their windows and seeing a solitary man pushing a white-haired old lady in a wheelchair. They cannot know how I feel seeing her reduced to this condition now, she who had been Mother of the Community, Sister of the Memorial Wheat, Queen of the Red Cross.

Tonight after dinner I came back up to my study in an effort to work, but I am tired, and the thought of sitting at my typewriter again seems overwhelming. Tomorrow...one more day.

July 14
The writing continues to go well, each day adding eight to ten more pages to the book. That push forward brought me yesterday to the fall of Tripolitza and the massacre of the Turkish inhabitants by the Greeks. Only an epilogue of some kind remains, with Xanthos, wounded in the battle, recuperating in the monastery which will set the scene with the children, utilizing the Kazantzakis story of the thrush.

This morning, knowing I would be working on the final pages, I was nervous, reluctant to begin. I considered going to play tennis with John. Finally, about eleven, I came up to my study prepared to suffer over every line. Then one of those miracles happened that makes writing a joy as well as anguish. For two hours my typewriter quivered and steamed, the union between myself and the machine intimate, endearing, fierce, and lovely. The scenes poured out, rough but rich—the creation of a monk, Brother Foolish, the monastery, the children, Xanthos, everything falling artfully and seamlessly into place. Scenes came to me from my journey to Greece, the little crypt where the bones of the monks were stored at Aghia Lavra, the wind wailing across the monument to the Greeks murdered by the Nazis...even Mother's face at the nursing home the other afternoon....

I am on page 505 in this draft now and near the end of the book. An immense revision of these final pages still lies before me, but the cycle of the book is complete, ending the journey that began in the village of Kravasaras almost three years ago.

Tonight I wrote Sandy telling him I could not make the July 20 deadline but that I need no more than another ten days to two weeks. Short of some calamity, I told him that I have the book in my grasp and spirit now.

After writing those pages this morning, I did not try to work again. All day I have been mustering my spirit and girding my body for the final assault. In the morning I will begin again...in the morning...with the almost miraculous delight of knowing the end isn't far away.

July 20
The good writing continues! I am inching forward, but I am pleased with the results. Starting from the beginning of chapter thirteen, working five, six pages a day through eight or nine drafts, I have reshaped and altered the momentum and material on the siege. The historians write that in the final days before the fall of the city, the heat was searing. I am making a special effort to evoke that sizzling climate, and show its effects on the starving inhabitants. The heat also aggravates the anger and bitterness of the Greek soldiers who each day were witness to the treasures of the fortress bartered away to the captains. When the city falls, they will take their frustration and rage out on the inhabitants.

Today was to have been my deadline, but I am no more than two weeks or so away. I will rewrite these first pages of the siege again, trying to tell less and show more, making sure that all the elements are there...the plague in the city and the heat, the greed of the Greek captains, the separate treaty signed between the Albanian mercenaries and the Greeks. When these scenes have been done as well as I can write them, I will move on to the final pages in the monastery.

I have been playing some tennis again the last few days and that always makes me feel better. John seems better these days, as well, and is playing tennis with me. The weather is hot and the sun feels therapeutic as I walk along the water's edge. Afterwards I shower and come up to my study cooled by the air conditioner to read and work on notes and write a little and listen to the lovely, melancholy music of Liszt.

I have avoided visiting Mother this last week, not wanting my edge of excitement dulled or depressed by seeing her now. But Diana has gone in my place a couple of times. I will begin visiting her again soon. That woman who never forgot others must not be forgotten.

How will I feel when I have finished the book? I know I will need a rest, but there won't be time for rest since on August 10 I must leave for Ball State University for a week's writing conference. Following that session I have another college conference in Cleveland.

How will readers react to the book? I have tried not to favor the Greeks more than the Turks. I think I have remained neutral in my portrayal of both sides. More important, the writing of the book has sharpened my own feelings about the suffering, cruelty, and brutality of any war.

July 25
These have been really splendid days of work and, that fine writing rhythm established, I have that sense of the book at work, so that whatever I am doing, a part of me is fashioning and creating. When I am bicycling or watching the news on television or talking to Diana or one of the boys, character and scene revelations burst into my thoughts.

The last chapter became so long and unwieldy I have made it two chapters. Fourteen will be the end instead of thirteen, and allow me to exercise greater control. There are fine, moving scenes in both chapters and after twelve to fourteen drafts I think I have caught some of the frenzy of the capture of the city and the massacre that followed.

Chapter thirteen now sets the stage for the attack on Tripolitza. Chapter fourteen describes the massacre in the city and its aftermath. I have written a scene in which Xanthos rescues a young Turkish girl and tries to save her. He finds Balalas, the old veteran, wounded in the fighting who promises to help him. But during the night Balalas dies. The girl is stolen from Xanthos and raped and murdered. In his fury, and I am not sure how the scene will finally work out, Xanthos kills her assailant. That, too, is significant, proving Xanthos' own capacity for hatred and violence.

Sandy sent me a good letter telling me how eager they are to have the completed book. No more eager than I am to finish it! I think that is possible by the first week in August. The next few days will tell the tale.

Feeling this mesmerizing draw of the book, I am tempted to remain at the typewriter longer than I should. Part of me begrudges time spent away from the writing, but I have learned that the quality falls off after a number of hours. The spirit is willing but the thought processes and the shaping of words and images grows faulty. It is better to be patient.

Tonight Dean and I drove in to see Mother, and again on our arrival I heard her calling for help. She calms down slightly when she sees us. We wheeled her to the terrace and then to the basement shop for ice cream and coffee. Afterwards I put her to bed. The little nurse closed her light and Mother, fearful, called so I would turn on the light again.

I have the feeling after each visit that there are small ways we could make her more comfortable. She still retains some of her old habits, like reading the Greek paper, although I am not sure how much she comprehends. She is always calmer when friends or family are with her. But so few people visit her now. I understand where it is depressing and it becomes easier to write her off and just stay away. I resent and resist that conclusion. Yet I am caught in fulfilling it and I think now it may be too late to do anything about bringing her home.

Tonight, watching Dean at seventeen listening to the old women scream, one clutching his arm desperately, made me aware how remote and alien a world this must be to him in the springtime of his life.

Time now to sleep a good night's rest so I will be fresh to start writing early in the morning. I will return to the doomed city with Xanthos, who has become in so many ways the character I feel closest to. I think he will be an important guide if I ever write a sequel to this book.

August 4
I have spent a series of hot, sunny days at my typewriter, wonderful working days averaging seven to nine hours of writing. I have completed a final draft of chapter thirteen, and the last few days have been working through numerous drafts of chapter fourteen. Today I finished the section of the chapter where Xanthos is attacked by the hunchback who rapes and murders the young Turkish girl.

Tomorrow I will work on the epilogue, shaping up the difficult ending of the book. Time is growing tight before I have to leave for the conference and I would love to finish and must finish before I leave on Sunday. I hope to God I can do it.

I am truly tired but am pleased because I have been working so well. When I am finished, when the final chapters have been packaged and sent away, then I will look back over the span of time that has passed since the first words went on paper. For three years there has been the slow, often tortuous sequence of the chapters, the angry, bitter, sometimes resigned way my life hammered upon the work.

This journal has been a record of all those anguishes, efforts, detours, and small triumphs. And now journal and novel are coming to an end together.

August 8
So close to finishing. . . .

Last night I stopped after fourteen hours of writing on the final pages of the book, Xanthos divining the miracle in the song of the thrush. I am still not satisfied that I have captured the essence of what I want the end of the book to be like, but that will only become attainable through additional drafts.

There are endless revisions of pages through joyous, productive days. In the last four days I have averaged ten to twelve hours of writing and then fourteen hours yesterday. I feel a weariness but an iridescent exhilaration as well. Last night, working on the final pages, I felt that even if I were to die during the night, the book was finished, cannot be taken from me now, will make its way to print.

And these last few days when I have been locked up in the study have been magnificent ones of flawless weather, humidity and heat eased, the skies cloudless and serene. For a couple of days the water was rough, churning and foaming, carrying a roar up to my room where I am working furiously, my spirit roaring. At times like these, contrary to the way I often feel, I envisage myself a merry and holy man!

Seeking to sharpen and enrich those final scenes that take place in the cloister, tonight I am reading Thomas Merton.

I will rise early in the morning, drink my orange juice, eat my muffin with coffee, ride my bike in the circuitous course around my yard, shower, and come up to work.

By this time tomorrow evening I may be finished. How lovely and infinite a word! Finished! There are other meanings for the word, perhaps, at other times, but for this one moment in my life, the connotation is a majestic one!

August 9 (10:55 P.M.)
I am finished!

I have been working today since almost eight this morning, stopping for a while at seven this evening for dinner with my niece, Barbara, and her family who were visiting. They had delayed the dinner which was to be a celebration until, finished or not, we decided to eat. I came up soon afterwards to start writing again. The problem was that the final section seemed to go to pieces on me. I wrote and rewrote pages 525 to 530 twelve, fourteen times, altering them a little each time, having a disordered feeling they were still not right. Then I finally divined the error.

The scene with the monk Brother Foolish taking Xanthos to the crypt and speaking to him of the bones of the monks who had died was a splendid scene. That was the problem because it was too rich, almost a climax, so that the allegory of the thrush seemed anticlimactic. I kept trying to save the crypt scene, kept rewriting furiously, trimming a little more away each time, reducing it but not eliminating it. Then, after the break for dinner, I became aware that the whole scene had to be thrown out. The scene was lovely, but was also superfluous in the smooth, unimpeded flow to the end. When I finally cut it away completely, the chapter recovered.

Now these final chapters are packaged, a note to Sandy enclosed, the envelope sealed. God, I am tired now, my body aching, my back sending vibrations of pain through me. But I have a majestic feeling of accomplishment, as well. I read the last pages aloud and reread them and cried, yes, and cried!

Tomorrow morning I leave for Ball State. I don't need the conference now, and they may not need the dregs of what I have left. But I must go, and meanwhile Sandy will be reading the book

If I have any reservations at this moment, I think the over-writing needs to be trimmed in places. But that can be done. The important thing is that the cycle of the book, the totality of the life I began nearly three years ago, is finished. And I am grateful. Grateful! That is the word that comes to mind now. God help me, I think it is lovely, perhaps flawed and overdone in places, but mighty and epical too.

We shall see if other readers agree.

Afterword

When *The Hour of the Bell* was published the book received many good notices, including one which said, ''Petrakis wrote as if he had lived through the Greek Revolution.'' Another reviewer complained the book read too much like history and not enough like fiction. In the following years I received letters about the book from Greeks and non-Greeks, moved by the story of the conflict. In some of the parishes where I traveled to lecture, I met a few old Greek patriots who thought I had glossed over the obviously greater brutality of the Turks. Those complaints suggested to me that I had achieved my intention of remaining fair. There is no humanity in any war.

In the next few years two more novels and a collection of my short stories were published. *A Petrakis Reader—27 Stories and a Novella* was published in 1978, *Nick the Greek* in 1979 and *Days of Vengeance* in 1983. Meanwhile, like an old firehorse quivering to make another run into danger, I have begun another book.

The depressing truth is that the writing doesn't become any easier no matter how many books one writes. Part of this burden has reference to the ascending years of my life. There are times now when I approach my day's work assaulted by the infirmities of Falstaff, the decreased leg, the shortened wind, the double chin and whitening beard, and other parts from my stem to my stern blasted by antiquity. Yet there are also other moments when I feel in the vigorous springtime of my senility, convinced a few more good books might accrue from this final flowering before I need succumb to my dotage.

In reviewing the often precipitous journey of my life to this point, I marvel how often I have been a fool without the redeeming wisdom of Lear's jester. I have wasted so much time, expended energies uselessly, chosen the less challenging course, evaded responsibilities, committed acts of insensitivity. Indeed there have been many instances when I have acted with astounding stupidity. Yet, in fairness, I also believe there have been times when I have been a considerate son, a tolerable husband, a fair father, and a good writer. How all of these might finally balance off requires the wisdom of an ancient sage.

If the blunders in my life outweigh the moments of sagacity, nothing can diminish the peerless, pristine wisdom of my having chosen Diana as my wife thirty-seven years ago. That action alone should pluck a few feathers from the fool's cap I have always worn. I wish those friends who share her warmth and friendship now also had the delight of knowing her as a young girl. Her hair was sable-black and longer then, her skin flawless and smooth, her dark eyes reflecting, as they still do now, her good, gentle soul. Her black hair is greying now, of course, but I am awed how she still holds that beauty some women retain as they grow older. Through the upheavals and eruptions, small triumphs and bitter disappointments of our years together, we have shared everything. Our joy when the finished copy of my first novel arrived and our grief as we sat holding my mother's hands in the last few hours of her life. One of the marvels of our closeness is that in spite of hearing me lecture and read a hundred times, she will still laugh and cry again at the things she almost knows by heart. I love her for her devotion and for that sense of renewal she brings to our days. There is an old Cretan parable that says, ''Poverty and nakedness mean nothing if a man has a good wife.''

We also have three sons. They have provided me a great deal of joy and pride. Perhaps it is in the nature of parents to expect a little more than sons and daughters can provide. Remembering how much my father loved me—I sensed with some remorse, a little more than I loved him—I didn't understand until years later how fathers (and mothers) live in their children in a way the children cannot possibly live in their parents. That is the pervasive lesson of the generations. I am the father now although it seemed so short a time ago when I roamed the alleys of my childhood with my rag-tailed friends. To prove how far I have come from those halycon days, sometimes catching my reflection in a mirror, I see staring back at me the face of my father's ghost.

When someone asks me which of my books is my favorite, I can no more answer that question than I could say which son is my favorite. Each son and each book hold a special, treasured place for me. Watching them grow from being dark-haired, handsome children, passing from childhood through the awkward anguish of adolescence, into dark-haired handsome men intent on fulfilling their destinies, I feel my own excitements in life grown young again.

Mark, the oldest, is an actor and a mime with a beguiling charm that makes it easier for us all to laugh. John, the middle son, aspires to make fine films and to write. His first short story, sent to me from the snowbound exile of a winter he spent in Minneapolis, moved me intemperately not only because he was my son but also because I have been teaching writing for years and can recognize the vision and imagination of talent. Dean, the youngest, works at acting, improvisational theatre and mime, as well. He regards art and life with the unflinching gaze of Starbuck, a steadfastness of character that he has revealed, in spite of his youth, through all our family trials.

Mark has also proven his sagacity by bringing into our family lovely Julie Hébert, a sensitive director and writer. They have provided Diana and me the experience of becoming grand-parents to a miniature Aphrodite they have chosen to name Alexis. I will restrain myself until some future essay and not attempt to further describe my first grandchild here. Since each child is unique and beloved, grandparents will understand the sanity of my silence

All of these now are personal observations that could be matched by numerous other parents and grandparents. We are no more and no better than any of them. That evidence of family love links our fate in many durable ways with families of other races and nationalities across the world. I cannot believe that Russian or Turkish grandparents love their grandchildren any less than we do. That commonality of destiny is essential to remember now that we exist under the terror of weaponry that would make a graveyard of our earth. We must find a way to live even with those with whom we argue and disagree because the alternative is too dreadful to contemplate. All the bristling arsenals and nuclear warheads in the world are insane as instruments of offense or defense because their use would mean the death of life as we have known it thus far. If God cannot help us, then, by God's grace, we must help ourselves

I can sign petitions and join in a few demonstrations but most

of the time I feel as helpless as others must feel about altering
the course of events. The leaders in the White House and in the
Kremlin don't phone to ask my opinion. Like millions of others I
have to rise to begin my day believing somehow that our earth
will survive. I would like to make a greater, more active
contribution to that survival, but I think I have seared into me
now the knowledge that my existence and my sanity consists of
sitting at my typewriter, typing words on paper, forming those
words into sentences and paragraphs and, finally, into stories.
That is, in the end, what I think I am and how I would like to be
remembered. A storyteller in the tradition of those old tellers of
tales whose voices lingered in firelights as they conjured for
their listeners another life more real, for a while, than the one
they were living. As a storyteller visiting libraries and many
schools, I have been witness to the delight of young and old
audiences at stories. I am certain that as long as men, women
and children survive, stories will go on.

In the writing classes where I teach, I try to pass on to my
students my belief that writing is an act of faith. For to write
today, to seek to create good work in a climate where so much of
the spurious and the mediocre is acclaimed, requires fortitude
and dedication. It is hard to be young and have talent and work
hard in the arts only to have one's contribution neglected. But,
in the end, one creates a quality of life as much for oneself as for
others. One who feels the need to write must write. The Nobel
poet of Greece, George Seferis, recorded in one of his journals,
"Sometimes it crosses my mind that the things I write here are
nothing other than images that prisoners or sailors tattoo on
their skins."

Now, just a few weeks from my sixtieth birthday, as I review
the possessions in my house and study, file cabinets full of
correspondence, bookcases filled with books, bureaus and
closets and boxes crammed with the memorabilia of a lifetime, I
remember my mother's last years in the nursing home. In her
earlier years her possessions had filled six trunks, six bureaus,
and fifty boxes. By the end all had been compressed into one
narrow closet and two shallow drawers in her room. I think of
her and I also remember the story of the sage who confronted
Alexander the Great, asking why he had traveled so far to
possess so much when all he could ever really own was the
ground on which he stood and a little more than that to be

buried in one day. I long suddenly to strip away so many of the things around me that do not seem significant.

With that stripping away I would also like to make still another effort to reform myself, and pledge anew to work harder, avoiding either undue optimism or excessive despair. My dappled past suggests these reforms will remain aspirations. Living wisely cannot be measured out as an apothecary measures ingredients for a prescription. We live and love with disorder and excesses because they remain parts of our human flaws, because we often don't even understand ourselves. I think I know myself better than others know me but I haven't yet achieved that moment Borges speaks of when ''a man discovers who he really is.''

I understand I am too much concerned with myself, feeling my rise and decline cosmic in dimension. There are many moments when I cannot conceive of an earth where I do not exist. That is simply why the poet of Ecclesiastes calls, ''Vanity, vanity...all is vanity.''

In more tranquil moments I am able to accept the ancient truth that all men and women begin their journey toward death the moment they are born. That individual province of life wherein we dream, love, hope, celebrate and create, laugh and cry, that province is simply a miniature particle of the world. Our eventual end, so overwhelming to us, becomes the embedding away of a single life in the sediment of rubble and the layers of earth, as the strata of epochs that have passed contain the impressions and imprints of fossils, the shells of lizards and the dust of kings. Someday then, I console myself in those moments of faith and trust, I will be drawn closer to the eyes of Homer, the vision of Eiseley, the soul of Kazantzakis, and the spirits of my departed parents and brother. That will crown the marvel and wonder of the journey I have made on this earth, loving, laughing and crying, writing my books and telling my stories.

So, good reader, who has stayed with me this far, this is where I am now, trying to write and tell my stories, while seeking an accomodation with my frailties and with those I love and the dear friends and strangers whose lives touch mine. When the surface is stripped away, there isn't any such thing as an ordinary life because each solitary human being reaffirms the magical, revelatory nature of life.

Harry Mark Petrakis

What we must remember is that we are also all fools. But even fools deserve some mercy and compassion. For that reason I wish us well and that we experience those essences the old blind storyteller Homer desired for his friends, "the banquet, the song and the harp, friendship, warm baths, sleep and love."